Edge Learning for Distributed Big Data Analytics

Discover this multi disciplinary and insightful work, which integrates machine learning, edge computing, and big data. It presents the basics of training machine learning models, key challenges and issues, as well as comprehensive techniques including edge learning algorithms and system design issues. The volume describes architectures, frameworks, and key technologies for learning performance, security, and privacy, as well as incentive issues in training/inference at the network edge. It is intended to stimulate fruitful discussions, inspire further research ideas, and inform readers from academia and those having an industry background. It is an essential read for experienced researchers and developers, as well as for those who are just entering the field.

Song Guo is a Full Professor in the Department of Computing at the Hong Kong Polytechnic University. He is an IEEE Fellow and the editor-in-chief of the *IEEE Open Journal of the Computer Society*. He was a member of the IEEE ComSoc Board of Governors and a distinguished lecturer of the IEEE Communications Society.

Zhihao Qu is an assistant researcher in the School of Computer and Information at Hohai University and in the Department of Computing at the Hong Kong Polytechnic University.

The authors of this book would like to acknowledge the following contributors: Jie Zhang for contributing materials to Chapter 6 (Efficient Training with Heterogeneous Data Distribution), Qihua Zhou for contributing materials to Chapter 8 (Edge Learning Architecture Design for System Scalability), Haozhao Wang for contributing materials to Chapter 5 (Computation Acceleration), Yufeng Zhan for contributing materials to Chapter 9 (Incentive Mechanisms in Edge Learning Systems), and Chenxi Chen for contributing materials to Chapter 7 (Security and Privacy Issues in Edge Learning Systems).

Edge Learning for Distributed Big Data Analytics

Theory, Algorithms, and System Design

SONG GUO

The Hong Kong Polytechnic University

ZHIHAO QU

Hohai University and The Hong Kong Polytechnic University

CAMBRIDGE
UNIVERSITY PRESS

CAMBRIDGE
UNIVERSITY PRESS

University Printing House, Cambridge CB2 8BS, United Kingdom

One Liberty Plaza, 20th Floor, New York, NY 10006, USA

477 Williamstown Road, Port Melbourne, VIC 3207, Australia

314–321, 3rd Floor, Plot 3, Splendor Forum, Jasola District Centre, New Delhi – 110025, India

103 Penang Road, #05–06/07, Visioncrest Commercial, Singapore 238467

Cambridge University Press is part of the University of Cambridge.

It furthers the University's mission by disseminating knowledge in the pursuit of
education, learning, and research at the highest international levels of excellence.

www.cambridge.org
Information on this title: www.cambridge.org/9781108832373
DOI: 10.1017/9781108955959

First published 2022

Printed in the United Kingdom by TJ Books Limited, Padstow Cornwall

A catalogue record for this publication is available from the British Library.

ISBN 978-1-108-83237-3 Hardback

Contents

Figures

Tables

1 Introduction

This chapter introduces the background and motivations of edge learning. We also specify the main challenges faced by edge learning ranging from challenges in data and computation, to communication.

1.1 Background

Machine learning has demonstrated great promises in various fields - e.g., smart healthcare, smart surveillance, smart homes, self-driving, and smart grid - which are fundamentally altering the way individuals and organizations live, work, and interact. Big data is one of the key promotion factors that boosts machine learning development, following the significant successes and progress of machine learning models (especially deep learning models) in many domains in recent years. Big data and machine learning are enabling technologies for smart decision making, automation, and resource optimization. These technologies collectively promote intelligent services from concepts to practical applications. Traditionally, to develop these intelligent services and applications, big data should be stored and processed in the cloud data center in a centralized mode. Due to the powerful capabilities of the cloud, it has enabled great achievements in learning from big data, especially for applications that allow long response delay and all data aggregated to the cloud - e.g., e-commerce services and recommendation systems.

However, with the growing workloads related to 5G, the Internet of Things (IoT), and real-time analytics, traditional centralized learning frameworks require all training data from different sources to be uploaded to a remote data server, which incurs significant communication overhead, service latency, as well as security and privacy issues. According to a report by Cisco, nearly 847 ZB of data will be generated at the edge while the storage capability of data centers will only reach to 19.5ZB by 2021. Moreover, plenty of emerging applications require a strict guarantee of response latency, e.g., self-driving and Industry 4.0 usually require millisecond-level or even microsecond latency.

Meanwhile, traditional distributed machine learning usually ignores the privacy and security issue. In recent years, with the development and wider application of artificial intelligence (AI) technology, data privacy protection has also received more and more attention [81]. The European Union has introduced the first data privacy protection bill - the General Data Protection Regulation (GDPR), which clarified certain provisions on data privacy protection. The "Cyber Security Law of the People's Republic of China" and "General Principles of the Civil Law of the People's Republic of China," which were implemented in 2017 also state that "network operators must not disclose, tamper with, or destroy the personally collected information, and when conducting data transactions with third parties, it is necessary to ensure that the proposed contract clearly stipulates the scope of the proposed transaction data and data protection obligations." In view of these legislations, the collection of user data must be open and transparent between enterprises and institutions. Data cannot be exchanged without user authorization [357]. The challenge that brings to traditional machine learning is: if the data cannot be communicated between institutions, a company has a limited amount of data, or a few giant companies monopolize a large amount of data. It is difficult for small companies to obtain data, which results in data islands. To tackle this problem, many researchers pay much attention to studying the design and implementation of machine learning on the edge.

Therefore, it is urgent to shift model training and inference from the cloud to the edge. In fact, the wide deployment of edge devices promotes the significant increase of computing capacity in the edge environment, far exceeding the increasing speed of network bandwidth. From this aspect, edge devices can be viewed as the extension of the cloud because of the huge computing capacity. By taking the advantages of both cloud and edge, big data analytics could be more efficient. The edge learning paradigm - i.e., distributed machine learning over edge devices - enables distributed edge nodes to cooperatively train models and conduct inferences with their locally cached data.

To explore the new characteristics and potential prospects of edge learning, we will provide a comprehensive and systematic introduction of the recent research efforts on edge learning. We hope that this book will elicit escalating attention, stimulate fruitful discussions, and inspire further research ideas in this field.

1.2   From Cloud Learning to Edge Learning

In this part, we discuss the development of edge learning.

1.2.1   From Cloud Computing to Edge Computing

In the past decade, cloud computing has become a mature computing paradigm for providing powerful computation as well as various standardized services. Traditional cloud-based methods have enabled great achievements in learning from big data, especially for those that allow long response delay and data aggregation from edge to cloud [174]. However, with the growing workloads related to 5G, autonomy, the IoT, and real-time analytics, businesses are beginning to look elsewhere for their computing needs. In addition, the cloud has unsolvable challenges in communication, computation, and storage that cannot satisfy the requirement in explosively increasing data.

These trends change the end-user experience and introduce new requirements and demands on data center and cloud-based infrastructures [81, 154, 170, 205, 209, 221, 298, 357, 386, 406].

As a result, users and service providers are likely moving toward the edge environment; the basic concept is to reduce the amount of data sent to the cloud and to provide computation at the place nearby [42]. Recently, plenty of edge servers are deployed at the network edge. Meanwhile, mobile devices are equipped with increasingly powerful Central Processing Units (CPUs) and Graphic Processing Units (GPUs), which have capabilities to perform complex computing tasks. Thus, offloading some tasks into the network edge can mitigate the cloud burden and improve the performance of services in terms of latency and resource utilization.

1.2.2   From Distributed Machine Learning to Edge Learning

At its beginning, the machine learning model was trained in a single machine with limited hardware resources. The training algorithms of many machine learning models - including most neural networks, graphical models, etc. - can be abstracted into an iterative-convergent process, which takes a lot of computing resources to complete. Studies have shown that a CPU clocked at 2.0 GHz training a VGG-16 model on the ImageNet dataset will take several years, which is totally incompatible with the real-time nature of the model application! Due to the limited computing power of a single machine and the decentralized big training data itself, machine learning is developing in a distributed scenario, known as distributed machine learning. In distributed machine learning, multiple workers cooperate with each other with communication and train the model in parallel.

Though traditional cloud-based methods have made great achievements in learning from the big data, the cloud has limitations due to heavy resource cost, privacy issues, high latency, etc. On the other hand, the principle of edge computing naturally facilitates edge learning by leveraging resources of edge devices and mobile devices. Edge learning is a paradigm complementary to the cloud-based methods for big data analytics in the cloud-edge environment. It has been proposed and developed for moving the training and inference to the edge environment to serve delay-sensitive and privacy-sensitive applications, for which the data cannot be gathered in the cloud. In Fig. 1.1, we illustrate the cloud-edge environment. With the promotion and popularization of edge devices - e.g., smartphones, autonomous vehicles, sensors, and wearable devices - data generated at the network edge are exponentially increasing. Thus, performing the training tasks and the inference tasks of machine learning model at the network edge can mitigate the cloud burden and improve the performance of intelligent services in terms of latency and resource utilization. Distributed big data analytics in cloud-edge environments has become a new trend.

Notably, federated learning is a typical example of edge learning. Since first introduced by Google, federated learning has demonstrated to be a promising solution for future AI applications with strong privacy protection [198]. Federated learning allows users to collaboratively train a global model without sharing their own data,

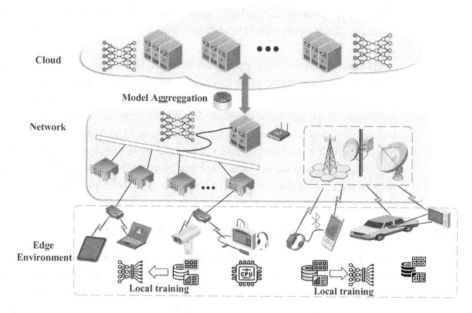

Figure 1.1 Illustration of the cloud - edge environment.

thus alleviating the risk of their privacy exposure. As such, federated learning can serve as an enabling technology for machine learning model training at mobile edge networks [170, 174, 221, 357].

1.3　　Edge Learning and Edge Intelligence

The integration of edge computing and machine learning results in a new interdiscipline, named edge AI or edge intelligence, which is beginning to receive a tremendous amount of interest.

Edge learning is the enabling technology to achieve edge intelligence. It is a paradigm complementary to the cloud-based methods for big data analytics in the cloud-edge environment. It is proposed and developed for moving the training and inference to the edge environment to serve delay-sensitive and privacy-sensitive applications, of which the data cannot be gathered to the cloud. This fusion of big data, edge computing and machine learning is an enabling technology for edge intelligence.

In regard to training, edge learning exploits pervasive data generated not only by user devices but also by other sensing devices and that stored in the cloud/edge servers (e.g., data from social networks). It leverages various computing entities (all the devices with computing capabilities ranging from cloud and edge servers to various edge devices) in an efficient, reliable, and robust manner. In regard to inference, trained models are properly deployed and updated in edge networks by taking into account both resource constraints and inference latency. It should also guarantee the privacy and security of training data and machine learning models as required. Compared with the traditional cloud-centric approaches to training machine learning models, edge learning has the following advantages.

- *Enabling various dispersed computing entities in the cloud-edge environment for learning collaboratively.* Edge learning enables the use of numerous edge servers and end devices in a collaborative manner, which is expected to increase the total computing power by multiple orders of magnitude.
- *Supporting the learning of multi-source data in a resource-efficient manner.* Edge learning supports communication-efficient learning of data not only generated by mobile users and edge sensors but also data that has been collected in the cloud, which can produce much more consistent, accurate, useful information and can greatly reduce the processing delay. In addition, there is no need to upload the raw data to the edge learning server for aggregation in the locally training process; instead, just upload their model updates, which significantly improves the communication efficiency.
- *Providing privacy and security as demanded.* Edge learning strikes a quite good balance between learning accuracy and data privacy by establishing privacy policies that the full exploitation of data while guaranteeing the security and privacy of different data as required.

1.4   Challenges of Edge Learning

While edge learning has great potential for many intelligent applications e.g., smart cities and self-driving cars - , it is quite challenging to realize it in an efficient and secure manner due to the inherent characteristics of the cloud-edge environment. We summarize the main challenges in edge learning in Fig. 1.2. First, the training efficiency is hard to achieve not only because of the distinctive methods of data storage

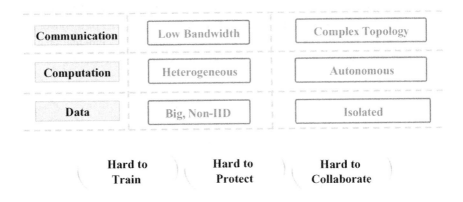

Figure 1.2 Summary of the main challenges in edge learning.

and communication of the edge facilities but also due to the greatly limited communication resource and the dynamicity of the edge environment. Second, learning on the edge needs to access data with various privacy protection requirements, posing a challenge in achieving learning accuracy while satisfying all the privacy requirements. Third, scalability is an important issue in edge learning, but it is difficult to manage a huge number of heterogeneous devices in the complex edge environment. Finally, edge devices utilize their resources and data to train a global model in edge learning. Without an appropriate incentive mechanism, edge devices may not participant in the training process.

1.4.1   Hard to Train Due to Constrained and Heterogeneous Edge Resources

The devices that participate in edge learning have heterogeneous characteristics, such as data distribution, computation abilities, and cooperation availability. There is also a much broader necessity to put forward effective methods to maximize the efficiency of the distributed learning process. In Fig. 1.3, we illustrate the challenges of edge learning from the perspective of communication, computation, and data.

First, communication is a critical challenge in edge learning. A typical learning system usually consists of a large number of mobile devices, such as mobile phones. In this scenario, the communication speed may be several times slower than local computation on most of the devices [117] [300]. In edge learning, the training process generally contains iterative transmission and aggregation of local updates - i.e., the gradient computed upon local samples -, while energy and communication resources are rather limited in edge devices. It is of great significance to achieve communication efficiency when a large number of edge devices regularly transmit local updates with millions or even billions of dimensional parameters. Thus, how to accelerate the learning process by incorporating various edge devices with resource and energy constraints is a challenging issue.

Second, edge devices are equipped with various processing units with different computing capabilities. How to make edge learning adapted to different hardware environments is challenging. Device heterogeneity significantly affects system performance due to variability in hardware (CPU, memory). For the given condition and resource constraints of each device, how to manage the computational and hardware resources to maximize the training process efficiency is crucial for us to explore.

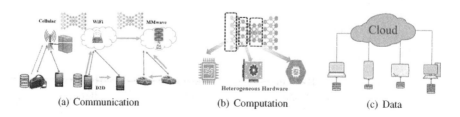

(a) Communication   (b) Computation   (c) Data

Figure 1.3 Challenges of edge learning from the perspective of communication, computation, and data.

Third, traditional centralized learning frameworks require to upload all training data from different sources to a remote data server, which relies on an unrealistic assumption that their training data are independent and identically distributed (IID). This assumption is sometimes not reasonable in the real world; it is common for users' data to have a dependence relationship, so the data in each device may have different probability distributions. The data distributions generated in different devices are vary from one another, which will degrade the model accuracy under traditional distributed training algorithms. The problem of non-IID data is difficult because mobile devices usually hesitate to share their data, and it is hard to get information about data distribution.

1.4.2   Hard to Protect Due to Vulnerable Edge Devices

Security and privacy issues are drawing more and more attention. We illustrate the privacy and security challenges of edge learning in Fig. 1.4. In the cloud-edge environment, security and privacy are far more difficult to guarantee than in the cloud. Since the data are generated and stored in users' own devices, privacy and security are important issues that should be considered in edge learning. The training data may contain privacy-sensitive information, such as location, health records, and manufacturing information. In traditional machine learning, directly uploading the original datasets to the centralized server or exchanging the training data among edge devices can have a high risk of privacy leakage. Although many studies have proposed sharing model updates instead of the raw data [198], edge learning still faces sensitive information leakage when communicating model updates during the training process.

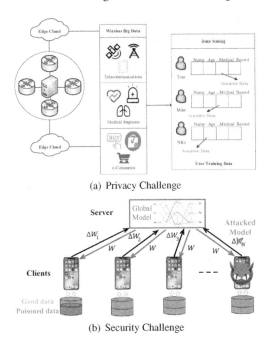

(a) Privacy Challenge

(b) Security Challenge

Figure 1.4 Challenge of edge learning from the perspective of privacy and security.

For instance, a third-party or centralized server may extract memory information of worker nodes from the uploaded model weights. How to guarantee the communication security throughout the training process is a significant problem to be resolved. Furthermore, the trustworthiness of the worker nodes needs to be considered to avoid malicious attacks.

1.4.3 Hard to Manage Due to Complex Edge Environment

Collaborative learning architecture enables learning beyond the cluster environment. Edge learning enables the use of all the cloud, edge servers, end devices in a collaborative manner, which is expected to increase the total computing power by multiple orders of magnitude.

In the scenario of big data analytics, operating large-scale machine learning applications often results in distributed processing and parallel computing, and handling the collaboration between edge nodes - especially in the heterogeneous environment - has become a promising research direction for both algorithm design and system implementation. We intend to elaborate an efficient distributed platform, which is compatible with the heterogeneous environment and fully exploits the capacity of edge devices when conducting machine learning applications. To achieve this goal, the major challenge is managing a huge number of heterogeneous devices in the complex edge environment to achieve a scalable edge learning system.

1.4.4 Hard to Collaborate Due to Lack of Participant

Another main challenge in edge learning is data islands, i.e., each client maintains its local data and has no incentive for contributing data to model training if no reward is granted. Thus, we must motivate a large number of clients to participate in edge learning to break the limitations inherent in isolated data islands. The power of the existing edge-based machine learning systems relies heavily on the quality of worker nodes' local model updates. Therefore, a fair incentive mechanism needs to be developed to achieve reliable participation.

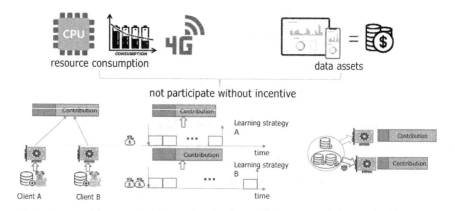

Figure 1.5 Challenges in edge device collaboration.

How to build a beneficial ecosystem for sustainable development of edge learning is a crucial issue. In Fig. 1.5, we illustrate the difficulty of collaboration due to lack of incentive. We face two main challenges: (1) from the worker nodes' perspective, how to recruit and retain more participants to improve the model efficiency, and (2) from the server-side perspective, how to evaluate each participant's contribution during the training process.

1.5 The Scope and Organization of This Book

In this section, we discuss the scope and organization of this book. An overview of organization is shown in Fig. 1.6.

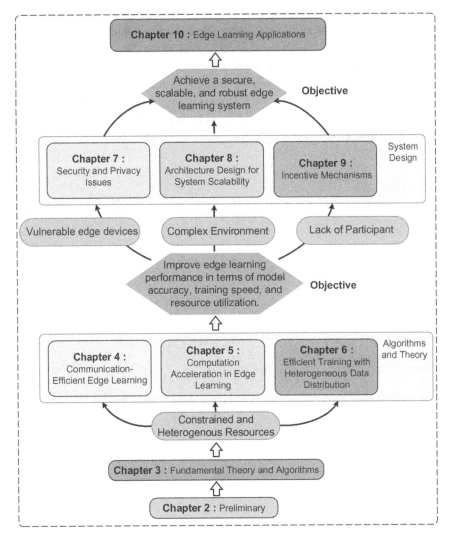

Figure 1.6 The scope and organization of this book.

Specifically, we first introduce the preliminary knowledge about edge learning, including the deep learning models, basic optimization algorithms, architectures, and synchronization modes (in Chapter 2). Then, to solve the basic optimization problem in edge learning, some fundamental theory and advanced training algorithms are explored in Chapter 3.

To deal with the constrained and heterogeneous resources in the edge environment, we introduce the edge learning technologies from the following aspects: communication-efficient technologies (Chapter 4), computation acceleration (Chapter 5), and heterogeneous data distribution (Chapter 6). Mainstream approaches are proposed to improve edge learning performance in terms of model accuracy, training speed, and resource utilization.

Apart from the investigation of algorithms and theory, we also present the details about the system design. Security guarantees and privacy protection mechanisms dealing with vulnerable edge devices are summarized in Chapter 7. In order to adapt to a complex environment, data parallelism, model parallelism, and hierarchical architecture are used in training procedure (in Chapter 8). Moreover, we explore the incentive mechanisms for edge learning to motivate the edge nodes to contribute to model training (in Chapter 9). After introducing how to design a secure, scalable, and robust edge learning system, we discuss the popular programming frameworks for edge learning and present the inspiration of how to implement learning into realistic scenarios (Chapter 10).

2 Preliminary

In this chapter, we first introduce the background of edge computing and the deep learning models that are widely used in edge learning. Then, we introduce the basic machine learning algorithms, architectures, and synchronization mode for edge learning.

2.1 Background of Edge Computing

With the rapid development of IoT, mobile computing, and big data technology, and the rapid popularization of the intelligent services, cloud computing can no longer meet the high requirements for low latency in scenarios such as autopilot, virtual reality / augmented reality, industrial control, and smart manufacturing. With the continuous improvement of the perception ability of mobile devices, the scale of its perception data and the computational complexity of data processing are growing exponentially. All data must be uploaded to a centralized server in the cloud and returned to the corresponding device after calculation. The explosive growth of data has also aggravated the network load, which seriously affects service quality and results in delays in response, network congestion, and other issues. In summary, the centralized cloud computing model cannot meet the explosive growth of data processing requirements in the terminal environment.

In order to solve these problems, a new computing paradigm, edge computing, is proposed. The basic idea of edge computing is to process data closer to where the data is generated or used, and to provide service functions near the edge of the network. The edge of the network can be any entity equipped with an edge computing platform from the data source to the cloud computing center. These entities have computing, storage, network, and application service capabilities to provide users with reliable, real-time, and intelligent computing services. By converging edge resources and providing services nearby, edge computing can reduce network traffic, provide real-time services, and reduce the load of cloud computing centers.

2.1.1 Edge Computing Paradigms

Computing task processing in the edge environment usually requires edge devices to perform computations based on distributed collaboration. Its core is efficiently allocating computing, storage, and network resources in the edge environment to realize the dynamic deployment of tasks and data and meet the needs of users for service quality. To achieve the effective integration of resources and adapt to the diverse service needs of users, researchers have conducted research on computing, storage, and network resources from the perspective of collaborative optimization, and have made a series of breakthroughs. In the following, we will introduce some edge computing paradigms and technologies of edge computing.

The core concept of the edge computing can be traced back to peer-to-peer (P2P) computing and content distribution networks (CDN). CDN is an Internet-based cache network. CDN deploys cache servers in various places and provides load balancing, content distribution, scheduling, and other functional modules on the central platform. The user is directed to the nearest cache server by the CDN to reduce network congestion and improve user access response speed and hit rate. CDN emphasizes content (data) backup and caching, while edge computing emphasizes computing capabilities. Furthermore, CDN is limited to CDN cache servers, while edge computing includes any entity equipped with edge computing platforms from the data source to the cloud computing center.

Cloudlets: As resource portals, cloudlets provide real-time interaction and cloud service gateway functions for mobile computing applications. We illustrate the architecture of a cloudlet in Fig. 2.1. Cloudlets support resource-intensive mobile applications that interact in real time, such as augmented reality applications, remotely rendered video games, etc. The cloudlet location is usually a one-hop wireless connection from the end user, such as deployed on a cellular network base station or Wi-Fi base station. It can provide a low-latency response to end users' computing tasks. In a network composed of multiple cloudlet self-organizing connections, computing tasks can be executed locally, directly connected to micro-clouds, or routed to other cloudlets for execution to achieve load balancing.

Micro data center: A micro data center is a miniaturized or modular data center architecture at the edge of the network, as shown in Fig. 2.2. It is deployed closer to the data source to reduce the communication delay and bandwidth cost of the IoT and

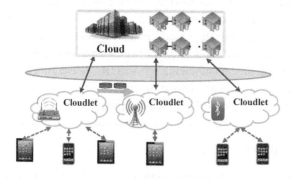

Figure 2.1 The architecture of a cloudlet.

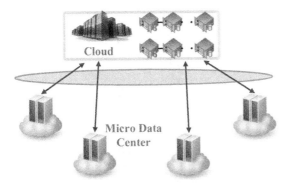

Figure 2.2 Illustration of a micro data center.

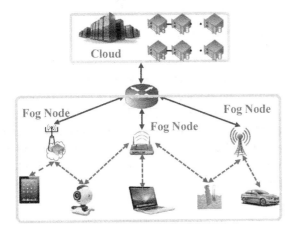

Figure 2.3 Illustration of a fog computing framework.

CDN. Solving different types of workload has different requirements for traditional cloud computing architecture software and hardware resources.

Fog computing: Cisco proposed the concept of fog computing in 2012. Subsequently, Cisco teamed up with ARM, Dell, Intel, Microsoft, and Princeton University to establish the OpenFog in 2015. The fog computing node is composed of fog nodes with relatively weak performance but widely dispersed geographical locations, as shown in Fig. 2.3. As an extension of cloud computing, fog computing emphasizes the distance between the end user and the computing bearer node, delay, backbone network bandwidth overhead, adaptive mobility, and location awareness. This makes it possible to obtain better service quality experience and edge data feature analysis. In recent years, researchers have studied fog computing from the aspects of basic architecture, resource management, task scheduling, energy saving, and data security, and have achieved promising research results.

Mobile edge computing: Mobile edge computing (MEC), also known as multi-access edge computing, was first proposed by the European Telecommunications Standards

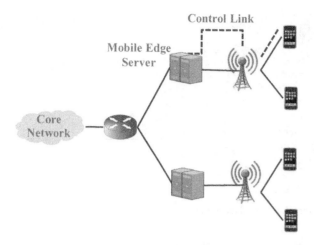

Figure 2.4 Illustration of mobile edge computing.

Institute (ETSI). We illustrate the architecture of MEC in Fig. 2.4. The core idea of MEC is to provide computing and storage resources in the base stations of the radio access network (RAN), which can respond to user computing tasks and data requests at a closer location. Also, MEC has led to the rapid development of research in a series of related fields and has been officially incorporated into the 5G standard. Combined with the Internet of Everything, it has produced many promising technological leaps and widely deployed application platforms.

2.2   Deep Learning Models and Collaborative Training Approaches

2.2.1   Deep Learning Models

Many machine learning models - e.g., naive Bayes, logistic regression, K-nearest neighbors, decision tree, and support vector machine (SVM) [103] - have been developed to hone the prediction abilities of machines. Some ensemble learning methods such as boosting are widely used in many data mining competitions and industrial applications [238]. The boosting algorithm works by sequentially applying weak learners to update the parameters and then combining the high performance of these sequential weak learners as strong learners.

As large-scale datasets such as ImageNet datasets [52], COCO datasets [176], SUN-RGBD [271] are obtained in industry and research, deep neural networks (DNN) are widely used in computer vision, natural language processing, recommendation systems, and other areas. Convolutional neural network (CNN) is one of the typical DNN models, which is a combination of a convolutional layer, activation functions, and pooling layers. Since AlexNet [147] greatly improved in the ImageNet LSVRC-2010 contest, a CNN has been explosively developed. A lot of studies focus on improving the performance of CNN architecture. A simple but useful idea is to add several base modules - e.g., VGG [267] and GoogleNet [282] - which makes the networks go deeper and wider. However, increasing network depth purely would make DNNs more difficult to train and cannot always improve the performance of the model. Recently, some other CNN architecture optimization methods have been proposed. Hu et al. [114] focused on channel relation and introduced SENet, which consists of squeezing global spatial information by global average pooling to generate channel-wise information and using adaptive recalibration to activate the information aggregated by previous squeeze operations. SKNet [165] applies multiple kernel sizes to generate different local receptive fields (RFs) of input, fuses the multiple sizes of RFs, and aggregates the feature maps in selection weights. In addition, a large number of recurrent neural networks (RNN) and variant RNN - such as Clockwork RNN [146], Grid LSTM [137], and FastGRNN [149] - have been introduced in the last decade.

The attention mechanism is an innovation in neural network architecture and has achieved huge success in natural language processing and computer vision [108, 296, 330]. After the attention mechanism was introduced, many efficient and effective variants have been proposed, such as XLNet [360] and Bert [55]. Transformer-relative methods promote the development of a pretrained model that can be fine tuned with a few additional layers to achieve state-of-the-art models for varied tasks, such as question answering.

Although such deeper CNN models can work at high performance level, these models contain a huge number of parameters that do not work well on devices. Researchers have paid great attention to designing DNNs to support on-device training and inference. SqueezeNet [122] replaces 3×3 filters with 1×1 filters, decreases the number of input channels to 3×3 filters, and downsamples late in the network, to cut down the size of the model and maintain the same level of accuracy as AlexNet on the ImageNet dataset. MobileNet v2 [247] has been proposed by inverting residual connections and replacing the nonlinear activation function with linear bottleneck layers in a low-dimensional manifold of interest. GhostNet [92] applies a series of linear operations to generate more feature maps, which is normally generated by convolutional operation and pooling operation, and archives state-of-the-art performance of lightweight deep convolution neural network.

2.2.2   Collaborative Training Approaches

Nowadays, with the rapid growth of training data as well as the size of machine learning models, traditional single-machine-based methods cannot learn efficiently due to their limited hardware resources. Distributed machine learning is promising, as computation can be parallelized in multiple nodes. For large-scale machine learning, one key issue is how to configure these distributed machines efficiently and robustly. There are two pertinent parallelism schemes to handle distributed machine learning applications: data parallelism and model parallelism [236]. In data parallelism, data are distributed over multiple nodes, and a global machine learning model is cooperatively optimized. In model parallelism, a neural network is divided into several pieces, and these pieces are separately trained at distributed workers. Workers are organized in parameter server architecture [156] and/or peer-to-peer (P2P) architecture (also known as decentralized architecture) [48, 299]. Parameter server architecture consists of two types of node named server and worker, and the learning process proceeds by iteratively conducting update aggregation and model synchronization. In P2P architecture, each worker has neighbors and can communicate with its neighbors. Each worker aggregates its parameters with its neighbors and then updates parameters locally. This will be discussed in greater detail in Chapter 6.

Recently, federated learning has been proposed to enable mobile devices to collaboratively train models without exposing their data. Federated learning involves the participation of heterogeneous devices that have different dataset characteristics, computation capabilities, energy states, and cooperation availability. Thus, it alleviates the cost of computation and communication of the traditional centralized learning paradigm. However, there are still some challenges in federated learning - for example, training data are non-independent identically distributed (non-IID), and workers are heterogeneous and vulnerable.

2.3   Basic Machine Learning Algorithms

2.3.1   Learning Problem Statement

The aim is to solve the sum optimization problem, which is the general objective in the field of machine learning. In particular, we use $f(\omega, \xi_i)$ to represent the loss of model ω fitting sample ξ_i, equivalently $f_i(\omega)$ for short. Then, the machine learning problem is to find a model ω to minimize the fitting loss of all samples in the whole dataset.

$$\min_{\omega} F(\omega) = \frac{1}{N} \sum_{i=1}^{N} f_i(\omega). \tag{2.1}$$

Then we introduce smooth and convex properties of the objective function. These properties are generally applied to analyze the convergence rate and the generalization ability of the training algorithm.

DEFINITION 2.1 (*L-Smooth Function*)   *The objective function $F(\cdot)$ is L-smooth ($L > 0$), if $\|\nabla F(\omega_1) - \nabla F(\omega_2)\| \leq L\|\omega_1 - \omega_2\|, \forall \omega_1, \omega_2$, i.e.,*

$$F(\omega_2) - F(\omega_1) \leq \nabla F(\omega_1)(\omega_2 - \omega_1)^T + \frac{L}{2}\|\omega_2 - \omega_1\|^2. \tag{2.2}$$

DEFINITION 2.2 (*Strongly Convex Function*)   *The objective function $F(\cdot)$ is μ-strongly convex ($\mu > 0$) if*

$$F(\omega_2) - F(\omega_1) \geq \nabla F(\omega_1)(\omega_2 - \omega_1)^T + \frac{\mu}{2}\|\omega_2 - \omega_1\|^2. \tag{2.3}$$

DEFINITION 2.3 (Convex Function)   *The objective function is convex, if*

$$F(\omega_2) - F(\omega_1) \geq \nabla F(\omega_1)(\omega_2 - \omega_1)^{\mathrm{T}}. \tag{2.4}$$

We present some examples of loss functions of popular machine learning models. Let $\xi_i = (x_i, y_i)$, where x_i denotes the features of the i-th training data sample, and y_i denotes the label. In linear regression, the loss function is $f_i(\omega) = \frac{1}{2}\|y_i - \omega^{\mathrm{T}}x_i\|^2$. In logistic regression, the loss function is $f_i(\omega) = \log(1 + e^{-y_i \mathbf{a}_i^{\mathrm{T}}\omega}) + \frac{\lambda}{2}\|\omega\|^2$. In CNN, the loss function is cross-entropy on cascaded linear and nonlinear transforms. The objective functions are strongly convex in linear regression and logistic regression and nonconvex in CNN and deep learning models.

2.3.2   Basic Machine Learning Algorithms

In this section, we mainly focus on optimization algorithms for edge learning that will work as local optimizers in each device or server. The gradient descent (GD) optimization algorithm is the most widely employed black-box optimizer for training a machine model. Currently, there are three main types of gradient descent methods: batch gradient descent (GD / Batch GD), stochastic gradient descent (SGD), and mini-batch stochastic gradient descent (Mini-batch SGD). The most popular Gradient Descent optimization algorithm is SGD [131, 319, 409], which was first proposed in 1951.

2.3.2.1   Gradient Descent

GD is also called batch gradient descent because the gradient of the objective function is calculated by using all the training data before starting the backward propagation pass to adjust the weights. This is called one epoch or iteration. The update process can be expressed as,

$$\omega_{t+1} = \omega_t - \eta_t \nabla F(\omega_t), \tag{2.5}$$

where ω_t denotes the model parameter vector in the tth iteration and η_t denotes the learning rate (also called step size) in the tth iteration.

However, with the rise of big data analytics, the efficiency of deterministic optimization algorithms has become the bottleneck of application processing speed. In order to clearly understand this challenge, we will use the GD algorithm to solve the linear regression problem as an example.

The objective function of a linear regression problem can be formulated as:

$$F(\omega) = \frac{1}{N}\sum_{i=1}^{N} f(\omega, \xi_i) \tag{2.6}$$

$$= \frac{1}{N}\sum_{i=1}^{N}(\omega^{\mathrm{T}}x_i - y_i)^2, \tag{2.7}$$

where $w \in R^d$ represents the model parameter and $\{(x_i, y_i) : i = 1, 2, \ldots, N$, and $x_i \in R^d\}$ are the training samples. If we employ the GD algorithm to optimize this objective function, the update rule can be described as:

$$\omega_{t+1} = \omega_t - \eta \nabla F(\omega_t) \tag{2.8}$$

$$= \omega_t - \frac{2\eta}{N} \sum_{i=1}^{N} x_i((\omega_i)^\mathsf{T} x_i - y_i). \tag{2.9}$$

We can observe that the per-iteration computational overhead for model update will linearly increase, following the growth of data amount n and data dimension d. When training more complex models (e.g., the neural network) and optimization scenarios (e.g., the second-order methods), deterministic optimization algorithms will suffer from huge computation overhead, leading to performance bottlenecks. Fortunately, we can conquer this challenge by using statistics. Intuitively, although the amount and dimensions of data are are very large, we can still figure out the approximation or obtain the alternative by sampling the dimensions randomly. Therefore, we can employ different kinds of stochastic optimization algorithm to improve these deterministic optimization methods. We will discuss one of the most widely used algorithm, the SGD [245] method, in the next subsection.

2.3.2.2   Stochastic Gradient Descent

The SGD [245] method employs the random sampling of the training data, and the corresponding update rule can be formulated as

$$\omega_{t+1} = \omega_t - \eta_t \nabla f_{i_t}(\omega_t), \tag{2.10}$$

where i_t is the data index of the random sampling in the t-th iteration and η_t is the learning rate in the current iteration. The concept of learning rate is very similar to the step length of different kinds of optimization method (e.g., the *steepest descent* method and *Newton's* method). Also, $f_{i_t}(w_t)$ can be the value the loss function after conducting regularization, based on the i_t-th data sample and the model w_t. The details of regularization will be introduced in the next chapter. In addition to this formulation, we will present the algorithm of SGD (Algorithm 2.1).

According to the algorithm of SGD, it is reasonable to transfer the experience loss function to the average value of the sampling loss function. As SGD employs the bootstrapping (i.e., random sampling with replacement) for the gradient calculation, we can obtain the unbiased estimation of standard gradients calculated by all the data-, i.e., $\mathbb{E}_i \nabla f_{i_t}(w_t) = \nabla f(w_t)$.

Meanwhile, as SGD only chooses one sample from the entire dataset, the corresponding computational overhead is significantly reduced. Consequently, it is natural to replace the traditional GD by using the SGD method, so as to improve the training efficiency of the DNN model.

Algorithm 2.1 Stochastic Gradient Descent Method

Input: Training dataset $\mathbb{X}$

Output: Updated model parameters w_T

1: **procedure** SGD(Training dataset $\mathbb{X}$)

2:     Initialize model parameters as w_0;

3:     **for** $t = 0, 1, \ldots, T - 1$ **do**

4:         Randomly select a sample x_i from $\mathbb{X}$, where $i_t \in \{1, \ldots, n\}$;

5:         Calculate the gradient $\nabla f_{i_t}(w_t)$ based on x_i ;

6:         Update the model parameters by using $w_{t+1} = w_t - \eta_t \nabla f_{i_t}(w_t)$;

7:     **end for**

8:     **return** the latest model parameters w_T;

9: **end procedure**

2.3.2.3 Mini-Batch Stochastic Gradient Descent

There is a common revision of SGD, called the mini-batch SGD, which is widely used in optimization of modern machine learning applications. Its key difference from SGD is that mini-batch SGD uses a a batch of samples in each iteration, instead of just using one sample of data. The number of samples contained in the batch is called *batch size* [158]; this is a very important hyper-parameter that impacts the training efficiency and convergence speed. In order to give a clear demonstration of mini-batch SGD, we present the corresponding algorithm (Algorithm 2.2).

Algorithm 2.2 Mini-Batch Stochastic Gradient Descent Method

Input: Training dataset $\mathbb{X}$

Output: Updated model parameters w_T

1: **procedure** SGD(Training dataset $\mathbb{X}$)

2:     Initialize model parameters as w_0;

3:     **for** $t = 0, 1, \ldots, T - 1$ **do**

4:         Randomly select a mini-batch of samples S_t from $\mathbb{X}$, where
         $S_t \in \{1, \ldots, n\}$;

5:         Calculate the corresponding gradients: $\nabla f_{S_t}(w_t) = \frac{1}{|S_t|} \sum_{i \in S_t} \nabla f_i(w_t)$;

6:         Update the model parameters by using $w_{t+1} = w_t - \eta_t \nabla f_{S_t}(w_t)$;

7:     **end for**

8:     **return** the latest model parameters w_T;

9: **end procedure**

2.3.2.4   Convergence Analysis

The training efficiency by using different optimization methods is not only related to the computational overhead in each iteration, but also relies on the convergence speed in theory. Similar to the GD method, SGD owns different convergence speeds under different configurations of the objective function. Therefore, we will present a brief convergence analysis of the SGD method. Understanding the convergence performance can help us better understand to paper's topic of *stochastic compositional optimization* [316, 317].

THEOREM 1   *The objective function $f : R^d \rightarrow R$ is convex, continuously differentiable, and L-Lipschitz continuous with the constant $L > 0$-, i.e., $w^* = \arg\min\limits_{\|w\| \leq D} f(w)$.*

Under the condition of step length $\eta_t = \sqrt{\frac{D^2}{L^2 t}}$, the SGD method owns the following sublinear convergence speed:

$$\mathbb{E}\left[\frac{1}{T}\sum_{t=1}^{T} f(w_t) - f(w^*)\right] \leq \frac{LD}{\sqrt{T}}. \tag{2.11}$$

THEOREM 2   *The objective function $f : R^d \rightarrow R$ is α-convex and β-smooth. Assume the second moment of stochastic gradient is upper bounded-, i.e., $\mathbb{E}_{i_t}\|\nabla f_{i_t}(w_t)\|^2 \leq G^2$, under the condition of step length $\eta_t = \frac{1}{\alpha t}$, the SGD method owns the following linear convergence speed.*

$$\mathbb{E}\left[f(w_T) - f(w^*)\right] \leq \frac{2\beta G^2}{\alpha^2 T}. \tag{2.12}$$

Compared to the GD method, we can observe that the convergence speed of SGD is slower. This is because the stochastic gradient is the unbiased estimation of standard gradients based on the entire dataset, where the estimation introduces variance and uncertainty, leading to the decrease in the algorithm convergence speed.

However, regarding the gradient calculation in each iteration, the GD method requires the calculation of the full gradient of all the n samples, while the SGD method only requires the calculation of one sample's gradient. This property guarantees that the SGD method has a much lower computational complexity than the GD, especially with a very large number of data samples.

2.4   Learning Architectures: Parameter Server and Decentralized Learning

There are two types of edge learning architectures: parameter server and decentralized learning architectures. A typical distributed architecture is the parameter server structure. In this architecture, the nodes are divided into two categories: the parameter server, which takes charge of the storing and management of the global model parameters, and the worker, which only need to communicate with the parameter server to pull or push updates and has no need to be aware of other participating machines. This means that the computation task of a worker is independent of other

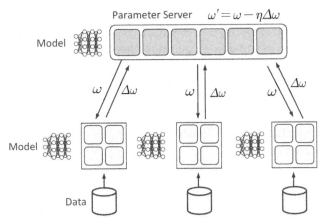

(a) Illustration of the architecture of parameter server.

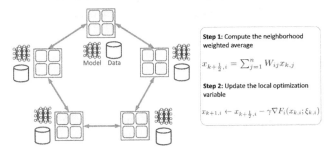

(b) Illustration of the decentrlized architecture.

Figure 2.5 Example of different architectures.

participators, so asynchronous working is possible [157]. An example of this scheme is shown in Fig. 2.5-(a).

The decentralized architecture has no central node, all the nodes are organized in a decentralized topology, and they only communicate with their neighbors [171] instead of with the parameter server. In the decentralized architecture, each node maintains its own local model; decentralized algorithms can usually be applied to any connected topology of network. Fig. 2.5-(b) shows the key steps of decentralized parallel stochastic gradient descent (D-PSGD) algorithms. Assume that the decentralized communication topology can be defined with an undirected graph with weights: (V, W), V denotes the set of n computational nodes: $V := \{1, 2, \ldots, n\}$. $W \in \mathbb{R}^{n \times n}$ is a symmetric doubly stochastic matrix, which means (i) $W_{ij} \in [0, 1], \forall i, j$; (ii) $W_{ij} = W_{ji}$ for all i, j; and (iii) $\sum_j W_{ij} = 1$ for all i. W_{ij} is used to encode how much node j can affect node i, while $W_{ij} = 0$ means node i and j are disconnected. The D-PSGD algorithm is a synchronous parallel algorithm. All nodes are usually synchronized by a clock. Each node maintains its own local variable and runs the protocol concurrently. In each iteration k, all the nodes compute the stochastic gradient $\nabla F_i \left(x_{k,i}; \xi_{k,i} \right)^2$ using the current local variable $x_{k,i}$, where k is the iteration number and i denotes the node index. When the synchronization barrier is met, each node exchanges local information with its neighbors and averages the local variables and received variables via the following expression (**Step 1** in Fig. 2.5-(b)):

$$x_{k+\frac{1}{2},i} = \sum_{j=1}^{n} W_{ij} x_{k,j}^{b} \qquad (2.13)$$

Then each node updates its local variable using the average and the local stochastic gradient (**Step 2** in Fig. 2.5-(b)):

$$x_{k+1,i} \leftarrow x_{k+\frac{1}{2},i} - \gamma \nabla F_i \left(x_{k,i}; \xi_{k,i} \right)^{c}. \qquad (2.14)$$

Compared with parameter server, on one hand, decentralized learning architecture can outperform the parameter server by avoiding the communication traffic jam; on the other hand, the cost of synchronization may be more complicated to analyze.

2.5   Synchronization Modes

There are three main modes for edge learning to update and synchronize the model parameters: bulk synchronous parallel (BSP), asynchronous parallel (ASP) and stale synchronous parallel (SSP). The synchronization processes are illustrated in Fig. 2.6.

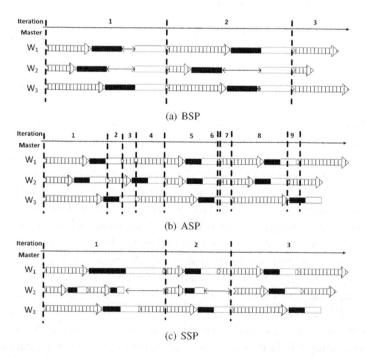

Figure 2.6 Illustration of different synchronization modes.

2.5.1   Bulk Synchronous Parallel (BSP)

BSP is a widely used synchronization method in distributed machine learning. In each iteration, all workers compute the gradients via their local datasets and send the gradients to the parameter server for synchronization. Then the parameter server updates the global model based on the average of gradients and transmits the updated model to all workers before the next iteration. This process repeats until the model converges.

In this synchronization mode, the workers can achieve high convergence quality in each iteration. Because of the inconsistent progress of each worker, faster workers need to wait for slower workers when aggregating the results-, i.e., the slow workers will slow down the training progress and incur wasted computational resources [345, 409]. To further improve the training performance of BSP, overlap synchronization parallel (OSP) [310] has been proposed to reduce the waiting time of fast workers by allowing multiple steps of local computation and conducting computation and communication in an overlapped manner.

2.5.2   Asynchronous Parallel (ASP)

ASP is a totally asynchronous mode in which all workers compute gradients and pull/push updates in an independent manner. They do not need to wait for each other during the training process. The worker who finishes first will continue on to the next iteration of training. In this way, the time waiting for a slow worker is eliminated, which will speed up the training convergence. Compared to BSP, it is faster for ASP to train a given number of epochs. However, some slower workers would send delayed or outdated updates to the parameter server, and download a different version of the global model form parameter server, resulting in degraded performance, lower accuracy, and poor convergence rate [315]. To this end, ASP is not stable in terms of model convergence.

2.5.3   Stale Synchronous Parallel (SSP)

In SSP, a certain degree of progress inconsistency is allowed, but there is a threshold s to this inconsistency, which we call the staleness value. SSP guarantees that the number of iteration between the fastest worker and slowest worker cannot exceed a specific value s. To some extent, the SSP can be regarded as a combination of BSP and ASP. This synchronous mode ensures that the difference in the number of iterations between workers is no larger than s. Therefore, there is no waiting time among workers unless the number of iterations between the fastest worker and the slowest worker exceeds the threshold [45]. From the preceding analysis, it is easy to understand that the convergence quality of each iteration is worse than BSP, and SSP may take more iterations to achieve the same convergent rate.

3 Fundamental Theory and Algorithms of Edge Learning

In this chapter, we first provide convergence results of SGD methods that are usually adopted to solve the machine learning problem. Then we introduce advanced training algorithms, including momentum SGD, hyper-parameter-based algorithms, and optimization algorithms for deep learning models. Finally, we give theoretical frameworks about how to deal with the staleness gradient incurred by ASP or SSP.

3.1 Distributed Machine Learning and the Convergence Theory

In this part, we first focus on the distributed SGD method under the parameter server architecture, which is applicable to various model optimizations with proven efficiency in terms of scalability and convergence rate. As discussed in the preliminary chapter, parameter server architecture consists of two types of nodes, named server nodes and worker nodes. Specifically, the learning process proceeds by iteratively running two procedures – i.e., pushing the local gradients and pulling the global model. In the push operation, each worker computes the local gradient separately according to its own dataset, and then sends the gradient to the server for aggregation. In the pull operation, after receiving gradients from workers, the server updates the global model and sends back the parameters of the global model for the next step of computation, also known as model synchronization.

The general machine learning problem is to solve the sum optimization problem that derives a model parameter best fitting the training data samples. Specifically, we consider a training dataset with N data samples $\{(\mathbf{x}_i, y_i)\}_{i=1}^{N}$ and use $f_i(\omega)$ to represent the loss value of model ω fitting the ith sample, where $\omega \in \mathbb{R}^d$ denotes the model parameter vector with dimension d. Then, the machine learning problem is to find a model ω that minimizes the fitting loss of all samples in the whole dataset.

$$\min_{\omega \in \mathbb{R}^d} F(\omega) = \frac{1}{N} \sum_{i=1}^{N} f_i(\omega). \tag{3.1}$$

Generally, most popular machine learning models have the property smoothness. Here are some examples of loss functions. For the ith data sample $(\mathbf{x}_i, y_i)$, $\mathbf{x}_i$ denotes the feature of the ith training data samples, and y_i denotes the label. In linear regression and logistic regression, the loss functions can be formally written as follows.

$$f(\omega, \xi_i) = \frac{1}{2}\|y_i - \omega^{\mathrm{T}} x_i\|^2 \tag{3.2}$$

$$f(\omega, \xi_i) = \log(1 + e^{-y_i a_i^{\mathrm{T}} \omega}) + \frac{\lambda}{2}\|\omega\|^2 \tag{3.3}$$

In CNN, the loss function is cross-entropy on cascaded linear and nonlinear transforms. The objective functions in linear regression and logistic regression are strongly convex, while in CNN and deep learning models, the objective functions are nonconvex.

SGD methods are usually adopted to solve the machine learning problem. Instead of using the whole dataset to compute the gradient, SGD randomly draws a mini-batch of data samples and computes stochastic gradient $\mathbf{g}(\omega; \xi)$. Compared to the batch method, the stochastic method is more efficient for large-scale learning problem according to practical and theoretical analysis. In SGD, the model is updated in iteration $t, t \in \mathbb{N}$ as

$$\omega_{t+1} = \omega_t - \eta_t \mathbf{g}(\omega_t; \xi_t). \tag{3.4}$$

For GD and SGD based optimization algorithms, we make the following assumptions that are widely used to establish the convergence rate of the algorithms.

ASSUMPTION **1.1 L-Smooth:** *The objective function $F : \mathbb{R}^d \to \mathbb{R}$ is continuously differentiable, and the gradient function of F is Lipschitz continuous with Lipschitz constant $L > 0$; i.e., for any $\omega_1, \omega_2 \in \mathbb{R}$, we have*

$$\|\nabla F(\omega_1) - \nabla F(\omega_2)\| \leq L\|\omega_1 - \omega_2\|.$$

ASSUMPTION **1.2 Bounded Value:** *In the sequence of iterations, the global synchronized parameters $\omega_1, \omega_2, \cdots$ are contained in an open set over which F is bounded below by a scalar F_{inf}, i.e., for any iteration t, $F_{inf} \leq F(\omega_t)$.*

ASSUMPTION **1.3 Unbiased Gradient:** *The stochastic gradient is unbiased for any parameter ω,*

$$\mathbb{E}_\xi[g_\xi(\omega)] = \nabla F(\omega),$$

where ξ is a random variable represented the selected mini-batch.

ASSUMPTION **1.4 Bounded Variance of Gradient:** *The variance of stochastic gradient is bound by a constant σ^2, i.e.,*

$$\mathbb{E}_\xi\left[\|g_\xi(\omega) - \nabla F(\omega)\|^2\right] \leq \sigma^2.$$

In a distributed learning framework, datasets are distributed over a large number of workers. In each iteration of distributed SGD, each worker i independently computes the local stochastic gradient and pushes the gradient to the server. After receiving gradients from all workers, the server computes the average of them and updates global model as the following:

$$\omega_{t+1} = \omega_t - \frac{\eta_t}{P} \sum_{i=1}^{P} g(\omega_t^i; \xi_t^i), \tag{3.5}$$

where $g(\omega_t^i; \xi_t^i)$ is the local gradient computed from random sample ξ_t^i and parameter ω_t^i.

In what follows, we provide insights into the behavior of a distributed SGD by establishing its convergence properties and worst-case iteration complexity bounds. A preview of such properties was given in the preliminary chapter, but now we prove these and other interesting results in detail, all within the context of a generalized distributed SGD algorithm. We start by analyzing our distributed SGD algorithm when it is invoked to minimize a strongly convex objective function, where it is possible to establish a global rate of convergence to the optimal objective value. This is followed by analyses when our distributed SGD algorithm is employed to minimize a generic nonconvex objective.

THEOREM 3.1 (Convergence Rate of Distributed SGD with Strongly Convex Objective) *Under Assumption 1, when $F(\cdot)$ is μ-strongly convex and distributed SGD is running with fixed learning rate η for all iterations, and satisfying*

$$\eta \leq \frac{1}{L}, \tag{3.6}$$

then, the expected optimality gap satisfies the following inequality for all $t \in \mathbb{N}$:

$$\mathbb{E}F(\omega_{t+1}) - F(\omega^*)$$

$$\leq (1 - \eta\mu)^t \left[F(\omega_1) - F(\omega^*) - \frac{3L\eta\sigma^2}{2P\mu} \right] + \frac{3L\eta\sigma^2}{2P\mu}. \tag{3.7}$$

Discussion. Based on this result, when $T \to \infty$, we have

$$\mathbb{E}F(\omega_{T+1}) - F(\omega^*) \leq \frac{3L\eta\sigma^2}{2P\mu}, \tag{3.8}$$

which proves the convergence property of distributed SGD. Under the fixed learning rate and based on this equation, we know that a smaller learning rate makes the convergence slower down, but allows one to arrive closer to the optimal value. For sufficiently large T, by setting $\eta = o(1/T)$, we have

$$\lim_{T \to \infty} [\mathbb{E}F(\omega_{t+1}) - F(\omega^*)] \preceq \frac{1}{PT}, \tag{3.9}$$

where the inequality follows according to $\lim_{T \to \infty}[(1 - o(T))^T] = 0$. It implies that if the objective function is strongly convex, distributed SGD admits a linear convergence rate – i.e., $O(1/T)$ – which is same order as SGD under fixed learning rate.

THEOREM 3.2 (Convergence Rate of Distributed SGD with Non-Convex Objective) *Bound of the Expected Average-Squared Gradient: Under Assumption 1, suppose that distributed SGD is running with fixed learning rate η for all iteration. Then, the* *expected average-squared gradients of general objective function $F(\cdot)$ satisfies the following inequalities for all $T \in \mathbb{N}$:*

$$\frac{1}{T}\sum_{t=1}^{T}\mathbb{E}\|\nabla F(\omega_t)\|^2 \le \frac{2|F(\omega_1) - F(\omega^*)|}{\eta T} + \frac{3L\eta\sigma^2}{P}. \qquad (3.10)$$

This result suggests that distributed SGD essentially admits the convergence rate $O(1/\sqrt{T})$. More specifically, distributed SGD runs with the convergence rate $O(1/\sqrt{PT})$, which means it has the linear speedup property and high efficiency in large-scale distributed learning.

Theorem 3.1 illustrates the interplay between the step sizes and bounds on the variance of the stochastic directions. When we apply distributed SGD to train a machine learning model, there exists noise in the gradient computation and we cannot obtain a convergence to the optimal value. However, we can choose a small step size in SGD such that the expected objective value could converge linearly to a close point of the optimal value. Also, one can design a decreasing step size in the SGD process to achieve a more efficient convergence rate.

3.2 Advanced Training Algorithm and Corresponding Theory

In this section, we will first introduce the regularization technology for the loss function. Then we state the mainstream of optimization algorithms from the perspective of optimization direction and hyper-parameters. Finally, we will introduce the specific techniques for DNN.

3.2.1 Regularization and Loss Function

For prediction tasks and classification tasks, the object of machine learning is usually to find the model parameter that minimizes the loss function, which measures the difference between true label and the prediction label. The parameter in the learning learning is denoted as ω. Then, for the ith sample, $\xi_i = (x_i, y_i)$, x_i denotes the feature of the training data samples, and y_i denotes the label. Given a parameter ω and the features x_i, the machine learning model gives the prediction label of x_i, denoted by $\hat{y}_i$. The loss function measures the difference between y_i and $\hat{y}_i$.

The loss function includes two parts: the experience risk loss and structure risk loss. The experience risk loss is the measurement of the difference mentioned earlier, while the structure risk loss is called regularization. Regularization is widely used to improve the generalization performance. Specifically, the model tends to overfit the training dataset when the model is more complex, leading to the bad performance in the test dataset. Then the objective of the machine learning based on loss function with regularization can be formulated as

$$f_i(w) = \ell(w; x_i, y_i) + \lambda R(w), \qquad (3.11)$$

where λ is the regularization constant, $\ell(w; x_i, y_i)$ measures the difference between the prediction $\hat{y}_i$ and the true label y_i, and $R(f)$ is the regularization function. In this section, we first introduce the experience risk loss, namely the loss function. Then we discuss various regularization methods that are widely applied to improve the performance of model training.

3.2.1.1   Loss Function

As the machine learning develops, there are some frequently used loss functions such as mean squared error (MSE), mean average error (MAE), and cross entropy loss. MSE is defined as

$$MSE = \frac{\sum_{i=1}^{n}(y_i - \hat{y}_i)^2}{n}. \tag{3.12}$$

And the MAE is defined as

$$MAE = \frac{\sum_{i=1}^{n}|y_i - \hat{y}_i|}{n}. \tag{3.13}$$

For MSE, due to the term of squared error in the expression, the loss value is more sensitive to the incorrect prediction label than MAE. In some situations, the error may be overestimated. MAE uses $|y_i - \hat{y}_i|$ to denote the difference between the prediction $\hat{y}_i$ and the true label y_i, but it is hard to derive the gradient.

For SVM, the widely used loss function can be formulated as

$$f_i(\omega) = \frac{1}{2}\max\{0; 1 - y_i\omega^T x_i\}^2 + \frac{\lambda}{2}\|\omega\|^2, \tag{3.14}$$

where λ is a constant. The SVM loss function is convex and shows good performance in the maximum-margin classification, but it is undifferentiable.

For most CNN models, the loss function is formulated based on the cross-entropy between cascaded linear and nonlinear transforms, which gives strong punishment to the incorrect prediction labels. One example is shown as follows.

$$f_i(\omega) = -(y_i \log(\hat{y}_i)) + (1 - y_i)\log(1 - \hat{y}_i). \tag{3.15}$$

Many basic loss functions use Euclidean distance to characterize the difference between the prediction label and the true label, which performs poorly when the distance is large. Considering the effect of features on the training performance, some loss functions based on the distance of features have been proposed. These methods can achieve entanglement of features by forcing the features of the same classes into a cluster and dispersing features of different classes [169], [170]. For example, interclass angular loss can enlarge the intraclass angle to decrease the confusion level to make learning much easier [121]. These methods can also give a clearer graph interpretation than Euclidean distance. Moreover, to address the mismatch of loss metric, adaptive loss alignment was proposed as a method to choose the hyper-parameters of loss function [115].

3.2.1.2 Regularization

The basic advantage of regularization is the improved generalization of models. The model tends to overfit the training dataset when it is more complex, leading to the bad performance in test dataset. The most widely used regularization method is adding the norm into the objective function – i.e., the L_1 and L_2 norm of the parameter vector. Let $\omega \in R^d$ be the parameter vector with d dimensions, and let ω_i denote the ith element in the parameter vector. In this case, the L_1 norm is

$$R(\omega) = \|\omega\|_1 = \sum_{i=1}^{d} |\omega_i|, \tag{3.16}$$

and the L_2 norm is

$$R(\omega) = \|\omega\|_2 = \sqrt{\sum_{i=1}^{d} \omega_i^2}. \tag{3.17}$$

On the other hand, another kind of method is designed specially for deep neural networks; it uses dropout to repress some neurons to reduce complexity. Previous works find that common optimization methods are very costly when the dataset is large; therefore, some new regularization methods were proposed to improve the convergence speed of training in addition to generalization [7]. As well as speeding up the training, a few algorithms were presented to give a new approach for the regularizations of a complex model such as DNN[334]. And a kind of fast clustering algorithm has a good performance even with small sample size [20]. There are also some methods using brain information or neural networks to make the model more robust to noise and new datasets [243], [168], which gives us new inspiration on how to design new regularization. Such methods try to find the explict regularization of model itself – for example, the model with large initial learning rate [167]. Additionally, an approach to find the optimal linear regularizer by computing hyper-parameters was also presented [278].

3.2.2 Direction Based Optimization

In Chapter 2, we introduce three types of Gradient Descent methods: batch gradient descent (GD/Batch GD), stochastic gradient descent (SGD), and mini-batch stochastic gradient descent (mini-batch SGD). Based on SGD, many variants have been proposed to improve the training efficiency by exploiting momentum and reducing variance. In this part, we first review the basic process of GD and then discuss the advanced SGD-based method.

The most frequently used first-order algorithm is based on GD, which is the most basic and common method to perform optimization. The main idea of GD is to use gradients to update parameters iteratively; then the objective function can converge to an optimal point. The GD method will repeat following two steps until it converges:

(1) Compute the gradient of loss function:

$$\frac{\partial L(\omega)}{\partial \omega_j}, \tag{3.18}$$

where ω_j is the jth element of the parameter vector ω.

(2) Update the parameter with the gradients in its opposite direction:

$$\omega_j := \omega_j - \eta \frac{\partial L(\omega)}{\partial \omega_j}, \tag{3.19}$$

where α is called learning rate or step size.

The advantages of GD is that global optimal can be achieved with enough iterations. However, it costs huge computation resources to calculate all the samples, which may lead to a low convergence rate. In order to speed up the convergence, SGD is proposed to use only one sample for each update, which means that we use an example of the dataset to approximate all the samples.

3.2.2.1   Momentum-Based Algorithms

When using GD or SGD, it does not update to the minimum straightly. Instead, it oscillates beside the best route in parameter space, which slows down the convergence of objective function. To solve this problem, a basic idea called Momentum SGD was proposed. Momentum SGD improves the gradient direction by computing the exponential moving average of all stochastic gradients.

Then the update of Momentum SGD is as follows:

$$m_t = \gamma m_{t-1} + \eta \nabla_{w_{t-1}} F(w_{t-1}),$$
$$w_{t+1} = w_t - m_t, \tag{3.20}$$

where γ is called the momentum factor. The Momentum method cannot only accelerate the convergence especially when learning rate is small; it can also help to get rid of the local minimum.

3.2.2.2   Other Variant Algorithms

After investigating the related work of SGD and stochastic compositional optimization, we summarize the common features of the GD-based optimization as the following: *the objective can be written in a finite-sum or an online expectation structure, where the variance-reduced gradient can be employed to improve the theoretical convergence properties of classical first-order algorithms.*

Motivated by these observations, we present the potential improvement space of these stochastic optimization algorithms mainly in two directions: (1) increasing the data utilization by reducing the variance of the stochastic optimization methods; (2) accelerating the algorithm convergence speed by combining the stochastic optimization methods with other optimization algorithms. As a result, many variant algorithms have been proposed.

Here, we will briefly discuss some widely used variants of the SGD algorithms, including the accelerated gradient descent (AGD) [74], variance reduction algorithms [135] (e.g., stochastic average gradient (SAG) [252], SAGA [50] and Stochastic variance reduced gradient (SVRG) [338]), stochastic coordinate descent [217] and stochastic quasi-Newton method [36]. We take the three pertinent algorithms of SVRG, SAGA and SAG as the example and present their iteration rules of the optimization procedure via Eqs. (3.21)–(3.23).

$$\text{SVRG: } w_{t+1} = w_t - \eta \left(\nabla f_{i_t}(w_t) - \nabla f_{i_t}(\tilde{w}) + \frac{1}{n} \sum_{i=1}^{n} \nabla f_i(\tilde{w}) \right), \tag{3.21}$$

$$\text{SAGA: } w_{t+1} = w_t - \eta \left(\nabla f_{i_t}(w_t) - \nabla f_{i_t}(\phi_i^t) + \frac{1}{n} \sum_{i=1}^{n} \nabla f_i(\phi_i^t) \right), \tag{3.22}$$

$$\text{SAG: } w_{t+1} = w_t - \eta \left(\frac{\nabla f_{i_t}(w_t) - \nabla f_{i_t}(\phi_i^t)}{n} + \frac{1}{n} \sum_{i=1}^{n} \nabla f_i(\phi_i^t) \right). \tag{3.23}$$

In order to better understand the rationale of these methods, we also present the corresponding algorithms via Algorithm 3.1 (for SVRG) and Algorithm 3.2 (for SAGA

Algorithm 3.1 SVRG Method

    Input: Training dataset $\mathbb{X}$

    Output: Updated model parameters w_S

1: **procedure** SVRG(Training dataset $\mathbb{X}$)

2:      Initialize model parameters as $\tilde{w}_0$;

3:      **for** $s = 0, 1, 2, \cdots, S-1$ **do**

4:          $\tilde{w} = \tilde{w}_{s-1}$;

5:          Calculate the precious gradient by using $\tilde{u} = \frac{1}{n} \sum_{i=1}^{n} \nabla f_i(\tilde{w})$;

6:          $w_0 = \tilde{w}$;

7:      **end for**

8:      **for** $t = 0, 1, \cdots, M-1$ **do**

9:          Randomly select a sample x_i from $\mathbb{X}$, where $i_t \in \{1, \cdots, n\}$;

10:         Update the model parameters by using $w_{t+1} = w_t - \eta_t \left(\nabla f_{i_t}(w_t) - \nabla f_{i_t}(\tilde{w}) + \tilde{u} \right)$;

11:      **end for**

12:      **return** $\tilde{w}_S = w_M$;

13: **end procedure**

Algorithm 3.2 SAG and SAGA Methods

Input: Training dataset $\mathbb{X}$

Output: Updated model parameters w_T

1: **procedure** SAGA & SAG(Training dataset $\mathbb{X}$)

2:      Initialize model parameters as w_0 and create the gradient table ϕ^0;

3:      **for** $t = 0, 1, 2, \cdots, T - 1$ **do**

4:          Randomly select a sample x_i from $\mathbb{X}$, where $i_t \in \{1, \cdots, n\}$;

5:          Let $\phi_{i_t}^{t+1} = w_t$ and save $\nabla f_{i_t}(\phi_{i_t}^{t+1})$ in the gradient table;

6:          Update the model parameters;

7:          **if** SAGA **then**

8:              $w_{t+1} = w_t - \eta \left(\nabla f_{i_t}(\phi_{i_t}^{t+1}) - \nabla f_{i_t}(\phi_{i_t}^t) + \frac{1}{n} \sum_{i=1}^n \nabla f_i(\phi_{i_t}^t) \right)$;

9:          **end if**

10:         **if** SAG **then**

11:             $w_{t+1} = w_t - \eta \left(\frac{1}{n} \left(\nabla f_{i_t}(\phi_{i_t}^{t+1}) - \nabla f_{i_t}(\phi_{i_t}^t) \right) + \frac{1}{n} \sum_{i=1}^n \nabla f_i(\phi_{i_t}^t) \right)$;

12:         **end if**

13:      **end for**

14:      **return** the latest model parameters w_T;

15: **end procedure**

---

and SAG), respectively. It is worth noting that the evaluation metric of stochastic optimization algorithms is different from that of deterministic optimization algorithms. The main difference is the focus on the expectation of the stochastic samples.

Besides, SAGA, SARAH, and Spider are all basic variance methods. But they all have some drawbacks. SAGA is with inflexibility and a large oracle complexity, so Momentum is used to accelerate SAGA and decrease its oracle complexity [180]. SARAH++ and a modified version of SARAH were proposed to decrease total complexity and get sublinear convergence [220]. Spider uses an accuracy-dependent step size which slows down the convergence, and performance is not so good when objective function is nonsmooth. With large, constant step size, SpiderBoost was proposed to process nonsmooth objectives with convergence and obtain best oracle complexity [324]. In addition, to analyze the effect of random reshuffling, it is proven that variance reduction methods, such as SAGA, with random reshuffling can get linear convergence, and a new algorithm called amortized variance reduction gradient (AVRG) was presented with balanced gradient computation [25].

3.2.3   Algorithms Based on Hyper-Parameters

In addition to the update directions, the hyper-parameters, including batch-size and learning rate, are also of great importance for the training acceleration.

3.2.3.1　Algorithms for Learning Rate

In (8), we note the learning rate or step size as α, which characterizes how much it descend toward the negative direction of the gradient in GD. Learning rate always has a great effect in the generalization and accuracy of models. With a small learning rate, it always uses more time to get convergence and is more likely to sink into the local minimum. And models with small learning rates are also likely to overfit. On the contrary, large learning rate often leads to gradient explosion and oscillation when training. A large learning rate makes it hard to converge.

To get balance from such problems, instead of using a constant learning rate, a common method is to use a learning rate with decay – i.e. exponential decay, formulated as $\eta = 0.95^t \cdot \alpha_0$ or $\eta = \frac{k}{\sqrt{t}}$, where t is the index of the iteration. Another method is to set the learning rate as $\eta = \frac{\eta_0}{1+rt}$, where r is a constant indicating decay rate. The basic idea of learning rate decay is to use a larger learning rate in the beginning and use a small learning rate when near convergence. However, these methods introduce new hyper-parameters and are not able to get rid of the saddle point. To solve such problems, a method called AdaGrad is proposed to take advantage of the information in historical gradients. It works as follows:

$$g_t = \frac{\partial L(\omega_t)}{\partial \omega},$$

$$V_t = \sqrt{\sum_{i=1}^{t}(g_i)^2 + \varepsilon}, \tag{3.24}$$

$$\omega_{t+1} = \omega_t - \alpha \frac{g_t}{V_t},$$

where g^t is the gradient at tth iteration, an V^t is the accumulation of historical gradients until tth iteration.

By computing V^t, AdaGrad uses historical gradients to tune the learning rate automatically. However, AdaGrad still has two weakness. The first is that one still need to manually choose a global learning rate α. The second is that, as the training goes, the accumulation of gradients will be larger and larger, so the learning rate will become zero. To avoid the second problem, RMSProp and AdaDelta are proposed to use a time window and exponential average to give up gradients a long time ago.

So far, many variants and theoretical analyses of AdaGrad has been presented. Some proposed the nonconvex and nonsmooth versions of AdaGrad, making it more robust to the noise in gradients [327], [164], and [336] also gives a generalized version of convex and nonconvex, with the sufficient conditions of convergence. To improve the convergence rate of polynomial decay, [88] proposed to use bounds to design the adaptive learning rate. All the methods improve performance and the convergence rate.

With new techniques coming out, many different adaptive learning rate schedules were presented. [212], [233], and [5] give methods to use the adaptive learning rate in deep learning, distributed machine learning, and ISTA, which is often used in sparse coding problems. Also, there is proof of advantages of reshuffling in SGD with constant step size and that first order with learning rate decay can avoid a saddle point [366], [225].

3.2.3.2   Algorithms for Batch Size

In (7), we show the objective function of our model, where n is the number of training samples. Here n is called the batch size. It represents how many samples we use in the computation of loss function at each iteration. If the batch size is too large – e.g., $n = \#\ training\ samples$ – we can get higher accuracy, but the computation cost is also high. While we can use a smaller batch size, which is easy to compute gradients and do gradient descent, it will introduce more noise and will need more time to converge. A typical example of a small batch size is SGD, where $n = 1$:

$$F(\omega) = \ell(\omega, x_i, y_i) + R(\omega), \tag{3.25}$$

where the only sample $(x_i, \ y_i)$ is chosen randomly. By using SGD, we can get faster convergence than GD with more noise and oscillation. To balance between GD and SGD, Mini-batch SGD is proposed. Mini-batch SGD uses b samples, which are IID to update parameters in each iteration. With relatively high computation efficiency, Mini-batch SGD can reduce the noise of gradient and oscillation in descent.

With the introduction of SGD and mini-batch SGD, batch size becomes another important hyper-parameter. However, it is unlikely the adaptive method would be used on batch size, so we often fix batch size at the beginning of training. Then what we need to do is choosing an appropriate batch size for the training. To balance the choice between learning rate and batch size, [99] proposed that a good ratio of learning rate and batch size can lead to a good generalization. They also prove that the PAC-Bayes generalization bound is a positive correlation to the ratio of learning rate and batch size. [387] and [70] presented that whether batch size is good is related to its bound and expected smoothness constant in JacSketch methods. And they find acceleration can lead to larger bound and give a closed-form formula to compute the smoothness constant. [386] shows that less similar data points in each batch can lead to better performance and proposed the active mini-batch sampling has less variance and high efficiency.

Some also presented some batch schedules for new learning algorithms. [309] improved two basic methods for choice of samples in BMAL based on analysis of their weakness. To reduce communication constraint, distributed training often uses a layer-by-layer schedule. However, it is inefficient on parameter communication and forward computation overlap. So [321] uses an iBatch schedule to improve scalability of distributed training, by making batch parameter communication and forward computation.

3.2.4   Co-designed Algorithms

We have introduced some algorithms for machine learning in terms of direction – e.g., Momentum – and adaptive learning rate – e.g., AdaGrad and RMSProp. In this section, we will introduce some algorithms that combine algorithms in both direction and adaptive learning rate – i.e., co-designed algorithms.

A basic and classical co-designed method is Adaptive Moment Estimation (Adam). Adam uses adaptive learning rate by an exponentially decay average of past squared gradients like AdaDelta and RMSProp, and it also uses an exponentially decay average of past gradients like Momentum. Adam works as follows:

$$g_t = \nabla F(\omega_t, \xi_t),$$

$$m_t = \beta_1 m_{t-1} + (1 - \beta_1)g_t,$$

$$v_t = \beta_2 v_{t-1} + (1 - \beta_2)g_t^2,$$

$$\hat{m}_t = \frac{m_t}{1 - \beta_1^t}, \tag{3.26}$$

$$\hat{v}_t = \frac{v_t}{1 - \beta_2^t},$$

$$\omega_{t+1} = \omega_t - \frac{\alpha}{\sqrt{\hat{v}_t} + \varepsilon}\hat{m}_t,$$

where g_t get the gradient with respect to the parameter ω_t and ξ_t in the tth iteration, β_1 and β_2 are the exponential decay rate for the moment estimates, m_t is 1st moment vector, and v_t is 2nd moment vector at tth iteration. According to experiments, a good default setting for Adam is $\alpha = 0.001, \beta_1 = 0.9, \beta_2 = 0.999$, and $\epsilon = 10^{-8}$. The training process with Adam is always stable and can get good performance in most nonconvex optimization problems. However, Adam sometimes connot converge.

Because we have seen that Nesterov accelerated gradient is better than Momentum, there is a good variant of Adam called Nesterov-accelerated Adaptive Momentum Estimation (Nadam) that combines NAG and Adam [59]. It works as follows:

$$g_t = \nabla F(\omega_t, \xi_t),$$

$$m_t = \beta_1^t m_{t-1} + (1 - \beta_1^t)g_t,$$

$$v_t = \beta_2 v_{t-1} + (1 - \beta_2)g_t^2,$$

$$\hat{m} = \left(\beta_1^{t+1} m_t \Big/ \left(1 - \prod_{i=1}^{t+1} \beta_1^i\right)\right) \tag{3.27}$$

$$+ \left((1 - \beta_1^t)g_t \Big/ \left(1 - \prod_{i=1}^{t} \beta_1^i\right)\right),$$

$$\hat{n} = \beta_2 n_t / (1 - \beta_2^t),$$

$$\theta_t = \theta_{t-1} - \frac{\alpha_t}{\sqrt{\hat{n}_t} + \varepsilon}\hat{m}_t.$$

Nadam can improve the speed of convergence and the quality of learned models. Another problem is that Adam is not suitable for solving black-box optimazation problems, where we cannot get explicit gradients easily. So a method called zeroth-order Adam method (ZO-AdaMM) is proposed to generalize Adam to a gradient-free schedule [40]. ZO-AdaMM shows faster convergence and higher accuracy than six state-of-art ZO optimization methods. At the same time, an understanding of adaptive learning rate methods for nonconvex constrained optimization is proposed.

Adam is a good method for nonconvex optimization, so there are some analyses on the behavior of Adam in nonconvex situation [273]. They analyze Adam as a preconditioned SGD, which can rescale the stochastic gradient noise to be isotropic near stationary points to escape saddle points. They also pointed out that the advantage of Adam is it can escape saddle points faster than SGD and converge faster to second-order stationary points. However, Adam still has a problem that it cannot converge in some cases. Based on that, some given analysis and variants have been proposed. The YOGI method enlarges the effect of the mini-batch to enable convergence and can improve the effective learning rate and decrease the tune of hyper-parameters [380]. NosAdam and AMSGrad are presented to solve the non-convergence of Adam by using a long-time memory of past gradients, and they show that one important reason of non-convergence is the use of exponential moving average in Adam [241], [116]. Then, as an improvement of AMSGrad, ACADG is proposed to solve the problem of AMSGrad that its convergence speed is slow and it is easy to find oscillations in training. ACADG can eliminate some negative effects of the previous gradients and reduce the oscillations to accelerate training [283]. Finally, some simple sufficient conditions for the convergence of Adam and RMSProp were presented to support global convergence in large-scale nonconvex stochastic optimization [410]. And a new idea that Adam is essentially a weighted AdaGrad with exponential moving average momentum is proposed to analyze the divergence.

To eliminate the generalization gap between SGD and Adam, new methods such as AdaBound, AMSBound, and AdamWR were proposed [182], [185]. AdamWR presents that weight decay with additive constant factor will limit the benefit of weight decay regularization, so AdamWR decouples weight decay and the optimization steps taken with respect to the loss function. As for AdaBound and AMSBound, they use dynamic bounds on the learning rate to realize a gradual and smooth transition from adaptive methods to SGD, and are proven to converge. With high learning speed, it can solve problems from extreme learning rate. AdaBound works as follows:

$$
\begin{aligned}
m_t &= \beta_{1t} m_{t-1} + (1 - \beta_{1t}) g_t, \\
v_t &= \beta_2 v_{t-1} + (1 - \beta_2) g_t^2, \\
V_t &= diag(v_t), \\
\hat{\eta}_t &= Clip\left(\alpha/\sqrt{V_t}, \eta_l(t), \eta_u(t)\right), \\
\eta_t &= \hat{\eta}_t/\sqrt{t}, \\
x_{t+1} &= \prod_{\mathcal{F}, diag(\eta_t^{-1})} (x_t - \eta_t) \odot m_t,
\end{aligned}
\tag{3.28}
$$

where η_l is the lower-bound function, η_u is the upper-bound function, and $Clip(\cdot)$ is a clipping operation to constrain learning rate to be in $[\eta_l, \eta_u]$. Chiefly, $\eta_l(t)$ is a non-decreasing function that converges to α^*; while $\eta_u(t)$ is a non-increasing function that converges to α^*. Another idea about improving generalization of Adam is

Hyper-Adam, which uses an adaptive combination of multiple updates to perform the parameter update, where weights and decay rate depend on specific tasks [323].

3.2.5 Optimization Algorithms for DNN

As the size of data and parameters increases, DNN becomes more and more important, because it has the ability to process large computation. Due to the large scale of deep learning networks, there are many specific optimization and regularization methods for DNN.

The most useful and common regularization method is dropout, protecting DNNs from overfitting. The basic idea of dropout is to make part of neurons deactive in a certain probability. Every time we delete some neurons, we will train a different neural model in each iteration. And with fewer neurons, we can train our models faster. In the test process, each neuron is active, and corresponding weights should be multiplied by probability. Another useful method is batch normalization. In machine learning, we often use feature scaling to make the training easier. Feature scaling is to make features with zero mean, while variance is 1. Batch normalization is to use feature scaling in each layer; i.e., the output of each layer is scaled. Batch normalization is often used to eliminate internal covariate shift and avoid gradient vanish. It also makes sense in regularization. Weight normalization (WN) is used to make optimization space of objective function smoother. With weight θ, WN decouples it into $\theta = \frac{g}{\|\mathbf{v}\|}\mathbf{v}$, where g is a scale and $\mathbf{v}$ is a vector. Then we will optimize two things. WN is more robust and often used in RNN and Generative Adversarial Networks (GAN). Another method for RNN is layer normalization (LN). Normalization in LN is based on each neuron in one layer, or to say each channel in an image.

Many new methods concentrate on the gradients in DNN. To avoid the pathological curvature, a natural gradient is proposed. [23] gave the exact expression in linear networks, and based on the analysis of convergence speed, the authors find loss can decrease exponentially to a global minimum in parameter space. To avoid the setting for sensitive hyper-parameters, P2SGrad was designed by using adaptive methods [395]. P2SGrad is stable in training and robust to noise. Most importantly, it is free for hyper-parameters. There is also a regularization method using gradients called Gradient Centralization [367]. GC centralizes gradients to have zero mean to regularize weight space and output feature space. What's more, it can also improve the Lipschitzness of the loss function to make training stable.

Hyper-parameters also affect the performance of DNNs. Large batch size often leads to problems in memory and computation, while small batch size has a worse performance. So there are new frameworks and schedule proposed to make the model more robust and improve accuracy for small batch size and noisy gradients [396], [377]. [368] analyzed the effect of another hyper-parameter learning rate on DNNs. It shows that an initial high learning rate can prevent model from memory of noisy data, while a low learning rate can improve the learning of complex pattern; i.e., learned pattern with low learning rate will be more complex and less transferable. Additionally, [60] presented a new parameter that influences the convergence rate.

It shows that with a wider layer, it is much easier for DNNs to converge to a global minimum with a linear rate.

3.3   Theoretical Framework for Flexible Synchronization in Edge Learning

ASP is a totally asynchronous mode such that all workers compute gradients and pull/push updates in an independent manner. It is not necessary to wait for each other during the training process. The worker who finishes first will continue to the next iteration of training. In this way, the time of waiting for a slow worker is eliminated, which will speed up the training convergence. Compared with BSP, it is faster for ASP to train a given number of epochs. However, some slower workers send delayed or outdated updates to the parameter server, and download a different version of the global model form parameter server , resulting in degraded performance, lower accuracy, and poor convergent rate.

In a totally ASP scheme, a lot of workers may compute the gradient with respect to the old parameter, which is known as staleness and severely degrades the convergence rate. To tackle this problem, SSP has been proposed. There is a staleness threshold in SSP to limit the lag between local version of model in worker and the global version of model in the server. Gradients computed by the stale model have a serious impact on convergence properties, which has been widely investigated. Instead, the number of bounded iterations is designed to restrict the number of internal updates in a worker, aiming to reduce the variance of local gradients and the diversity of searching directions between workers to guarantee the convergence rate of the algorithm. In the following, we establish the convergence rate for ASP with a staleness threshold τ.

THEOREM 3.3 (Convergence Rate for ASP with a Staleness Threshold τ)   *Under the assumptions of unbiased and bounded variance of the stochastic gradient, when the objective function $F(\cdot)$ is nonconvex and L-smooth, and SGD-based algorithm is running with fixed learning rate η for all iterations and satisfying $2L^2\eta^3\tau^2 + 2L\eta^2 - \eta \leq 0$, where τ is the threshold of staleness, the expected average-squared gradients satisfies the following inequality for all $T \in \mathbb{N}$:*

$$\frac{1}{T}\sum_{t=1}^{T}\|\nabla F(\omega_t)\|^2 \leq \frac{2[F(\omega_1) - F(\omega^*)]}{\eta T} + 2L\eta\delta^2 + 2L^2\eta^2\tau^2\delta^2, \qquad (3.29)$$

where T is the number of iterations and δ^2 is the upper bound of the variance of stochastic gradient.

The model parameter is updated in iteration t as follows.

$$\omega_{t+1} = \omega_t - \eta g(\omega_{t-\tau_t}, \xi_{t,i}), \qquad (3.30)$$

where τ_t denotes the staleness of the current updated worker in iteration t and $\xi_{t,i}$ denotes the mini-batch selected by ith worker of in iteration t. In the following, we present the detailed proof of Theorem 3.3.

Based on the L-Smooth assumption and the update policy of model parameter, we have:

$$F(\omega_{t+1}) - F(\omega_t) \leq \langle \nabla F(\omega_1), \omega_2 - \omega_1 \rangle + \frac{L}{2}\|\omega_{t+1} - \omega_t\|^2$$

$$= \langle \nabla F(\omega_t), -\eta g(\omega_{t-\tau_t}, \xi_{t,i}) \rangle + \frac{L}{2}\| - \eta g(\omega_{t-\tau_t}, \xi_{t,i})\|^2$$

$$= -\eta \langle \nabla F(\omega_t), g(\omega_{t-\tau_t}, \xi_{t,i}) \rangle + \frac{L\eta^2}{2}\|g(\omega_{t-\tau_t}, \xi_{t,i})\|^2. \quad (3.31)$$

For the first part of (3.31), by taking the expectation with respect to $\xi_{t,i}$, we obtain

$$\mathbb{E}\left[-\eta \langle \nabla F(\omega_t), g(\omega_{t-\tau_t}, \xi_{t,i}) \rangle \right]$$

$$= -\eta \langle \nabla F(\omega_t), \nabla F(\omega_{t-\tau_t}) \rangle$$

$$= -\frac{\eta}{2}[\|\nabla F(\omega_t)\|^2 + \|\nabla F(\omega_{t-\tau_t})\|^2 - \|\nabla F(\omega_t) - \nabla F(\omega_{t-\tau_t})\|^2]$$

$$= -\frac{\eta}{2}\|\nabla F(\omega_t)\|^2 - \frac{\eta}{2}\|\nabla F(\omega_{t-\tau_t})\|^2 + \frac{\eta}{2}\|\nabla F(\omega_t) - \nabla F(\omega_{t-\tau_t})\|^2. \quad (3.32)$$

where the first equality comes after that, all $\xi_{t,i}$ are IID and the unbiased gradient assumption, and the second equality holds according to $\langle a, b \rangle = \frac{1}{2}(\|a\|^2 + \|b\|^2 - \|a - b\|^2)$. Then, we have to obtain the upper bound of $\|\nabla F(\omega_t) - \nabla F(\omega_{t-\tau_t})\|^2$.
Since

$$\omega_t = \omega_{t-1} - \eta g(\omega_{t-1-\tau_{t-1}}, \xi_{t-1,i}) = \omega_{t-\tau_t} - \sum_{k=1}^{\tau_t} \eta g(\omega_{t-k-\tau_{t-k}}, \xi_{t-k,i}),$$

$$(3.33)$$

we obtain that

$$\|\nabla F(\omega_t) - \nabla F(\omega_{t-\tau_t})\|^2$$

$$\leq L^2\|\omega_t - \omega_{t-\tau_t}\|^2$$

$$= L^2\eta^2 \left\| \sum_{k=1}^{\tau_t} g(\omega_{t-k-\tau_{t-k}}, \xi_{t-k,i}) \right\|^2$$

$$\leq L^2\eta^2\tau_t \sum_{k=1}^{\tau_t} \left\| \sum_{i\in\mathcal{C}_{t-k}} g(\omega_{t-k-\tau_{t-k}}, \xi_{t-k,i}) \right\|^2$$

$$\leq L^2\eta^2\tau_t \sum_{k=1}^{\tau_t} \|g(\omega_{t-k-\tau_{t-k}}, \xi_{t-k,i})\|^2$$

$$= L^2\eta^2\tau_t \sum_{k=1}^{\tau_t} \|g(\omega_{t-k-\tau_{t-k}}, \xi_{t-k,i}) - \nabla F(\omega_{t-k-\tau_{t-k}}) + \nabla F(\omega_{t-k-\tau_{t-k}})\|^2$$

$$\leq 2L^2\eta^2\tau_t \sum_{k=1}^{\tau_t} \left[\|g(\omega_{t-k-\tau_{t-k}}, \xi_{t-k,i}) - \nabla F(\omega_{t-k-\tau_{t-k}})\|^2 + \|\nabla F(\omega_{t-k-\tau_{t-k}})\|^2 \right]$$

$$\leq 2L^2\eta^2\tau_t\sum_{k=1}^{\tau_t}\left[\delta^2 + \|\nabla F(\omega_{t-k-\tau_{t-k}})\|^2\right]$$

$$= 2L^2\eta^2\tau_t^2\delta^2 + 2L^2\eta^2\tau_t\sum_{k=1}^{\tau_t}\|\nabla F(\omega_{t-k-\tau_{t-k}})\|^2 \qquad (3.34)$$

where the first inequality comes after the L-smooth assumption, and the last inequality holds based on the bounded variance assumption. Combining (3.32) and (3.34), we bound the first part of (3.31) as:

$$\mathbb{E}\left[-\eta\langle\nabla F(\omega_t), g(\omega_{t-\tau_t},\xi_{t,i})\rangle\right] = -\frac{\eta}{2}\|\nabla F(\omega_t)\|^2 - \frac{\eta}{2}\|\nabla F(\omega_{t-\tau_t})\|^2$$

$$+ L^2\eta^3\tau_t\sum_{k=1}^{\tau_t}\|\nabla F(\omega_{t-k-\tau_{t-k}})\|^2 + L^2\eta^3\tau_t^2\delta^2.$$

$$(3.35)$$

For the second part of (3.31), we have

$$\frac{L\eta^2}{2}\|g(\omega_{t-\tau_t},\xi_{t,i})\|^2 \leq L\eta^2\delta^2 + L\eta^2\|\nabla F(\omega_{t-\tau_t})\|^2 \qquad (3.36)$$

Replacing the first and second parts of (3.31) by the previously obtained bounds immediately yields that

$$\mathbb{E}\left[F(\omega_{t+1}) - F(\omega_t)\right] \leq -\frac{\eta}{2}\|\nabla F(\omega_t)\|^2 + \frac{2L\eta^2 - \eta}{2}\|\nabla F(\omega_{t-\tau_t})\|^2$$

$$+ L^2\eta^3\tau_t\sum_{k=1}^{\tau_t}\|\nabla F(\omega_{t-k-\tau_{t-k}})\|^2 + L\eta^2\delta^2 + L^2\eta^3\tau_t^2\delta^2.$$

$$(3.37)$$

By summing the both sides of (3.37) from $t = 1$ to T, we obtain:

$$\mathbb{E}\left[F(\omega_{T+1})\right] - F(\omega_1)$$

$$\leq -\frac{\eta}{2}\sum_{t=1}^{T}\|\nabla F(\omega_t)\|^2 + \frac{2L\eta^2 - \eta}{2}\sum_{t=1}^{T}\|\nabla F(\omega_{t-\tau_t})\|^2$$

$$+ L^2\eta^3\sum_{t=1}^{T}\tau_t\sum_{k=1}^{\tau_t}\|\nabla F(\omega_{t-k-\tau_{t-k}})\|^2 + L\eta^2\delta^2T + \sum_{t=1}^{T}L^2\eta^3\tau_t^2\delta^2$$

$$\leq -\frac{\eta}{2}\sum_{t=1}^{T}\|\nabla F(\omega_t)\|^2 + \frac{2L\eta^2 - \eta}{2}\sum_{t=1}^{T}\|\nabla F(\omega_{t-\tau_t})\|^2$$

$$+ L^2\eta^3\tau\sum_{t=1}^{T}\sum_{k=1}^{\tau}\|\nabla F(\omega_{t-k-\tau_{t-k}})\|^2 + L\eta^2\delta^2T + L^2\eta^3\tau^2\delta^2T$$

$$\leq -\frac{\eta}{2} \sum_{t=1}^{T} \|\nabla F(\omega_t)\|^2 + \frac{2L\eta^2 - \eta}{2} \sum_{t=1}^{T} \|\nabla F(\omega_{t-\tau_t})\|^2$$

$$+ L^2 \eta^3 \tau^2 \sum_{t=1}^{T} \|\nabla F(\omega_{t-\tau_t})\|^2 + L\eta^2 \delta^2 T + L^2 \eta^3 \tau^2 \delta^2 T$$

$$= -\frac{\eta}{2} \sum_{t=1}^{T} \|\nabla F(\omega_t)\|^2 + \frac{2L^2 \eta^3 \tau^2 + 2L\eta^2 - \eta}{2} \sum_{t=1}^{T} \|\nabla F(\omega_{t-\tau_t})\|^2$$

$$+ L\eta^2 \delta^2 T + L^2 \eta^3 \tau^2 \delta^2 T \tag{3.38}$$

where the second inequality holds due to $\tau \geq \tau_t$ for any t, and the third inequality comes after the fact that for any $t = 1$ to T, the term $\|\nabla F(\omega_{t-\tau_t})\|^2$ appears, at most, τ times in $L^2 \eta^3 \tau \sum_{t=1}^{T} \sum_{k=1}^{\tau} \|\nabla F(\omega_{t-k-\tau_{t-k}})\|^2$.

Let $2L^2 \eta^3 \tau^2 + 2L\eta^2 - \eta \leq 0$. By rearranging and dividing both sides of (3.38) by $\frac{\eta T}{2}$, we have

$$\frac{1}{T} \sum_{t=1}^{T} \|\nabla F(\omega_t)\|^2 \leq \frac{2\left[F(\omega_1) - F(\omega_{T+1})\right]}{\eta T} + 2L\eta\delta^2 + 2L^2 \eta^2 \tau^2 \delta^2$$

$$\leq \frac{2\left[F(\omega_1) - F(\omega^*)\right]}{\eta T} + 2L\eta\delta^2 + 2L^2 \eta^2 \tau^2 \delta^2, \tag{3.39}$$

which completes the proof.

4 Communication-Efficient Edge Learning

Edge learning has enabled the training of large-scale machine learning models on a big dataset by implementing data parallelism in multiple nodes. However, the iterative interaction incurred by multiple learning nodes together with the considerable quantity of communication data on each interaction yields huge communication overhead, which greatly hinders the scalability of the edge learning. In this chapter, we introduce the mainstream approaches to achieve communication efficiency of edge training, including compressing communication data, reducing the synchronous frequency, overlapping computation and communication, and optimizing the transmission network. Specifically, we introduce two hybrid mechanisms for communication-efficient edge learning. The first one is Quantized Overlap Synchronization Parallel (QOSP), which integrates gradient quantization for communication compression and overlap synchronization parallel for simultaneous computation and communication. The second mechanism improves communication efficiency during the aggregation of client-side updates by quantizing the gradients and exploiting the inherent superposition of radio frequency signals. Finally, we discuss the future directions of communication-efficient edge learning.

4.1 Introduction to Communication-Efficient Edge Learning

Training a machine learning model in the edge environment is data-intensive since the gradient data should be transferred across the edge nodes. In the scenario where edge devices cooperatively train a machine learning model with SGD-based methods, participating nodes update the local model parameters or local gradients based on the calculation of local training data. The central processor or collaborator aggregates the intermediate results and synchronizes the model parameters. These steps run multiple times until an expected accuracy is achieved. However, with the complexity of intelligent application scenarios, the scale of parameters involved in the edge learning model has increased rapidly (for example, in typical application scenarios such as high-precision image recognition and natural language processing, the scale of parameters reaches millions or even billions). In addition, because the network environment of the edge terminal is dynamic and the communication performance is limited, it is difficult to meet the communication requirements of the convergence of intermediate results of edge learning and synchronization of model parameters, which reduce the learning efficiency. This becomes the key factor restricting the training accuracy of edge intelligent model precision and affecting the quality of edge intelligent service.

The communication overhead increases training latency, energy, and bandwidth consumption. Communication overhead is affected by the size of the gradient data, gradient synchronization frequency, the way of transmission, and the available bandwidth. Therefore, reducing the communication complexity and improving the communication efficiency in edge learning are the key factors that affect the training performance.

Various methods of reducing communication overhead have been studies, such as compressing communication data, reducing the synchronous frequency, overlapping computation and communication, and optimizing the transmission network. All these methods have demonstrated promising results in different scenarios. In the following four sections, we will discuss these methods and show how they achieve communication efficiency in edge learning.

4.2 Communication Data Compression in Edge Learning

Considering that the main concern of incurring large communication overhead is the huge amount of transmitted data in each single communication round, inherent to the machine learning model, it is natural that compression-based methods have been proposed. The core idea of compression is to reduce the size of data in each communication round. Three mainstream approaches are quantization, sparsification, and low-rank factorization.

4.2.1 Quantization

The data communicated between learning nodes is usually the gradient (or the locally accumulated gradients of each worker), the size of which is a 32-bit float. Quantization is proposed to discretize these floats such that each dimension could be expressed with lower bits - e.g., 2 bits [388]. We illustrate the basic idea of gradient quantization in Fig. 4.1, which shows the early work with quantization used to quantize the gradient on each round. The typical methods include SignSGD [253] with 1 bit, TernGrad [328] with $log3$ bits, and QSGD [12] with arbitrary bits. To investigate the impact of quantization, QSGD establishes a theoretical relationship between the number of discrete values and the convergence rate. QSGD focuses on understanding the trade-off between the communication cost of data parallel SGD and its convergence guarantees. The processor can weigh the number of bits communicated in each iteration and add the variance in the process. QSGD is based on two ideas. The first is an intuitive stochastic quantization scheme: given the gradient vector at the processor, we quantize each component by rounding randomly to a set of discrete values by preserving the statistical properties of the original data. The second is an effective lossless code for the quantized gradient, which uses its statistical properties to generate efficient encoding.

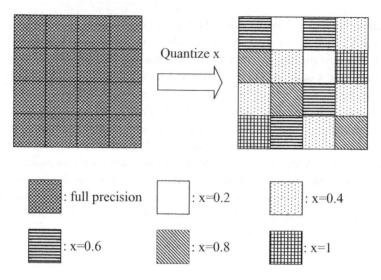

Figure 4.1 Gradient quantization method.

The quantization function of QSGD is denoted by $Q_s(v)$, where s is the adjustment parameter, which corresponds to the number of quantization levels, and s is defined as the level of uniform distribution between 0 and 1. The way to quantify each value can retain the expected value and introduce the smallest variance. For any $v \in \mathbb{R}_n$ with $v \neq 0$, $Q_s(v)$ is defined as

$$Q_s(v) = \|v\|_2 \cdot sgn(v_i) \cdot \xi_i(v, s), \tag{4.1}$$

where $\xi_i(v, s)$ are independent random variables, defined as follows. Let $0 \leq l \leq s$ be an integer such that $\|v_i\|/\|v\|_2 \in [l/s, (l+1)/s]$. That is, $[l/s, (l+1)/s]$ is the quantization interval corresponding to $\|v_i\|/\|v\|_2$. Then

$$\xi_i(v, s) = \begin{cases} l/s & \text{with probability } 1 - p\left(\dfrac{\|v_i\|}{\|v\|_2}, s\right); \\ (l+1)/s & \text{otherwise.} \end{cases} \tag{4.2}$$

Here, $p(a, s) = as - l$ for any $a \in [0, 1]$. If $v = 0$, then we define $Q(v, s) = 0$.

The distribution of $\xi_i(v, s)$ has minimal variance over distributions with support $\{0, 1/s, \ldots, 1\}$, and its expectation satisfies $\mathbb{E}[\xi_i(v, s)] = \|v_i\|/\|v\|_2$.

For any vector v, the output of $Q_s(v)$ is a tuple $(\|v\|_2, \sigma, \zeta)$, where σ is the vector of signs of the v_i and ζ is the vector of integer values $s \cdot \xi_i(v, s)$. The key idea behind the coding scheme is that not all integer values can be equally likely: in particular, larger integers are less frequent.

Assume there are K processors, and a parameter $m > 0$, where each processor i has access to functions $\{f_{im/K}, \ldots, f_{(i+1)m/(K-1)}\}$. The goal is to approximately minimize $f = \frac{1}{m} \sum_{i=1}^{m} f_i$. For processor i, let $h_i = \frac{i}{m} \sum_{j=im/K}^{(i+1)m/K-1} f_i$ be the portion of f that it knows, so that $f = \sum_{i=1}^{K} h_i$.

The algorithm description is as follows. Let $\tilde{Q}(v) = Q(v, \sqrt{n})$. Given arbitrary start-ing point x_0, we let $y^{(1)} = x_0$. At the beginning of epoch p, each processor broadcasts $\nabla h_i(y^{(p)})$ - that is, the unquantized full gradient, from which the processors each aggregate $\nabla f(y^{(p)}) = \sum_{i=1}^m \nabla h_i(y^{(p)})$. Within each epoch, for each iteration $t = 1$, $\ldots, T$, and for each processor $i = 1, \ldots, K$, we let $j_{i,t}^{(p)}$ be a uniformly random integer from $[m]$ completely independent of everything else. Then, in iteration t in epoch p, processor i broadcasts the update vector $u_{t,i}^{(p)} = \tilde{Q}(\nabla f_{j_{i,t}^{(p)}}(x_t^{(p)}) - \nabla f_{j_{i,t}^{(p)}}(y^{(p)}) + \nabla f(y^{(p)}))$. Each processor then computes the total update $u_t^{(p)} = \frac{1}{K}\sum_{i=1}^K u_{t,i}$, and sets $x_{t+1}^{(p)} = x_t^{(p)} - \eta u_t^{(p)}$. At the end of epoch p, each processor sets $y^{(p+1)} = \frac{1}{T}\sum_{i=1}^T x_t^{(p)}$.

QSGD is fairly general: it can also be shown to converge, under assumptions, to local minima for nonconvex objectives, as well as under asynchronous iterations.

Another quantization algorithm is GradiVeQ. It exploits the strong linear corre-lations between CNN gradients through principal component analysis (PCA) for substantial gradient dimension reduction. GradiVeQ can significantly reduce the com-munication load in distributed CNN training, and it is the first method that leverages both gradient compression and parallel aggregation by employing a vector compres-sion technique that commutes with gradient aggregation, hence enabling compressed domain gradient aggregation. The step of GradiVeQ is shown in Algorithm 4.1.

Algorithm 4.1 Parallelized GradiVeQ Gradient Compression and Ring All-Reduce Communication

---

1: N nodes, each with a local gradient vector g_n, $n \in [0, N-1]$;

2: Each node-n partitions its g_n into N equal segments $g_n(0), \ldots, g_n(N-1)$;

3: Every node-n compresses $g_n(n)$ to $g'_n(n)$, and sends $g'(n) \triangleq g'_n(n)$ to node-$[n + 1]_N$;

4: **for** $i = 1 : N - 1$ **do**

5:     Each node-n downloads $g'([n - i]_N)$ from node-$[n - 1]_N$;

6:     **At the same time,** each node-n compresses $g_n([n - i]_N)$ to $g'_n([n - i]_N)$;

7:     Once node-n has completed the above two steps, it adds $g'_n([n - i]_N)$ to $g'([n - i]_N)$, and send the updated $g'([n - i]_N)$ to node-$[n + 1]_N$;

8: **end for**

9: Each node-n now has the completely aggregated compressed $g'([n + 1]_N)$;

10: **for** $i = 0 : N - 1$ **do**

11:     Each node-n decompresses $g'([n + 1 - i]_N)$ into $g''([n + 1 - i]_N)$;

12:     **At the same time,** each node-n downloads $g'_n([n - i]_N)$ from node-$[n - 1]_N$;

13: **end for**

14: All nodes now have the complete g'';

Theoretical results exhibit an inverse linear relationship between the final conver-gence error and the number of discrete values. Empirically, all these methods have demonstrated a great improvement in reducing the communication overhead.

There are also some methods considering the quantization for some specific distributed architectures. For parameter server, the authors of [288] quantize the double-pass communication between the centralized nodes - i.e., parameter servers - and workers to further improve the communication efficiency. On the other hand, some work [184, 285] considers the decentralized architecture, in which each node only interacts the quantized model difference with its neighbors in each communication round.

4.2.2   Sparsification

Based on the fact that the communication data is usually composed of high-dimensional vectors, sparsification proposes compressing the communication data by only transmitting several dimensions of the vector. An important observation regarding machine learning algorithms is that the model parameters always converge to their optimal value in a nonuniform speed [344]. Inspired by such observation, some sparsification methods employ a significant filter to select the dimensions [111]. For example, Gaia [111] defines the filter function as the the update magnitude relative to the current parameter value. The authors of [291] propose a communication-efficient distributed estimation method for sparse linear discriminant analysis (LDA) in the high-dimensional regime. It distributes the data of size N into m machines, and estimates a local sparse LDA estimator on each machine using the data subset of size N/m. After the distributed estimation, this method aggregates the debiased local estimators from m machines, and sparsifies the aggregated estimator.

In addition, there are also some other sparsification methods - e.g., selecting random K, top K, and unbiased random K dimensions [325]. The key idea of [325] is to randomly drop out coordinates of the stochastic gradient vectors and amplify the remaining coordinates appropriately to ensure the sparsified gradient is unbiased. We show the basic idea of the sparsification method in Fig. 4.2. Apart from this, the gTop-k sparsification scheme has recently been proposed to reduce the communication complexity from $O(kP)$ to $O(k \cdot \log P)$, which significantly boosts the system scalability. Shi et al. [259] provides theoretical proofs on the convergence of the gTop-k scheme for nonconvex objective functions under certain analytic assumptions. They then derives the convergence rate of gTop-k synchronous SGD. However, it remains unclear whether the gTop-k sparsificaion scheme can converge in theory. These significant filter-based methods has omitted those insignificant dimensions leading to a performance degradation compared to non-compressed method.

Similar to that of quantization, sparsification also refers to the error compensation technique to reduce the negative impact on the convergence. These methods accumulate the unselected dimensions and compensate the future gradients. For example, the authors of [177] proposed deep gradient compression (DGC) to greatly reduce the communication bandwidth. To ensure no loss of accuracy, DGC employs momentum correction and local gradient clipping on top of the gradient sparsification to maintain model performance. DGC also uses momentum factor masking and warmup training to overcome the staleness problem caused by reduced communication. But

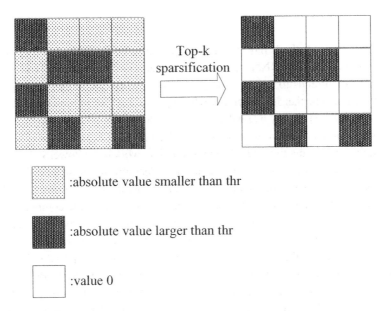

Top-k
sparsification

☐ :absolute value smaller than thr

■ :absolute value larger than thr

☐ :value 0

Figure 4.2 The basic idea of sparsification method.

the theory about the convergence of DGC is lacking. Zhao et al. [398] proposed a novel method, called global momentum compression (GMC), for sparse communication in distributed SGD. GMC also combines memory gradient and momentum SGD. However, in contrast to DGC, which adopts local momentum, GMC adopts global momentum. It theoretically proves the convergence rate of GMC for both convex and nonconvex problems. This is also the first work that proves the convergence of distributed momentum SGD (DMSGD) with sparse communication and memory gradient. Experimental results show that 99.9% or even more of the communication cost could be saved. In addition, convergence theories established for various loss functions - e.g., strongly convex functions [276], general convex functions, and nonconvex functions [15] - also exhibit the same order as non-compressed methods. [15] proves that, under analytic assumptions, sparsifying gradients by magnitude with local error correction provides convergence guarantees, for both convex and nonconvex smooth objectives, for data-parallel SGD. The main insight is that sparsification methods implicitly maintain bounds on the maximum impact of stale updates, thanks to selection by magnitude.

Due to the development of federated learning, in order to adapt to the need to train machine learning models using geographically dispersed data collected by local entities, the authors of [93] present a fairness-aware GS method, which ensures that different clients provide a similar amount of updates. Then, with the goal of minimizing the overall training time, they proposes a novel online learning formulation and algorithm for automatically determining the near-optimal communication and computation trade-off that is controlled by the degree of gradient sparsity. In this work, it also considered adaptive degree of sparsity and non-IID local datasets.

4.2.3   Low Rank

Recently, some methods have been specially designed for the currently popular deep learning models - i.e., DNNs. Inspired by the observations that the DNNs with good generalization tends to be low rank [166], some work finds that the performance of DNNs achieve further improvement when spectral regularization is added to the optimization update [82]. By using the fact that the low-rank matrix could be decomposed into small submatrices, some studies try to decompose the gradient of DNNs to obtain communication reduction [82]. The most efficient work is the PowerSGD [301], which decomposes the gradient with singular value decomposition method. The empirical results in [301] also exhibit that a higher final generalization accuracy is achieved by PowerSGD than the other compression methods under the same compression ratio.

Theoretically, all these communication data methods are in the same order in terms of the convergence speed. Among all methods, sparsification achieves the best compression efficiency that only one dimension - i.e., 4 bytes - required to be transmitted on each communication round in an extreme case [276]. However, the sparsification-based methods come at the cost of time of sparsifying itself, including selecting the dimensions and synchronizing all workers. Taking the most commonly used Top-K sparsification operator as an example, it requires selecting k dimensions with the largest magnitude of which the time is not negligible. Besides, the synchronization of the different dimensions from multiple workers also need to match the indexes in CPU, which also costs time. Compared to sparsification, quantization and low-rank-based methods have a smaller compression ratio but have better processing efficiency. For example, the authors of [301] show that PowerSGD is more suitable for current popular communication protocols - e.g., AllReduce. Recently, researchers have also attempted to combine these methods together to further reduce the communication overhead [22, 332].

4.2.4   Error Compensation Techniques for Communication Compression

Compression techniques such as quantization and sparsification have been proposed to reduce the communication overhead via sparsification or quantization. Since nodes only exchange a fraction or a low-precision representation of the whole model update (or the gradient), errors caused by compression will be accumulated, resulting in a severely degraded convergence rate. To tackle the challenge, error compensation techniques have been recently invented in centralized training and have shown to be effective in accelerating the convergence and tolerating a high compression ratio.

Error compensation, which is also called error feedback, is a method typically used to reduce the precision error incurred by compressing the gradients such as quantization and sparsification. Seide and colleagues [254] first introduced this concept for AllReduce 1Bit-SGD, which used the quantization error from the last iteration to compensate current gradients and then apply the quantization function to the compensated gradients. Their empirical study indicated that such a strategy has a minor influence on converge accuracy. However, they do not provide a theoretical analysis to prove its effectiveness.

Later, in [333], Wu et al. designed error-compensated SGD for quadratic optimization, which has two hyper-parameters to adjust the degree of compensation. But there are no theoretical advantages of using error compensation demonstrated in this paper. Stich et al. [277] theoretically proved that, for nonparallel and strongly convex loss functions, the error compensation strategy would greatly reduce the negative effect of the quantization. Their theoretical conclusions work for a specific type of compressing operators, of which expectation compressing error should be less than the magnitude of the original vector. Further, Alistarh et al. [16] studied error-compensated SGD for nonconvex loss functions. However, compared to the noncompensated method, it is more difficult to prove that the error-compensate method could achieve an acceleration in the convergence factor.

Algorithm 4.2 Centralized Compressed Stochastic Gradient Descent with Error Compensation

---

Initialize: point $x_{0,i} = x_0$, **learning rate** γ, **iterations** T, **accumulated error** $e_0 = 0$, **and compensation coefficient** α

Output: x_T

1: **procedure** CENTRALIZED COMPRESSION(Training dataset $\mathbb{D}$)

2:     Sample D_i from $\mathbb{D}$ for ith node;

3:     **for** $t = 0, 1, \cdots, T - 1$ **do**

4:         **On Worker** i:

5:             Randomly select a sample $d_{t,i}$ from D_i of the ith node;

6:             Calculate the local gradient $g_t^{(i)} = \nabla f_i(x_{t,i}; d_{t,i})$,$\forall i$ on all nodes;

7:             Correct the error: $p_t^{(i)} = g_t^{(i)} + \alpha e_t$

8:             Compress the corrected gradient $\tilde{g}_t^{(i)} = Compress(p_t^{(i)})$, send $\tilde{g}_t^{(i)}$ to the server;

9:             Update the residual error: $e_{t+1} = p_t - \tilde{g}_t^{(i)}$;

10:            Receive x_{t+1} from the server and set $x_{t+1,i} = x_{t+1}$;

11:        **On Server:**

12:            Receive $\tilde{g}_t^{(i)}$ from the workers and Decompress: $g_t^{(i)} = decompress(\tilde{g}_t^{(i)})$

13:            Update the model parameters: $x_{t+1} = x_t - \gamma \frac{1}{N} \sum_{i=1}^{N} g_t^{(i)}$

14:            Send x_{t+1} back to the workers;

15:    **end for**

16:    **return** the latest model parameters x_T;

17: **end procedure**

Algorithm 4.2 shows a typical example of error-compensation methods, which is proposed by Karimireddy et al. [138]. It is a similar idea to 1-bit SGD, but they proved that EF-SGD is compatible with arbitrary compression operators and achieves the same rate of convergence as vanilla SGD both nonconvex and weakly convex cases. The following work [289] has investigated error compensation for two-pass communication models, with error-compensated compression on both the parameter server and worker nodes. They not only showed that error compensation it is compatible with an arbitrary compression technique but also proved that it admits an improved convergence rate over the non-compensated compressed SGD such as QSGD [13]. Additionally, they first demonstrated that error compensation achieves linear speedup with respect to the number of workers. Finally, Zheng et al. [401] provided a distributed error-compensated compressed SGD with Netsterov's momentum, which is called dist-EF-SGD. Similar to Tang's work, they considered two-way compression. However, they also considered changing step size, blockwise compressor, and Nesterov's momentum. By partitioning the gradient into blocks, they introduced a blockwise compressor with a scaling factor such that each gradient block is compressed and converted in 1-bit format. This method results in significant communication cost reduction.

4.2.5   Communication Compression in Decentralized Training

In parameter server learning architecture, the servers could easily become the bottle-neck, especially when failures occur in some servers. To improve the robustness of distributed learning system, decentralized learning architecture has been proposed. In decentralized learning, there are no central servers, and each node only exchanges information with its neighbors. To reduce the communication overhead, communication compression specifically for decentralized learning is also necessary.

Gradient compression and network decentralization are two effective strategies to reduce the communication cost in distributed training. Gradient compression techniques suggest that each node only transmits compressed gradients. Typical compression techniques include including quantization [13, 329], sparsification [277, 326], and model averaging (local iterations) [198], which are designed for the standard distributed training case. Decentralized learning only requires each node to exchange its stochastic gradients to connected nodes and update its model parameters using the gradients it receives. Compared with centralized algorithms, the main advantage of decentralized algorithms is that they release the communication traffic in the central node. Therefore, decentralized algorithms could be much more efficient than centralized algorithms when the network bandwidth is small and the latency is significant.

Tang et al. [286] first proposed difference compression SGD (DCD) and extrapolation compression SGD (ECD) algorithms that combine the decentralized algorithms and quantization techniques. They have shown that both algorithms converge at the same rate as the centralized one, only for a constant compression ratio. They later suggested DeepSqueeze [287], a method that converges with an arbitrary compression ratio. Based on these, Koloskova et al. [143, 144] introduced CHOCO-SGD, which considers sparsification or quantization in decentralized learning for both convex and nonconvex functions. However, they did not consider momentum in theoretical analyses.

For momentum SGD, Wang et al. [311] studied the combination of local iterations and momentum under the decentralized network, but their algorithm does not compress the gradients. Another work [332] investigated quantized SGD with local iterations, but momentum techniques were not involved. Extending these studies, Singh et al. [268] proposed SQuARM-SGD, in which each node performs a fixed number of local SGD steps with Nesterov momentum and then sends sparsified and quantized information to its neighbours only when there is a significant change in its model parameters since the last communication.

4.3 Lazy Synchronization

The optimization methods adopted now for training machine learning models in edge environment are generally the iterative algorithms - e.g., SGD, which consumes a large number of iterations before reaching convergence. In each iteration, the data samples are distributed to multiple workers, computed in parallel, and then the computed results are synchronized among all workers. It can be seen that the number of communication rounds is equivalent to the number of iterations required to reach convergence that also yields large communication overhead. The original federated learning algorithm applies the lazy synchronization idea, since each client trains the local model through multiple epochs before the centralized server aggregates the local models.

In this section, we first introduce three methods of lazy synchronization: large batch size, periodic averaging, and fine-grained aggregation. Then we give an example in which periodic averaging and quantization method are combined to achieve communication-efficient edge learning.

4.3.1 Large Batch Size

Due to the large size of the dataset, stochastic optimization algorithms are generally used. In each iteration of the stochastic algorithms, a subset of dataset, namely a mini-batch of data, is sampled from the whole dataset to compute the optimization update. Though such mini-batch-based methods could reduce the computation cost, they yield noise (or variance) that results in more iterations to be convergent. Theoretically, the magnitude of the noise is in an inverse relationship with the size of mini-batch. Considering the significant computing resources but the limited communication bandwidth in distributed learning, an intuitive method is increasing the size of mini-batch. In this way, many methods employ the large batch size combined with the large learning rate [78, 371] to accelerate convergence. In practical implementation, such methods could make use of a large quantity of graphic processing units (GPUs) up to the order of a thousand. The experimental results also exhibit a promising performance - e.g., training Bert in only 76 minutes [369]. However, both theoretical and empirical findings indicate that the size of the mini-batch is limited for training deep learning models [365, 370]. In other words, the large batch size may deteriorate the generalization accuracy of the DNNs. Now, the generalization degradation incurred by the large mini-batch size is still a problem waiting to be solved [370].

4.3.2   Periodic Averaging

Different from traditional distributed learning algorithms that synchronize all workers in each iteration, periodic averaging locally iterates multiple times in each worker before synchronizing all workers [175, 405]. In this method, each worker possesses a separate data partition and iteratively updates its local model with the mini-batches sampling from the data partition. All workers synchronize their local models only when the given threshold to the number of local iterations is reached. The theoretical analysis established for strongly convex functions shows that this method could reduce the number of communication rounds up to a factor of $\sqrt{T}$, where T is the number of iterations [275]. Blake et al. [331] extends the analysis to quadratic and general convex objective functions by using the SGD algorithm. They say that the periodically averaging SGD, equivalent to local SGD, could always reduce the communication cost for the quadratic functions and at least sometimes show improvement for general convex functions. However, they also reveal that the local SGD does not dominate mini-batch SGD and that the lower bound on the performance of local SGD is worse than the mini-batch SGD. Farzin et al. [90] point out that this convergence error of local SGD arises from the variance among different data partitions on multiple workers. Therefore, they propose a redundancy-based method to reduce the convergence error of periodic averaging methods, where several copies of each data partition is made and allocated to different workers. Their theoretical results show that the convergence error could be linearly reduced with the number of copies. The extreme case of the periodic averaging method is the one-shot aggregation, where all workers are only synchronized once [257, 379].

4.3.3   Fine-Grained Aggregation

Considering that synchronization is composed of push and pull operation, fined-grained aggregation is to intermittently execute the two operations, which can be viewed as a fined-grained version of periodic averaging based methods. Taking the commonly used parameter server as an example, in each iteration, each worker can either push, pull or neither the model update to or from server. It can be seen that periodic averaging is a special case of fined-grained optimization where the push/pull operations are executed together every once in a while. The first work is done by Tianyi et al. [39], in which they propose a model called LAG. LAG aims at the parameter server architecture, in which the server only collects the gradients from partial workers and reuses the gradients of the rest workers. A variant of LAG is LAQ [279], which combines the quantization the LAG together. Their methods exhibit promising results on the deterministic optimization method - e.g., Gradient Descent with the full dataset using in each iteration - but are less efficient in the stochastic settings. Especially for reducing the number of pushing operations, Wang et.al. [186] propose excluding the updates of some workers that are outliers of the all updates. Under a non-IID setting of datasets between different workers - e.g., federated learning [197] - empirical results show that their method could reduce the number of pushing operations up to a factor of 50%. Further, Wang et al. [308] proposed a novel PRLC method in which only a portion of workers pull global model from servers in each iteration and those not pulling use their local updates to compensate the gap. It is also the first algorithm which analyzed the convergence rate of distributed SGD with pulling reduction and local compensation in both strongly convex and nonconvex cases. The method is shown in Algorithm 4.3.

Algorithm 4.3 Distributed SGD with PRLC

1: **Input:** Initialize $\omega_i^i = \omega_1$, learning rate η_0, pulling ratio r, and iterations T, mini-batch ξ;
2: **for** $t = 1$ to T **do**
3:    Each worker i computes $g(\omega_t^i; \xi_t^i)$ in parallel;
4:    $\omega_{t+1} = \omega_t - \frac{\eta_t}{P} \sum_{i=1}^P g(\omega_t^i; \xi_t^i)$;
5:    Each worker i updates its local model with the pulled global model or its local gradient:

$$\omega_{t+1}^i = \begin{cases} \omega_{t+1} & \text{with probability } r; \\ \omega_t^i - \eta_t g(\omega_t^i; \xi_t^i) & \text{otherwise.} \end{cases} ; \qquad (4.3)$$

6: **end for**

Currently, how to efficiently reduce the synchronization frequency still remains an ongoing problem to be solved. To this end, the large-batch-size-based optimization methods receive the most successful results, but such method tends to fall into the saddle point leading to performance degradation that raises concern of its application to practical settings. Recently, some work also tries to exploit the advantage of periodic averaging to further enhance the large-batch-size-based methods [57]. The established theories provide that the communication could be further reduced. In fact, to achieve better communication efficiency, the adaptive methods for different hyper-parameters - e.g., the period [89] - deserve considering.

4.3.4 A Communication-Efficient Edge Learning Framework with Quantized and Period Averaging

Edge training using the stochastic gradient descent (SGD) algorithm has been widely recognized as a promising approach. Considering the challenge that this approach frequently suffers substantial communication overhead in each iteration, previous work proposes two solutions - gradient quantization and parallel restarted techniques - which compress the communication data and reduce communication frequency, respectively.

In our previous work, we proposed a communication-efficient scheme that integrates gradient quantized and period averaging, which can be applied in distributed edge learning [332]. The underlying theoretical guarantee for the combination is nontrivial since the precision loss incurred by quantization and the gradient deviation incurred by period averaging interact with each other. Moreover, the accumulated errors would make the training difficult to converge if they are not strictly controlled. In this part, we introduce the basic idea and the theoretical results of this communication-efficient scheme in a parameter server learning architecture.

First, we present the details of period averaging. Here we adopt a simple period averaging method, also known as local SGD or K-AVG SGD, where all nodes make constant times of local updates before global synchronization. Generally, the flow of two successive global synchronizations in every node is described as follows:

- Step 1: Initialized the start point x_0, where x_0 is a vector that denotes the model parameter.
- Step 2: Repeat the following steps for K times.
  - Generate the IID realizations of the random ξ_k, which denotes the random mini-batch in SGD.
  - Compute the model parameter for the next iteration: $x_{k+1} = x_k - \gamma \nabla f(x_k; \xi_k)$, where $\nabla f(x_k; \xi_k)$ means the one-step gradient with respect to the the model parameter x_k and mini-batch ξ_k, and γ denotes the learning rate.
- Step 3: Output the model parameter x_K.

Quantization method compresses gradients that are exchanged through the network while generally preserving the model convergence performance of optimization. We adopt the QSGD scheme with an s-level uniformly distributed quantized function, as shown in the previous section of this chapter.

In a parameter server architecture, regardless of the transaction details of these two paradigms, each node works independently in every two successive synchronizations:

- (**Pull**): pull the parameter $\tilde{x}$ from the last update as initial state x_0
- (**Compute**): compute the gradient using period averaging SGD
- (**Push**): push the quantized variance g by $g = x_0 - x_K$
- (**Aggregate**): aggregate the averaging stochastic gradients g from all other nodes and summarize them into Δ
- (**Update**): update the parameter $\tilde{x}$ by $\tilde{x} = \tilde{x} - \Delta$

In Algorithm 4.4, we present the pseudo-code of quantized and period averaging SGD algorithm, which reduces the communication overhead by implementing two feasible ideas: reducing the number of synchronizations and compressing the gradient. Period averaging is the well-known solution, reducing the number of synchronizations and achieving a remarkable convergence rate. However, this method may not be available at a low-bandwidth network because the cost of each iteration remains unchanged. Although QSGD can fix this shortcoming, the effectiveness and efficiency of the combination depends on its convergence rate. In the following lemma and theorems, we establish the convergence rate of quantized and period averaging SGD in a parameter server architecture.

Algorithm 4.4 Quantized and Period Averaging SGD Algorithm (Worker m)

1: **Input:** Initial point $\tilde{x}_1$, learning rate series $\{\gamma_n\}$, the interval value K, and the number of total iterations N

2: **for** $n \leftarrow 1 \ N$ **do**

3: $\quad x_{n;0}^{(m)} \leftarrow \tilde{x}_n$

4: $\quad$ **for** $k \leftarrow 0 \ K - 1$ **do**

5: $\qquad$ Generate a realization of the random variable $\xi_k^{(m)}$

6: $\qquad x_{n;k+1}^{(m)} \leftarrow x_{n;k}^{(m)} - \gamma_n \nabla f_m(x_{n;k}^{(m)}; \xi_k^{(m)});$

7: $\quad$ **end for**

8: $\quad g_n^{(m)} \leftarrow \text{Quantize}(x_{n;0}^{(m)} - x_{n;K}^{(m)})$

9: $\quad$ Send $g_n^{(m)}$ to all other nodes

10: $\quad$ Receive $g_n^{(j)}, \forall j \in \{1, 2, ..., M\}$:

11:

$$\Delta \leftarrow \frac{1}{M} \sum_{j=1}^{M} g_n^{(j)}$$

12:

13: $\quad$ Update the gradient $\tilde{x}_{n+1} \leftarrow \tilde{x}_n - \Delta$

14: **end for**

The model update policy of quantized and period averaging SGD under a parameter server learning architecture can be expressed by the following recursion functions:

$$x_{n;0}^{(m)} = \tilde{x}_n,$$

$$x_{n;t}^{(m)} = \tilde{x}_n - \gamma_n \sum_{j=0}^{t-1} \nabla f_m\left(x_{n;j}^{(m)}, \xi_j^{(m)}\right),$$

$$\tilde{x}_{n+1} = \tilde{x}_n - \frac{1}{M} \sum_{m=1}^{M} Q_s\left(\gamma_n \sum_{k=0}^{K-1} \nabla f_m\left(x_{n;k}^{(m)}, \xi_k^{(m)}\right)\right). \tag{4.4}$$

where $\nabla F(\cdot)$ denotes the gradient of a function F, $|| \cdot ||_2$ denotes ℓ_2 norm of a vector in $\mathbb{R}^d$, γ_n denotes the learning rate in iteration n, and $Q_s(\cdot)$ denotes the quantization function that quantizes the gradient with s-level.

Since we apply an unbiased quantization method, to derive the convergence rate, the main distinction between this approach and tradition period averaging using AVG-K is the second moment of the quantized part. The following lemma gives a general boundary of this term.

LEMMA 4.1 (Bound the Quantized Gradient) *For any* $m \in \{1, 2, ..., M\}$ *and vector* $w^{(m)} \in \mathbb{R}^d$ *that is independent of others, we have*

$$\mathbb{E}\left[\left\|\frac{1}{M}\sum_{m=1}^{M} Q_s(w^{(m)})\right\|_2^2\right] \leq \frac{d}{4s^2 M^2}\sum_{m=1}^{M} \|w^{(m)}\|_2^2 + \left\|\frac{1}{M}\sum_{m=1}^{M} w^{(m)}\right\|_2^2. \tag{4.5}$$

Under the assumptions of L-smooth function, unbiased stochastic gradient, and bounded gradient variance introduced in Chapter 3, based on the bound derived in Lemma 4.1, the following theorem establishes the upper bound of convergence rate for nonconvex optimization with a fixed learning rate.

THEOREM 4.1 (Convergence Property of Quantized and Period Averaging SGD) *Consider a nonconvex optimization in distributed edge learning. Under assumptions of L-smooth function, unbiased stochastic gradient, and bounded gradient variance, when Algorithm 4.4 is running with a constant learning rate $\bar{\gamma}$ satisfying*

$$1 - 2L\bar{\gamma}K \geq 0 \quad and \quad L^2\bar{\gamma}^2K(K-1) \leq 1 - \delta \quad and$$

$$\frac{L\bar{\gamma}K}{\delta}\left(L\bar{\gamma}(K-1) + \frac{d}{2s^2}\right) \leq 1 - \varepsilon \quad \exists \varepsilon \in (0,1), s$$

then for all $N \geq 1$, we have

$$\frac{1}{N}\sum_{n=1}^{N}\mathbb{E}[\|\nabla F(\tilde{x}_n)\|_2^2] \leq \frac{K(K-1)(\sigma^2+2\kappa^2)}{2\varepsilon\delta}L^2\bar{\gamma}^2 + \frac{D_1}{M\varepsilon}KL\bar{\gamma} + \frac{2[F(\tilde{x}_1) - F_*]}{\bar{\gamma}K\varepsilon N}$$

$$(4.6)$$

where N is the number of iteration, M is the number of participating devices, δ^2 is the upper bound of gradient variance, s is the quantization level, and d is the size of gradient vector. Notation D_1 is a constant represented as follows.

$$D_1 := 2\sigma^2 + \frac{(\sigma^2 + 2\kappa^2)d}{4s^2\delta}$$

To clearly show the convergence result derived in Theorem 4.1, we select an appropriate learning rate in the following theorem to achieve a sublinear convergence rate and a linear speedup property.

THEOREM 4.2 (Convergence Rate of Quantized and Period Averaging SGD) *Under Theorem 4.1, take*

$$\bar{\gamma} := \sqrt{\frac{[F(\tilde{x}_1) - F_*]M}{D_1NLK^2}},$$ $$(4.7)$$

Then for any

$$N \geq \frac{L[F(\tilde{x}_1) - F_*]}{D_1} \cdot \max\left(4M, \frac{(K-1)M}{K(1-\delta)}\right)$$

$$N \geq \frac{L[F(\tilde{x}_1) - F_*]}{D_1} \cdot \max\left(\frac{4s^4(K-1)^2M}{d^2k^2}, \frac{d^2M}{2(1-\varepsilon)^2s^2\delta}\right)$$

$$N \geq \frac{L[F(\tilde{x}_1) - F_*]}{D_1} \cdot \frac{(K-1)^2(\sigma^2+2\kappa^2)^2M^3}{4\delta^2K^2(D_1)^2},$$

the output of Algorithm 4.4 achieves the following convergence rate:

$$\frac{1}{N} \sum_{n=1}^{N} \mathbb{E}[\|\nabla F(\tilde{x}_n)\|_2^2] \leq \frac{4}{\varepsilon} \sqrt{\frac{D_1 L [F(\tilde{x}_1) - F_*]}{NM}}, \tag{4.8}$$

where D_1 is the same as the one in Theorem 4.1.

For the detailed proofs for these lemma and theorems, please refer to [?], which also extend the quantized and period averaging SGD in AllReduce and Decentralized architecture. Since ε, D_1, L, and $[F(\tilde{x}_1) - F_*]$ are constant, this theorem claims that the convergence rate achieves $O(1/\sqrt{NM})$ when total iterations N is sufficiently large. With this result, we have the following observations:

Linear Speedup   Since the only term of the convergent rate is $O(1/\sqrt{NM})$, which has the same result as both period averaging SGD, this indicates that Algorithm 4.4 achieves linear speedup with respect to the number of workers.

This parts introduce quantized and period averaging SGD in a parameter server learning architecture, which is the seamless combination of two famous techniques – QSGD and PR-SGD. Based on theoretical analysis, the algorithm can achieve a sublinear convergence rate and show linear speedup property in parameter server architecture. Furthermore, it significantly saves the total communication overhead and preserves the convergence rate when compared to its prototypes.

4.4   Overlap Synchronization Parallel with Quantization

As stated before, all workers in the distributed SGD sequentially run two procedures - i.e., computing the gradients and synchronizing the gradients. In the synchronizing process, each worker has to send the gradient and receive the refined model, which is dominated by the communication. Since the synchronizing process has to be done in each iteration, when the size of the machine learning model is large, the communication process incurs a significant delay and becomes a prominent bottleneck for the efficiency of the training system. This problem becomes even more severe in the parameter server architecture where the servers have to synchronize all workers in each iteration [389].

To solve the bottleneck, previous work mainly focuses on two kinds of approach: compressing the communication data and designing the overlapping process. Compressing the communication data is to use quantization or sparsification to compress the gradient. Gradient quantization transforms the gradient from 32 bits to fewer bits - e.g., 1 bit [12, 328] - and gradient sparsification only transfers a subset of dimensions of the full gradient [9, 34]. On the other hand, in the overlapping process first proposed in [389], the parameters of a DNN are sent layer by layer in parallel with computing. The experimental results demonstrate a higher computation efficiency when compared to the previous non-overlapped methods. The extended work [322] takes both forward and backward process into account to further improve the overlapping rate. All preceding methods achieve great improvement in reducing the communication delay.

In this section, based on the preceding methods, we introduce a method that further reduces the delay incurred by the communication. The method called QOSP integrates the gradient quantization for communication compression and the Overlap Synchronization Parallel for simultaneous computation and communication. In QOSP, all workers calculate the gradient in a nonstop manner while synchronizing the gradients in parallel such that the communication delay can be significantly reduced.

4.4.1   Algorithm Description

In this subsection, we state the QOSP in the parameter server that integrates gradient quantization and overlap synchronous parallel.

4.4.1.1   Overlap Synchronization with Gradient Quantization

In traditial distributed SGD, each worker first computes the gradient and then transmits the gradient to the server. Next, based on the aggregation of all gradients, the server updates the global model and returns the updated model back to all workers. All these steps are executed in a sequential manner, of which the illustration of a three workers example is shown in Fig. 4.3. It can be observed that the computing units, e.g., GPU and CPU, are idle when the synchronization starts. We show that these idle time can be significantly reduced by using the overlap and quantization methods.

In QOSP, each worker creates two threads that are responsible for computing gradients and communicating gradients respectively. The two threads are run in parallel, so the huge delay incurred by synchronization could be totally eliminated. The illustration of the overall workflow is shown in Fig. 4.3(c). In each iteration, Thread 1 pulls the current global model and pushes the gradients to the master. Thread 2 employs the global model received by Thread 1 to compute the gradients. By communicating with Thread 1 of all P workers, the server can receive all gradients. The server aggregates them and returns the aggregated gradient back to all workers.

The workflow of the two threads are presented in the function *Comm* and *Comp*, which are shown in Algorithms 4.6 and 4.7, respectively. In each iteration t, worker i calculates the gradients $g_{t,k}^i$ by using the local model $\omega_{t,k}^i$ and accumulates the gradients into Δ_t^i. For updating the model, the worker employs the *Comp* function to replace the local model $\omega_{t,k}^i$ with the global model ω_t when the global model is pulled back. Otherwise, the *Comp* function will update the local model $\omega_{t,k}^i$ with the gradient calculated by itself. It proceeds to update its local model with gradients computed by itself until a bounded number of iterations τ are reached or a new global model are pulled back from the server. To collaborate with the server that enables distributed learning, the function *Comm* is responsible for the gradients pushing and model pulling operation. In corresponding with *Comp*, the function *Comm* pulls the global model ω_t from the server and pushes the local accumulated gradient to the server.

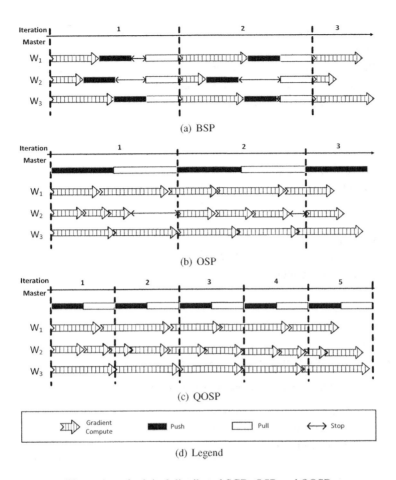

(a) BSP

(b) OSP

(c) QOSP

(d) Legend

Figure 4.3 Illustration of original distributed SGD, OSP, and QOSP.

Specifically, the quantization employed by QOSP reflects that the worker quantizes the local accumulated gradients to get $Q(\Delta_t^i)$ so that the communication data sent to server is compressed. In fact, the training process can be accelerated by quantization. Since the communication time is reduced due to the traffic compression, the frequency of refining the local model with the global model improves, which leads to better convergence efficiency.

It is worthwhile to note that the number of bounded iterations τ is designed to restrict the number of internal updates in a worker, aiming to reduce the variance of local gradients and the diversity of searching directions between workers to guarantee the convergence rate of the algorithm. To improve the ratio between computation time and total execution time, we could adjust the bounded iterations τ, the quantization level s, and the number of workers P. Because the computation and synchronization overlap, the ratio could reach 100%, as the computation time is no less than the synchronization time.

Algorithm 4.5 QOSP

1: **Worker** i:;
2: **Input:** learning rate η_t, compensated step size γ, iterations threshold τ;
3: **Initialize:** $k = 0$, $isPull = false$, $\Delta_0^i = 0$;
4: **Parallel** *Thread 1* and *Thread 2*:

5:
6: *Thread 1:*
7: **Repeat;**
8: 　　$Comm(isPull, \Delta_t^i)$;
9: **Until Convergence;**

10:
11: *Thread 2:*
12: **Repeat;**
13: 　　$Comp(\eta_t, \gamma, \tau, k, isPull, \Delta_t^i, \omega_t, t)$;
14: **Until Convergence;**

15:
16: **Server:;**
17: **Initialize:** $t = 0$, initialize ω_0 randomly;
18: **Repeat;**
19: 　　receives Δ_t^i from each worker i;
20: 　　computes global update $\Delta_t \leftarrow \frac{1}{P} \sum_{i=1}^{P} \Delta_t^i$;
21: 　　broadcasts Δ_t to all workers;
22: 　　updates global clock $t \leftarrow t + 1$;
23: **Until Convergence;**

Algorithm 4.6 Function *Comm*

1: **Input:** $isPull, \Delta_t^i$;
2: pulls $Q(\Delta_t)$ from the master;
3: **if** Δ_{t+1}^i is not 0 **then**
4: 　　copies the local update $\Delta^i \leftarrow \Delta_{t+1}^i$;
5: 　　sets the pulled flag $isPull \leftarrow True$;
6: 　　clears the local update $\Delta_{t+1}^i \leftarrow 0$;
7: 　　pushes quantized local update $Q(\Delta^i)$ to the master;
8: **end if**

4.4.2　Theoretical Results

Now, we establish the convergence rate of QOSP. The quantization scheme introduces a precision loss of accumulated gradient in each worker, which will be further aggregated at the server in the synchronization process. The convergence rate of QOSP is affected by the precision loss combined with the staleness incurred by overlapping and local updates. The relationship between these factors is complicated. To analyze their

---

Algorithm 4.7 Function *Comp*

1: **Input:** $\eta_t, \gamma, \tau, k, isPull, \Delta_t^i, \omega_t, t$;
2: **if** $k \geq \tau$ **then**
3:     wait until $isPull$ is $True$;
4: **end if**
5: **if** $isPull$ is $True$ **then**
6:     resets the flag $isPull \leftarrow false$;
7:     updates global model $\omega_{t+1} \leftarrow \omega_t - Q(\Delta_t)$;
8:     compensates local model $\omega_{t+1,k}^i \leftarrow \omega_{t+1} - \gamma\Delta^i$;
9:     resets the local clock $k \leftarrow 0$;
10:     updates global clock $t \leftarrow t + 1$;
11: **end if**
12: computes stochastic gradient $g_{t,k}^i \leftarrow \nabla f_\xi(\omega_{t,k}^i)$;
13: accumulates the local gradients $\Delta_t^i \leftarrow \Delta_t^i + \eta_t g_{t,k}^i$;
14: updates local model $\omega_{t,k+1}^i \leftarrow \omega_{t,k}^i - \eta_t g_{t,k}^i$;
15: updates local clock $k \leftarrow k + 1$;

---

relationship, here, we adopt QSGD [12] as the quantization method, which is one of the most popular communication quantization technology. The key idea is to quantize each dimension of a vector from the 32 bits to the smaller number of bits. QSGD first determines a quantization level $s(\geq 1)$ and then quantizes each dimension v_i of the vector $\mathbf{v}$ via an unbiased manner. Now, given the quantization level and local update policy, we derive the convergence properties of QOSP in the following theorem.

THEOREM 4.3 (The Convergence Property of QOSP)   *(QOSP, Nonconvex objective, fixed stepsize) Let the average of the number of local updates of all workers be $\bar{K}$. Suppose algorithm QOSP is run with a fixed learning rate $\eta_t = \bar{\eta}$ satisfying*

$$\frac{L\bar{\eta}K_{max}}{P}\left[P + P\bar{\eta}L(K_{max} - 1) + \min\left(\frac{d}{s^2}, \frac{\sqrt{d}}{s}\right) \right.$$
$$\left. + 2P\bar{\eta}L\bar{K} + 2\bar{\eta}L\min\left(\frac{d}{s^2}, \frac{\sqrt{d}}{s}\right)\bar{K} \right] \leq 1, \tag{4.9}$$

where $K_{max} = \max\{K_t^i, t = 1, 2, \ldots, N$ and $i = 1, 2, \ldots, P\}$. Then the expected average squared gradient norms satisfy the following bounds for all $N \in \mathbb{N}$:

$$\frac{1}{N}\sum_{t=1}^{N}\mathbb{E}\|\nabla F(\omega_t)\|_2^2 \leq \frac{2[F(\omega_1) - F(\omega_\star)]}{N\bar{\eta}\bar{K}} + \bar{\eta}L\sigma^2\left[\frac{(1 + \min(\frac{d}{s^2}, \frac{\sqrt{d}}{s}))}{P} + \frac{\bar{\eta}LM}{\bar{K}} \right.$$
$$\left. + \bar{\eta}L\bar{K} - \bar{\eta}L + \frac{2\bar{\eta}L(1 + \min(\frac{d}{s^2}, \frac{\sqrt{d}}{s}))\bar{K}}{P} \right]. \tag{4.10}$$

For the better understanding of Theorem 4.3, we further present the convergence result in the following corollary.

THEOREM 4.4 (The Convergence Rate of QOSP) *Under the condition of Theorem 4.3, if we set*

$$\bar{\eta} = \sqrt{\frac{(F(\omega_1) - F(\omega^\star))P}{\bar{K}L\sigma^2 N(1 + \min(\frac{d}{s^2}, \frac{\sqrt{d}}{s}))}},$$
(4.11)

then for any iteration number

$$N \geq \frac{(F(\omega_1) - F(\omega^\star))(\frac{M}{\bar{K}} + \bar{K} - 1 + \frac{2\bar{K}(1+\min(\frac{d}{s^2}, \frac{\sqrt{d}}{s}))}{P})LP^3}{\bar{K}L\sigma^2(1 + \min(\frac{d}{s^2}, \frac{\sqrt{d}}{s}))^3},$$
(4.12)

the output of QOSP algorihtm satisfies the following ergodic convergence rate

$$\frac{1}{N}\sum_{t=1}^{N} \mathbb{E}\|\nabla F(\omega_t)\|^2 \preceq O\left(\frac{1}{\sqrt{PN}}\right) + O\left(\frac{1}{N}\right),$$
(4.13)

where $\preceq$ denotes order inequality, which means less than or equal to up to a constant factor.

Proof The result of ergodic convergence rate is derived by replacing η in Eq. (4.10) according to (4.11). By combining with the constraint of (4.9), the inequality of (4.13) holds. □

Obviously, there always exists positive $\bar{\eta}$ that satisfies condition (4.9). This result of Theorem 4.4 suggests that QOSP essentially admits the same convergence rate as sequential D-SGD since it has the asymptotical convergence rate $O(1/\sqrt{N})$. More specifically, QOSP runs with the convergence rate $O(1/\sqrt{PT})$, which means that it has the linear speedup property with respect to the number of workers, resulting in high efficiency in large-scale distributed machine learning. Despite the fact that the quantization error and staleness affect the speed of training process, the order of convergence rate maintains and the staleness only introduce the higher order of N - i.e., $O(1/N)$. Consequently, the communication complexity could be significantly reduced due to quantization and local updates, and the synchronization delay could be almost eliminated due to overlapping computation and communication.

4.5 Wireless Network Optimization for Edge Learning

With the development of wireless communication techniques and the growing computation capabilities of mobile devices, a group of mobile devices cooperatively training a global model becomes practical in many intelligent applications - e.g., federated learning [196]. The communication cost is the main bottleneck in this on-device training scenario because mobile devices iteratively transmit the updates and synchronize the model parameter, especially when a large number of participants are training a large-scale model.

Many communication compression methods have been proposed for in-cloud training - e.g., quantization [14] and sparsification [260]. These compression methods can be directly applied in distributed training over mobile devices. Nevertheless, the communication cost is still proportional to the number of participants, and thus inefficient in large-scale edge training over mobile devices.

4.5.1 Scheduling Policy for Communication-Efficient Edge Learning in Wireless Environments

It is impractical to aggregate all the local updates in each round of edge learning. Firstly, large quantities of local devices will participate in the training process of edge learning. However, the radio resources, such as the spectrum and bandwidth, are too limited to support such a large number of devices at the same time. Secondly, because different devices have different computation and communication capabilities, one device may need a longer time to compute the local update and transmit it, which result in a longer round and greatly slowdown the whole training process. Finally, if the local devices upload model updates to the parameter server in every iteration, it will quickly drain the local devices, which carry very limited energy. Due to these reasons, it is very meaningful to design an efficient scheduling policy, which means to select the devices or allocate the radio resources properly [346, 353] in the process of edge learning, as shown in Fig. 4.4.

The goal of federated learning is often different as the application scenarios of federated learning change. Some scenarios prioritize the convergence time of learning. Some pay attention to the energy consumption of local devices. Some work prioritize the accuracy of the global model more. The application of scheduling strategy will reduce the number of devices participating in each round of iteration, which may reduce the energy consumption of equipment, and will inevitably affect the convergence time of edge learning and the accuracy of the global model. Therefore, it is worth studying if a suitable scheduling strategy is designed, In the following, recent studies about the scheduling strategies for different objectives are analyzed and discussed.

4.5.1.1 Convergence Analysis for Edge Learning in Wireless Environment

Most of the research focuses on the convergence of edge learning because it is the most basic requirement of an federated learning algorithm and to analyze it is the primary task of one study. In synchronous edge learning, the iteration time of each round depends on the device with the longest total computation and transmission time. Therefore, reducing the time of the slowest node in each iteration is a feasible strategy. In [237], Pilla proposes an algorithm, named Optimal Assignment of Tasks to Resources (OLAR), which can provide optimal scheduling by dividing the whole task into independent, identical, and automatic tasks and assigning them to heterogeneous resources with non-decreasing cost functions. Similarly, Yang, et al. in [354], propose

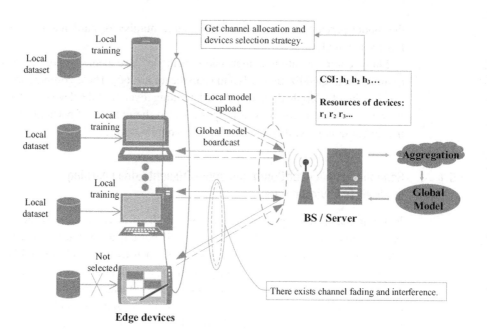

Figure 4.4 Illustration of scheduling policy and channel allocation for communication efficient edge learning in wireless environments.

an algorithm to decouple the global training model into different subproblems that local devices solve individually. They develop an analytical model that characterizes the performance of edge learning in wireless networks, and they compare the effectiveness of three different scheduling policies - i.e., random scheduling, round robin, and proportionally fair in terms of edge learning convergence rates in different scenarios.

The wireless channel state information and statistical characteristics of clients are not known in real applications while assumed perfect in most studies. To tackle this issue, in [337], W. Xia, et al. propose an online scheduling policy based on the multiarmed bandit algorithm for minimizing the total training time. In [18], M. M. Amiri, et al. use the data compression scheme proposed in their previous work [17], called the digital SGD quantization scheme, to employ digital transmission. To reduce the convergence time, four proposed scheduling algorithms - which are the best channel (BC), best L_2-norm (BN2), best channel-best L_2-norm (BC-BN2), and best L_2-norm channel (BN2-C) schemes - are then proposed.

The convergence rate of edge learning is very significant in the wireless environment, which are the limited energy and bandwidth. In [294], two trade-offs are described. One is between the computation and communication learning time while finding the optimal parameter of training accuracy; the other one is between the training time of edge learning and the energy of local devices consumed by communication and computation. In order to get the optimal allocation strategy while considering these two trade-offs, Tran, et al. propose an optimization problem and split this nonconvex problem into two solvable subproblems exploiting the particular structure of it in [294]. The optimal results from their rigorous mathematical proof are examined by simulation experiments.

4.5.1.2 Optimizing the Energy Consumption of Mobile Devices in Edge Learning

Most of mobile devices are equipped with a battery that can only last for a limited period of time.There are two parts in edge learning consume the battery of local devices; one is local model training, which needs a lot of computation, and the other one is transmitting local model updates to the parameter server. The energy consumed by downloading global model updates is negligible compared to the other two parts. Thus, it is necessary to consider the energy consumption during the training process of edge learning. The proposed greedy algorithm in [222, 264] attempts to complete edge learning in a shorter amount of time by selecting as many devices as possible in every iteration. However, the greedy algorithm may not find the global optimal solution. In addition, the rounds of edge learning are not only temporally interdependent but also have varying significance towards the final learning outcome due to the limited energy. Hence, in [347], Xu, et al. considering the bandwidth allocation and client selection from a long-term perspective, formulate this scheduling as an stochastic optimization problem. They regard the power consumption of mobile devices and the wireless conditions as the long-term constraints, and they propose an algorithm named OCEAN to solve this problem. In [382], Zeng, et al. aiming to minimize the sum energy consumption of local devices while warranting the convergence speed of edge learning, propose two novel radio resources management (RRM) strategies that can jointly allocate bandwidth and schedule devices to participate in training. In their proposed strategy, devices under good wireless conditions and powerful computation capacities will be allocated less bandwidth but scheduled with higher priority, while devices under poor conditions will gain more bandwidth.

Similarly, considering the problem of limited energy in local devices, Yang, et al. in [359], intend to minimize the weighted sum of total delay and energy consumption and then find the optimal time and resources allocation. They develop an iterative algorithm with low complexity to solve this minimization problem, which could obtain the optimal resource allocation scheme according to their theoretical analysis. This algorithm performs better than other regular edge learning algorithms in simulation experiments.

4.5.1.3 Model Accuracy Analysis under Resource Allocation in Wireless Environment

Because the data between devices in heterogeneous scenarios is usually very different in data size and distribution, the model generated by parameter server through edge learning can be high on average while may be very low in some devices whose data is far different from most devices. Considering the energy constraint, in [281], Sun, et al. propose an online scheduling policy, which can maximize the average number of workers per iterative scheduling gradient update under long-term energy constraints and achieve little short of optimal accuracy.

Considering the wireless resources allocation and clients scheduling, it is often assumed that the local devices perform the perfect transmission - i.e. ignore the packet errors. Therefore, in [38], Chen, et al. formulate the joint wireless resources allocation and client selection while considering the wireless factors and energy constraints as an optimization problem. The goal of it is to find the optimal radio resource allocation, optimal user selection, and optimal transmit power to minimize the value of the loss function of edge learning. Their proposed algorithm, which uses the Hungarian algorithm to find the optimal strategy, reduces the loss by about 15% from the simulation experiments. Likewise, a novel joint client scheduling and resource block allocation strategy for imperfect channel state information proposed in [303] also reduce the loss of accuracy. Non-Orthogonal Multiple Access (NOMA) allows multiple users to transmit simultaneously on the same channel. Therefore, in a NOMA setting, the scheduling problem can be treated as a maximum weight independent set problem and the proposed solution achieves higher accuracy [188].

In the Table 4.1, we summarize the optimization objectives and constraints considered in scheduling policies for communication-efficient edge learning.

4.5.2   MIMO and Over-the-Air Computation for Fast Aggregation in Edge Learning

Very recently, with the assistance of a central server equipped with a massive antenna array, new technologies have been proposed for massive multiple-input multiple-output (MIMO) communication systems - i.e., MIMO-based communication and over-the-air computation for efficient edge learning training.

The success of edge learning relies heavily on wireless communication. Efficient scheduling strategies and compression methods can make good use of the number and capacity of wireless channels. However, most of the previously mentioned studies are based on single-input and single-output systems while majority of devices and parameter servers are equipped with multiple antennas. There will be interference, called the multipath effect, between the wireless channels that are allocated to these antennas, which can be used for improving privacy [63, 142]. In traditional wireless network architecture, if no corresponding measures are taken to remove it, the signal may be distorted or wrong at the receiver due to the interference caused by the superposition of their respective phases. However, while applying edge learning in MIMO systems, if adopting complex signal processing techniques, this natural characteristic of wireless channels can be used to significantly enhance reliability, transmission range, and data throughput. Through these techniques, the transmitter can transmit multiple radio frequency signals at the same time, and the receiver can recover the data from these signals. If fully using these antennas, local devices can form a MIMO system with parameter servers, as shown in Fig. 4.5, to greatly improve channel capacity and hence the performance of edge learning. The other characteristic of MIMO system is its high spectrum efficiency. On the basis of making full use of the existing spectrum resources, the gain of reliability and effectiveness can be obtained by using space resources. MIMO also brings challenges to processing the data, just as in complex signal processing techniques mentioned before, to transmit both in

Table 4.1. Optimization objectives of scheduling policies in edge learning with constrained resources

Objectives	References	Energy	Convergence Time	Non-i.i.d.	Wireless Condition	Mobility	Heterogeneous	Asynchronous
Accelerate the convergence	[354]		✓	✓				
	[18]	✓	✓	✓	✓		✓	
	[294]	✓	✓	✓	✓		✓	
	[242]		✓	✓				
	[222]		✓	✓		✓		
	[264]		✓		✓			
Reduce the energy consumption	[318]	✓	✓	✓	✓	✓		
	[384]	✓	✓		✓	✓		
	[382]	✓	✓		✓			
	[359]	✓	✓	✓	✓			✓
	[347]	✓	✓		✓			
Improve the accuracy	[38]	✓	✓		✓		✓	
	[163]		✓	✓				

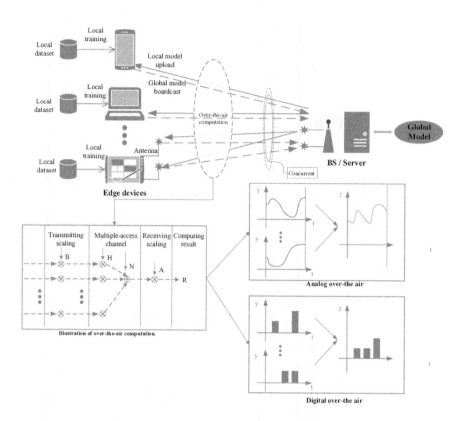

Figure 4.5 Illustration of over-the-air computation for fast aggregation in edge learning.

local devices and parameter servers, which is worth studying. High-performance, low-complexity signal detection methods or joint-detection methods have always been a hot topic for researchers.

Huang et al. [61, 408] discuss a case study of fast analog transmission and Grassmann learning over a MIMO communication system. They focus on improving the transmission efficiency of data samples located on a group of mobile devices, which are equipped with antenna arrays and forms a set of narrowband MIMO channels. By using linear analog modulation and quantization, they proposed a fast analog transmission (FAT) scheme, which allows CSI-free transmission and significantly reduces the transmission latency. Vu et al., propose a transmission scheme for cell-free MIMO networks to support federated learning over mobile devices [302]. They focus on minimizing the time of the training process and formulate a mixed timescale stochastic nonconvex optimization problem in a cell-free MIMO network. By capturing the complex interactions among the participants of the training, and the characteristics of transmission and computation in model training, the local training accuracy, the processing frequency of the mobile device, the transmission power, and the transmission rate can be jointly optimized. Huang et al. [119] propose an approach named Physical-Layer Arithmetic (PhyArith) that first applies physical-layer coding techniques in wireless networks featuring uplink multiuser multiple-input and multiple-output (MU-MIMO). The novelty lies in that the mobile devices encode and then send their gradients to the server simultaneously, while the server can directly recover the exact summation of these gradients by exploiting the inherent superposition of radio frequency (RF) signals. Obviously, PhyArith is compatible with traditional communication compression methods like quantization. Because there is no need to decode the gradient of every mobile device, PhyArith significantly accelerates the training process.

Considering the physical characteristics of wireless channels and that multiple antennas can be equipped in parameter servers, which means that in a massive multiple-input multiple-output (MIMO) system, developing appropriate reception techniques can significantly improve the capacity of wireless channels. While applying edge learning in a MIMO system, the central parameter server would use a proper reception technique to estimate the local gradient vectors calculated in and sent from local devices to build the global model. In order to reduce the error caused by estimation, in [127], Jeon et al. develop a new gradient-estimation method. The main idea of their method is to exploit the sparsity of the local gradient vector. The transmission strategy they adopted allows that multiple devices transmit their local gradient vectors simultaneously, only occupying one channel while still keeping the sparsity of the local gradient vector, which means that there are only few devices whose gradient are not zero. Based on this, they propose a novel gradient-estimation algorithm to find devices with non-zero gradients. Compared to existing methods such as linear minimum mean square error (LMMSE), it has lower complexity and better performance - complexity trade-off demonstrated by simulation results.

In addition, by exploiting the superposition nature of wireless communication, the over-the-air computation can greatly accelerate the update aggregation and facilitate communication-efficient machine learning in the wireless environment.

In traditional edge learning framework, local updates need to be transmitted via wireless channels and then the parameter server aggregates these updates and calculates their average for the next round of iteration. In order to avoid interference in wireless channels, each local device needs to be allocated orthogonal radio resources. So the whole calculation of averaging can be completed only after all the updates arrive, which causes a large time delay, as the number of local devices increases while the wireless resources are limited. Over-the-air computation is a new technology that takes advantage of the waveform superposition characteristic of wireless channels [179]. While adopting over-the-air computation in edge learning, all of local devices that need to transmit updates can transmit concurrently, and the parameter server can directly obtain the summation of local updates, in which only one wireless channel is needed. An over-the-air computation-based edge learning framework is developed for Intelligent IoT in [356] and proved to be effectively in reducing the communication load and aggregation error.

As shown in Fig. 4.5, there exists analog and digital over-the-air computation. In analog over-the-air computation [256], each local device does not encode its update in any form, but only does some preprocessing and then transmits. All updates are aggregated and processed by the parameter server. The uncoded analog over-the-air computation is simple but is easily affected by noise, especially when the transmitting power is lower than normal level, which may cause errors in aggregation and may even not be able to converge. Digital over-the-air computation [133] has good noise immunity, in which updates are coded through quantization or other code strategy and then transmits. The parameter can decode them after aggregation.

While applying over-the-air computation in edge learning, good scheduling policy and power control strategy can achieve high performance, which significantly reduces the convergence time of edge learning. And due to channel fading, power control is very important in over-the-air computation [393]. It is often not applicable in practical scenarios to normalized the updates when the distribution of updates is unknown for local devices. Therefore, a power control strategy that ignores the distribution of updates may perform poorly. To address this issue, Zhang, et al. in [392] try to get the optimal power control strategy to minimize the error occurring in aggregation to speed up the convergence and improve the accuracy of federated learning. At first, they derive the optimal power control strategy when the distribution is known, and they analyze the special cases where the data sets used for training are highly non-IID. Finally, the adaptive optimal power control strategy is proposed based on the estimation of updates distribution, which is obtained from historical updates.

Gunduz et al. [83] focus on physical layer optimization and over-the-air computation technologies for on-device training in the wireless environment. They summarize and discuss the major promises, the challenges, and some recent research advances in this field. Zhu et al. [407] propose a 1-bit broadband digital aggregation approach, which combines 1-bit gradient quantization , digital modulation at mobile devices, and a majority-voting-based decoding scheme at the server to improve the efficiency of wireless transmission for on-device training. Yang et al. [355] further consider the distribution of training data across mobile devices and propose an over-the-air computation based approach by joint optimizing device selection and beamforming design. Both theoretical results and simulation results demonstrate the effectiveness of the proposed algorithms.

4.6   Conclusion and Future Directions

In edge learning, the training process generally contains iterative transmission and aggregation of local updates - i.e., gradient computed upon local samples - while energy and communication resources are rather limited in edge devices. One issue that significantly slows down the training process is communication overhead. Recently, to pursue extreme accuracy and improve the generalization ability, more and more sophisticated machine learning models - e.g., deep learning models with millions or billions of dimensions - are adopted in various practical applications. Due to the limited bandwidth of the network, high communication cost is the main bottleneck for large-scale edge learning with SGD-based optimization.

In this chapter, we introduce the mainstream approaches to achieve communication efficiency of edge training, including compressing communication data, reducing the synchronous frequency, overlapping computation and communication, and optimizing the wireless transmission network. In the following, we discuss the future directions of communication-efficient edge learning.

4.6.1 Two-Pass Compression Method for Edge Learning

To alleviate communication overhead, various communication compression methods have been proposed recently. They can be classified into three categories - i.e., gradient quantization , gradient sparsification, and lazy gradient pushing. It has been shown that the previously discussed methods are effective in reducing the communication cost of the procedure of pushing the local gradient.

Because the gradient and the model are vectors with the same size, it has great significance to investigate two-pass compression methods. Very recently, a handful of studies propose efficient two-pass compression methods for both pushing and pulling [288, 378], which fall in quantization and sparsification categories.

Few studies consider the hybrid mechanisms for two-pass compression, such as quantized/sparsified gradient pushing and lazily model pulling. This idea comes from the fault-tolerance property of SGD that the training process could still converge under some tiny faults incurred by a fraction of workers [239]. Due to this property, it is not necessary for all workers to pull the global model. Workers that do not pull the global model from the server could utilize their local updated model to substitute the global model and thereby significantly reduce the communication overhead. However, the hybrid two-pass compression still faces challenges in both algorithm design and theoretical analysis. The reason lies in the difference between the compression for pulling operation and pushing operation. The error of pushed gradients incurred by quantization or sparsification can be viewed as noise because it could be naturally reduced in the pushing procedure that computes the average of quantized parameters from all workers, which does not apply to compression for pulling operation.

4.6.2 Gradient Compression Robust to Byzantine Workers

Distributed SGD enables the significant acceleration for training large models by parallelly computing the gradient in multiple workers. Gradient sparsification that only sends several dimensions of the gradient can further accelerate the training through reducing the communication cost. However, gradient sparsification has its limitations, the failures in the adversarial settings where some workers are Byzantine.

While the gradient sparsification has witnessed great achievements, its applicability highly relies on a key assumption - all gradients sent by workers are correct. This assumption, however, breaks in distributed learning systems with Byzantine workers, where gradients may be arbitrarily forged by malicious attackers. Although massive robust learning methods have been developed for tolerating Byzantine workers, including selecting good gradients or getting rid of wrong gradients from all gradients, they rely on a majority-based assumption that most of the values of each single dimension are sent by honest workers, which can hardly be satisfied by the existing gradient sparsificaition methods.

In the dimensional level, they require that most of the values for the same dimension are sent by honest workers. They implicitly require the gradient in server to be integral - i.e., containing all dimensions, such that the good majority can be guaranteed for each dimension that can hardly be satisfied by the current sparsificaition techniques.

Nowadays, massive works have been developed for the two problems respectively. On one hand, to guarantee the correctness of the aggregated gradient, various Byzantine tolerance operators that select good gradients or get rid of the bad gradients from all received gradients in server have been designed. This is because the current Byzantine tolerance operators used in server require the gradients sent from workers to be integral that contain all dimensions while existing gradient sparsification methods only transfer several dimensions of the original gradients. As a consequence, to enable the distributed SGD running with robust to Byzantine workers while retaining high communication efficiency, a novel method is in urgent demand.

4.6.3 Communication Compression for Two-Order Optimization Algorithm

The existing edge learning communication compression methods are based on SGD optimization framework and are in the empty stage of communication optimization and convergence analysis for the second-order optimization methods. In the first-order optimization framework based on SGD, parameter updating is based on gradient vector or linear combination iterative updating of past gradients. The parameter updating strategy of the second-order optimization method is: $\omega_{t+1} = \omega_t + H_t g_t$, where g_t is the gradient in iteration t and H_t is a second-order matrix, such as a Hessian matrix with second-order partial derivative in Newton method, and a correlation coefficient matrix between gradient and gradient in preconditioning method. The existing research results show that the second-order optimization method can greatly improve the convergence speed compared with the first-order optimization method. However, with the increase of model parameters in edge learning, the transmission of the second-order matrix will cause intolerable communication overhead. At the same time, the convergence speed and training accuracy of the second-order matrix compression and approximation methods lack theoretical guarantee.

Existing theoretical results show that the second-order optimization method can achieve the second-order convergence rate in single node training, which significantly outperform the first-order optimization method like SGD based methods. In the edge learning, the traditional first-order optimization method determines the direction of optimization by gradient, which can be directly aggregated by summation or averaging. However, the second-order optimization method usually determines the search direction according to the inverse matrix of Hessian matrix, the summation of inverse Hession metrics from multiple training nodes is different from the inverse summation of Hession metrics. Moreover, considering that the inversion operation of Hessian matrix is very complex, and there may be nonpositive definite cases, the existing single-node training methods usually use approximate methods to describe the forward direction of the search. The approximation of Hessian matrix can not only reduce the computational cost, but also reduce the dimension of effective information, which has the potential of communication compression. Therefore, one direction is to design communication compression mechanisms for second-order optimization in edge learning, and to analyze their convergence rate.

5 Computation Acceleration

5.1 Introduction to Computation Acceleration

Currently, machine learning methods can be implemented on distributed and heterogeneous computation units – e.g., CPUs, GPUs, neural processing unit (NPUs), field programmable gate array (FPGAs). In addition, the popularity of 5G communication systems and trusted execution environments (TEE) provide hardware support of high-capacity communication and private computation. However, due to the resource restraints as well as the mismatch between the structure of the algorithm and the architecture of hardware platforms, current solutions still suffer from low resource utilization and unnecessarily high energy costs. Moreover, the communication efficiency and privacy protection for distributed training and inference are still critical issues. Therefore, we propose a comprehensive review of computation acceleration technologies from both the algorithm level and hardware level.

This chapter will first focus on model compression and hardware acceleration for efficient, cost-effective, and privacy-preserving machine learnings. It will cover many aspects, including the learning algorithms, learning-oriented communication, distributed machine learning with hardware adaptation, TEE-based privacy protection, algorithm and hardware joint optimization, etc. The essential objective is to implement an integrated algorithm-hardware platform, in order to optimize the implementation of emerging machine learning algorithms, to fully explore the potential of modern computation hardware, and to promote novel intelligent applications for sophisticated services.

Then we introduce straggler tolerance schemes that can avoid the overall training performance seriously degraded by faulty nodes, and can efficiently utilize the computation power of slow nodes. Large-scale edge learning systems are usually composed of devices with unreliable low-performance hardware, and hence sudden failure of edge devices often occurs. At the same time, the completion time of the training task is difficult to predict and shows great fluctuations due to the dynamic edge environment, load imbalances, power limitations, shared resource competition, etc. Such slow or faulty edge devices, known as "stragglers", seriously drag down the overall training process. Therefore, we introduce straggler tolerance schemes and the corresponding migration strategies to guarantee the reliability of the edge learning systems.

Finally, we introduce computation acceleration technologies for inference at the edge. After the training of the machine learning model, the efficient implementation of model inference to classify, recognize, and process new inputs at the edge will be critical for enabling high-quality edge learning service deployment. The collected input data can be directly processed at the edge devices to derive the final outputs. Thus, we will introduce model deployment and update strategies to do model inference in the edge to achieve the best inference service experience.

5.2   Model Compression and Hardware Acceleration

On top of the theoretical analysis and algorithm optimization of the machine learning applications, fully accelerating the task processing speed requires the coordination of underlay hardware, which is the fundamental part that deploys all the distributed machine learning architectures. In this section, we will discuss the hardware implementation: (1) schduling of multiple computation primitives, (2) I/O connection optimization, (3) memory management and (4) dedicated hardware.

5.2.1   model compression

The training and inference of neural networks often yield a high amount of pressure on the computation primitives, data storage, memory footprint, and electric power. This phenomenon becomes more crucial when deploying modern machine learning applications in the resource-hungry GPU-based environment. Although it is possible to obtain more resources by handling the neural networks in a distributed manner, the previously mentioned challenges may still become the performance bottleneck of distributed machine learning systems. Therefore, it is urgent to study how to make machine learning applications work in the resource-constrained scenarios.

Fortunately, previous studies of neural network design have shown that neural networks are often trained in a over-parameterized way, where a great portion of neurons or network structures are redundant with trivial information and can be removed from the network without downgrading the model quality. This research discovery points out a promising direction to alleviate the huge resource requirements – i.e., reducing the network complexity by compressing the model. Recently, model compression has become a hot research topic in the area of neural network optimization. In this section, we will discuss three typical compression techniques: (1) low-rank factorization, (2) network pruning, and (3) data quantization.

5.2.1.1   Low-Rank Factorization

Low-rank factorization is a straightforward compression method that reduces the matrix size. Considering the property that the computation pressure of executing machine learning applications mainly comes from matrix operations, a natural idea to alleviate the overhead is to reduce the matrix complexity. As the matrices in the neural network are often sparse with many zero or near-zero elements, it is possible to factorize the primary sparse matrix into several low-rank vectors. Meanwhile, the multiplication of these vectors can be used to recover the original matrix.

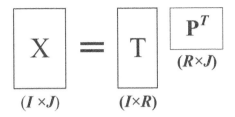

Figure 5.1 Low-rank factorization simplifies the matrix representation and reduces the memory footprint.

Specifically, we can use the *Singular Value Decomposition* (SVD) [150] method to simplify the computational operations of two-dimensional matrices. The core matrix transformation inside SVD can be formulated as: $\mathbf{M} = \mathbf{UAV}^T$, where $\mathbf{U}_{l \times m}$ and the conjugate transpose $\mathbf{top}_{m \times n}$ are orthogonal to each other. Note that $\mathbf{A}_{m \times m}$ is a diagonal $m \times m$ matrix with nonnegative elements. As to real-world DNNs, we can introduce the SVD-based methods to compress the weight matrices inside CONV layers and reduce the memory footprint to represent these parameters.

Moreover, as to the compression of parameter matrices in FC layers, the factorization method can be further simplified because the matrix rank is approximately to 1 or less than 3. Considering this matrix sparsity, it is possible to use the *Sufficient Factor Broadcasting* (SFB) [342], [341], [389] method, a special variant of SVD, to fully compress the matrix. The basic idea of SFB can be expressed as $\mathbf{M} = \mathbf{uv}^T$, where $\mathbf{u}_{1 \times m}$ and $\mathbf{v}_{m \times 1}^T$ are regarded as sufficient factors to reconstruct the original matrix $\mathbf{M}$.

Here, we use an example to better illustrate the effectiveness of low-rank factorization. As shown in Fig. 5.1, the matrix $\mathbf{X}$ represents the parameters of a given layer with the shape of $I \times J$. After conducting the matrix factorization, $\mathbf{X}$ will be factorized into two small matrices – i.e., $\mathbf{X} = \mathbf{TP}^T$ – where $\mathbf{T}$ and $\mathbf{P}^T$ are in the shape of $I \times R$ and $R \times J$, respectively. In general, R is far smaller than I and J. Therefore, the original shape $I \times J$ to represent matrix $mathbf{X}$ is is much smaller than the shape sum of matrices $\mathbf{T}$ and $\mathbf{P}^T$ – i.e., $I \times J \ll I \times R + R \times J$. We can observe that the corresponding memory footprint to cover the elements of matrix $mathbf{X}$ is significantly reduced. This is the key advantage of low-rank factorization to compress the model size. It is worth noting that matrix factorization mainly focuses on the memory-level optimization, but it cannot significantly improve the computational acceleration. In contrast, matrix factorization may lead to the operation mismatching of matrix calculation because $mathbf{X}$ is represented by two vectors instead of the original square matrix. As a result, low-rank factorization may face some issues in real-world deployment. In practice, network pruning and data quantization are two widely used techniques in modern machine learning applications. We will discuss them in what follows.

Overall, low-rank factorization is a simple but effective method to reduce the matrix shape for storing model parameters. By compressing the model size, the intermediate operations of neural networks are simplified, and the computational pressure is greatly alleviated.

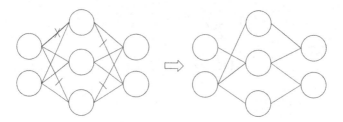

Figure 5.2 Network pruning.

5.2.1.2   Network Pruning

As the neural network complexity keeps growing, the model size and calculation pressure will exhaust the limited computational capacity of the machine. Consequently, simplifying the model structure is one of the most critical issues for the deployment of the real-world machine learning applications. Here, we will discuss the network pruning [193] techniques, which are effective at accomplishing the objective of model compression.

As shown in Fig. 5.2, the gist of network pruning is very straightforward– i.e., ignoring the parameters of the insignificant neurons and retraining the adjusted network until model convergence. Generally, there are five core steps for conducting network pruning: (1) correctly measuring the contribution or reflecting the impact of each neuron during the model training, (2) figuring out the insignificant neurons that can be removed from the network while not hurting the model quality, (3) setting the parameters of redundant neurons as zero or directly skipping these neurons, (4) retraining the compressed network and updating the parameters on all the remaining neurons to reach the model convergence, (5) keeping the pruning procedure until there are no redundant neurons left.

According to these five steps, implementing a high-performance network pruning method is not easy, where three critical factors should be carefully addressed first: (1) how to properly reflect the essential impact and significance of all the neurons or network structures, (2) how to precisely determine which portion of the network needs to be removed, (3) how to make the network pruning method online applicable. In general, there are two kinds of pruning methods to capture these factors: (1) neuron-level pruning [86], [193] and (2) structure-level pruning [349].

Neuron-Level Pruning. The neuron-level pruning is widely used in many approaches because of its straightforward implementation. Imagine the neural network as a tree with many leaves, each of which represents a neuron. The basic idea is to remove the useless "leaves" by setting the parameters of these neurons as zero. As shown in Fig. 5.2, the parameter matrices of the network will become much more sparse after pruning. Based on these sparse matrices, it is possible to efficiently handle and calculate them by using the sparsification-based methods [95]. However, there are also some limitations in neuron-based pruning. The most crucial issue is the degradation of the calculation efficiency, especially in the GPU-based computational environment. As the parameters of a part of neurons are set as zero, the parameter matrix is very sparse. It is hard to obtain performance improvements when training this sparse model by using GPU primitives or Compute Unified Device Architecture (CUDA)-based programming, In some serious cases, the system performance may even decrease, including the degradation of processing speed and forward propagation latency. This is mainly because calculating the sparse matrices may not fully exploit the parallelism superiority of GPU-based computations.

Structure-Level Pruning. Observing the limitations of neuron-level pruning, the structure-level pruning focuses on removing the entire channel or layer from the network, instead of simply adjusting the neuron parameters. Therefore, the structure-level pruning can essentially reduce the model complexity because it greatly changes the network structure. It is worth noting that the processing speedup from model simplification cannot hold a linear increase with the compression ratio of pruning. For example, it is hard to obtain a $3\times$ performance improvement even when we have pruned the network with the $1/3$ compression ratio of the original size. However, the structure-level pruning is easy to implement and is hardware friendly. The major superiority comes from the reduction of the memory footprint with the smaller model size. By using the structure-level pruning, the matrix operations based on memory storage and I/O access can be effectively accelerated.

Overall, these two kinds of network pruning are promising methods of reducing the model complexity and hardware overhead, so as to improve the execution efficiency of large-model applications.

5.2.1.3   Data Quantization

In real-world scenarios, the limited bandwidth capacity and expensive computational primitives may often restrict the system performance for handling large-scale machine learning applications. Besides, the size of parameter matrix is huge for common deep models. For example, the memory footprint is on the order of a hundred of megabytes for the VGG19 and ResNet models [101], [343]. A more serious concern is that, in the distributed processing environment, the parameters and corresponding gradients need to be exchanged among different machines, where a huge volume of network traffic will be generated. Thus, aggregating and scattering all the parameters are time-consuming operations that often slow down the model training progress. The network flow caused by inter-machine data exchange will yield plenty of long-tailed flows, which will significantly impact the communication efficiency.

Considering the arithmetic operations in model training, the digital numbers are often represented in the 32-bit floating-point format, which is called the FP32 type. The operations based on FP32 data type can provide good precision of matrix calculations and avoid introducing representation error [246]. Unfortunately, enabling this high-precision calculation will bring immense resource demands on computational primitives and memory footprint.

Low-Precision Tolerance. As mentioned in the discussion of network pruning, the neural networks are often over-parameterized, and the information covered by the model is highly redundant [183]. This property indicates that we do not have to represent the values of parameters in a very high precision because they are robust enough against slight numerical precision loss while not greatly degrading the model quality. Consequently, we can represent the values of parameters (e.g., weights and activations) and gradients in low data precision to essentially reduce the computational overhead and accelerate the processing speed.

In order to enable low-precision numerical representation without hurting the model accuracy, we need to deeply inspect the data representation in the machine first. There are two kinds of number formats widely used in modern machines: (1) floating-point numbers and (2) fixed-point numbers.

Floating-Point Numbers. Numbers expressed by a machine usually follow the IEEE-754 standard, where the floating-point number is represented by the sign s, mantissa m, exponent e, and bias b, within the 32 bit width. This data type is called the FP32 format. The decimal value V can be described as

$$V = (-1)^s \times 1.m \times 2^{e-b}. \tag{5.1}$$

The FP32 format holds a wide range with high precision, providing about 1.2×10^{38} different kinds of numbers. Therefore, FP32-based data can be regarded as almost continuous numbers.

Fixed-Point Numbers. Another number type used in data representation is the fixed-point format, which is controlled by two parameters: (1) the bit width for number representation and (2) the binary/decimal point position marking the number. Therefore, a n-bit fixed-point number holds 2^n different values, which are discrete data following the uniformed distribution. For example, the common 8-bit fixed-point number (INT8) can represent $2^8 = 256$ digital values. In general, number representation is about how to optimize continuous numbers via discrete variables.

Basically, the gist of data quantization is to reduce the bit width for number representation by mapping the original 32-bit floating-point (FP32) representation domain to a small range– e.g., 8-bit fixed-point (INT8) numbers. The direct advantages from this kind of quantization is the reduction of the computational overhead and memory footprint of matrix operations in neural networks. Therefore, shifting the numbers from FP32 to the INT8 data format is a hot research topic in both industry and academia. Compared to the aforementioned compression techniques of low-rank factorization and network pruning, data quantization has the following two advantages.

- Quantization jointly enables compression (for memory footprint) and acceleration (for computation) at the bit level, which can be used for the deployment of on-device/edge learning applications.
- Quantization can be implemented via the binary shifting operations, which are hardware friendly for both generic computation primitives (e.g., CPU/GPU) and domain-specific chips (e.g., FPGA and AI chips).

Overall, data quantization is a powerful method to jointly optimize the memory-level and computation-level overhead, which can be used to accelerate the training and inference speed for emerging machine learning applications.

5.2.2   Hardware Acceleration

Apart from the theoretical optimization of computation accelerations for model training, deploying all these algorithms requires the support of the corresponding hardware, including commodity computational primitives (e.g., CPU and GPU), data access (memory footprint and I/O links), and domain-specific accelerators (e.g., FPGA and AI chips). In order to give a comprehensive introduction of hardware-level acceleration, our discussion will cover the following three topics: (1) scheduling of multiple computation primitives, (2) topology optimization, and (3) dedicated hardware management.

5.2.2.1   Scheduling of Multiple Computation Primitives

Modern machine learning tasks often yield huge computational overhead and resource demands, which can be addressed by using the distributed training scheme. In this condition, the machine learning systems have multiple computation primitives to handle the resource-hungry calculations, where employing the CPU- and GPU-based programming is an effective way to implement the machine learning training in practice [373].

In order to obtain more powerful computational capacity, GPUs are often organized together to build a GPU cluster, where large-scale machine learning applications can be executed across the GPUs simultaneously. Therefore, we need to carefully schedule the machine learning tasks and assign moderate computation resources to most suitable tasks. This kind of GPU cluster management problem can be resolved into two objectives. The first object is to reduce the average time consumption to finish the machine learning jobs, under the limited computation primitives, memory, and network bandwidth. The second goal is to dispatch the machine learning tasks to the most proper machines or assign the hardware resources to a given job.

These two objectives are two basic factors designing a highly efficient GPU manager for distributed machine learning system. However, the potential issues involving incomplete prior knowledge of model properties and resource demands are the main challenges for real-world system implementation [235], which deserves future research to design more intelligent and automatic scheduling strategies.

5.2.2.2   Topology Optimization

As modern machine learning applications are often deployed in the distributed collaboration scheme, the intermediate data exchange will lead to frequent I/O access and yield a very large amount of synchronized parameters. The communication between multiple computation primitives (e.g., GPUs and CPUs) dominates the per-iteration time of model training, with complex and unpredictable communication patterns. These patterns make conventional flow-aware scheduling and link connection become ineffective, especially when the cluster is in a large scale. This phenomenon requires us to carefully design the collective communication mechanism and capture the computation primitives property so as to better manage the underlay network topology.

Basically, a high-performance distributed machine learning system should consider the topology characteristics when determining the job scheduling strategies. The basic optimization objective is to minimize the average machine learning training time while not downgrading the hardware and resource efficiency. As a result, it becomes the topology-aware task scheduler [66] that controls the multiple GPUs to make full use of the collective communication – e.g., NVIDIA Collective Communications Library (NCCL). Also, we can handle the communication programming via the Message Passing Interface (MPI) to enable elastic parameter synchronization across the cluster.

Moreover, with the rise of large-scale graph computing, it is possible to optimize the topology-aware scheduling by abstracting the communication pattern and network connections as dependency graphs. A promising research direction is to study how to improve the inter-GPU communication schemes via the learning-based methods, including deep reinforcement learning and graph embedding [295] neural networks.

5.2.2.3   Dedicated Hardware Management

Large-scale machine learning applications often reply on the rich expression capacity and precise feature extractor of large neural networks, which are resource-hungry and require high link speed for inter-machine communication. These practical properties bring critical challenges to the implementation of distributed machine learning systems. Fortunately, it is possible employ dedicated hardware to address this problem by carefully managing these scarce resources. In this section, we mainly focus on two kinds of hardware: memory management and neural accelerators.

In order to efficiently manage the limited memory, we need to capture the properties of the processing tiles and computation chips inside the memory. More precisely, as commodity clusters are often composed of different kinds of computation primitives with various processing capacity, it is also significant to make the memory management adapt to this heterogeneous scenario [100]. Also, during the distributed processing, the remote procedure calling should be considered, where the memory are shared across different machines. All the arithmetic operations and number representations need to match the computational pattern of the training procedure [229]. This requires us to carefully design the storage and access of each data segment and adjust the numerical precision to reduce the memory footprint. The network pruning and data quantization techniques are promising ways to achieve this target.

Apart from the memory management, we can employ dedicated neural accelerators to improve the computational efficiency. Considering the iterative calculation pattern of neural network training, the floating-point numbers are the major data type during the computation. Handling the matrix operations based on these floating-point numbers are the key to accelerating the processing speed. Recently, many industrial processing units have employed this dedicated hardware for higher learning efficiency. For example, the NVIDIA GPUs assemble plenty of tensor cores in the motherboard to obtain a powerful computation capacity to deal with floating-point numbers.

Meanwhile, in the academic area, many researchers have focused on using customized FPGA and multi-cores processors to increase the learning speed. A pertinent case is the Google *Tensor Processing Units* (TPUs) [136] based on special Application Specific Integrated Circuit (ASIC) instructions, which are used to handle the training of large-scale models in the data center networks, providing much higher processing speedups over the conventional GPUs.

5.2.2.4 Multi-task Oriented Resource Allocation

It is well known that the training and interference of DNNs are time-consuming, computation-intensive, and memory-intensive. A great number of distributed learning systems are introduced to tackle such resource-intensive training both in CPU and GPU clusters. Single task training can directly process in such a simple case. However, multi-tasking must take consideration of many resource-relative factors and work on accelerating DNN training and interference. How to assign tasks and how to place them in a suitable device are problems that need to be solved.

Hadjis et al. [91] propose an Omnivore system to allocate computational resources for DNN training in single-device and multi-device. The authors speed up throughput proportional both GPU and CPU by using batching and the data-parallel mechanism to optimize single-device case. The server architecture and execution strategy are the focused dimensions to accelerate DNN training in a multi-device case. Omnivore groups, computational devices assign single-batch data iteratively. The computation, like multiplication and computing gradients, executes in a synchronous manner inside a group and happens in asynchronization across the group. Gao et al. [67] derive the solution of placing deep learning tasks in optimal devices by new reinforcement learning algorithms based on proximal policy optimization because of the previous algorithm based on the policy gradient method, which is suboptimal. In this scenario, the device placement problem is modeled as a Markov decision process with multiple stages, and it can be proven mathematically and theoretically that it can archive performance improvement.

For GPU cluster management, Gu et al. [79] propose Tiresias, which efficiently and effectively schedules distributed Deep Learning (DL) training single or multiple jobs by two scheduling algorithms. Addanki et al. [6] propose a general device placement approach based on a reinforcement learning algorithm for distributed DNN training. It regards device placement tasks as a learnable strategy that can iteratively optimize placement performance. The key idea of placement policy is to encode the computation graph structure by applying graph embeddings, including computing per-group attributes, local neighborhood summarization, and pooling summaries. When the DNN training task is narrow, GPUs would suffer from underutilization problems due to the sensitivity of network latency. Yeh et al. [362] build a GPU runtime system to solve the aforementioned problems by creating MasterKernel, an OS-like daemon kernel. The narrow task system needs to minimize the communication overhead, because the short-running task would be sensitive to task-switching overhead, and to keep the overhead in task spawning and switching low. Moreover, the system needs to support the general function in GPU, including memory sharing usage and keeping efficient thread block synchronization. Considering that DNNs tasks are applied in heterogeneous environments with a mixture of computational devices, such as CPUs, GPUs, TPUs, NPUs, FPGA, Azalia Mirhoseini et al. [203] proposed a hierarchical model to place computational graphs effectively onto various heterogeneous devices without human intervention. The hierarchical model consists of two networks, Grouper and Placer, which are trained jointly using reinforcement learning to obtain a trade-off between computation speed and feasibility.

5.3   Straggler Tolerance

In distributed learning, BSP is the most popular parallel scheme that collaborates with all workers due to its improved generalization performance over the asynchronous schemes. However, in BSP, all workers are required to synchronize in each iteration. When some workers become the stragglers that cannot return the gradient within the reasonable deadline, as shown in Fig. 5.3(a), the performance of the synchronization is significantly degraded. Generally, the stragglers can be incurred by arbitrary reasons – i.e., fault occurrence and resource contention between processes, and are hard to predict. One of the most efficient methods for mitigating stragglers is the gradient coding method. We illustrate it by the following example.

Example 5.1 We consider the machine learning system with the same settings as that of the naive BSP in Fig. 5.3(a). As shown in Fig. 5.3(a), the whole dataset is uniformly partitioned into three parts, $\mathcal{D} = \{D_1, D_2, D_3\}$, and each data partition D_i is allocated to different two workers instead of the single worker in the naive BSP. Correspondingly, each worker computes the gradients from two data partitions – e.g., data partition D_1 and D_2 by worker $W1$. After that, to keep the same communication cost, each worker encodes the obtained two gradients into a single one and sends the encoded gradient to the server. As the worker $W3$ becomes the straggler, the server recovers the sum of all gradients by only using the two encoded gradients from worker $W1$ and $W2$. In fact, since each encoded gradient is composed of two gradients from two different partitions, the server can recover the sum of all gradients by using any two workers.

The example illustrates that the stragglers can be tolerated by employing the redundant workload allocation methods combined with encoding and decoding schemes. Throughout this section, we let m denote the number of workers, and the set of workers is denoted as $\mathcal{W} = \{W_1, \ldots, W_m\}$. The whole dataset is uniformly partitioned into k parts $\mathcal{D} = \{D_1, \ldots, D_k\}$. For any $r \in \mathbb{N}$, if we use $[r]$ to denote the set $\{1, \ldots, r\}$. Next, we specify the design of gradient-coding-based methods.

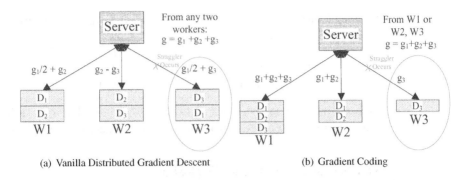

Figure 5.3 Illustration of gradient coding methods for tolerating stragglers.

5.3.1 Framework of Gradient Coding

In a gradient-descent-based algorithm, the gradient computed from the data partition D_i is denoted as $\mathbf{g}_i$ and the server seeks to aggregate the gradients computed from all data partitions $\mathbf{g} = \sum_{i=1}^k \mathbf{g}_i$. As illustrated in Example 5.1, to tolerate stragglers, each data partition has to be replicated into several copies and is allocated to different workers. Let $\mathcal{D}_i \subseteq \mathcal{D}$ be the set of data partitions allocated to worker i. Then the worker i encodes all the gradients $\{\mathbf{g}_j\}_{i \in \mathcal{D}_i}$ computed from these data partitions $\tilde{\mathbf{g}}_i = e_i(\{\mathbf{g}_j\}_{j \in \mathcal{D}_i})$ and sends the encoded gradient $\tilde{\mathbf{g}}_i$ to the server. After receiving enough results of workers $\tilde{\mathcal{W}} \subseteq \mathcal{W}$, the server recovers the summation of all gradients by applying the decoding function $\mathbf{g}^T = h(\{\tilde{\mathbf{g}}_i\}_{i \in \tilde{\mathcal{W}}})$.

Now, we introduce the framework of the typical gradient coding method [284]. Gradient coding adopts the linear encoding function and decoding function. For any vector $\mathbf{x} \in \mathbb{R}^k$, supp$(\mathbf{x})$ denotes its support – i.e. supp$(\mathbf{x}) = \{i | x_i \neq 0\}$. With a row vector $\mathbf{b}_i \in \mathbb{R}^{1 \times k}$, the encoding function of worker i can be written as

$$\tilde{\mathbf{g}}_i^T = e_i(\{\mathbf{g}_j\}_{j \in \mathcal{D}_i}) = \mathbf{b}_i \bar{\mathbf{g}}, \tag{5.2}$$

where supp$(\mathbf{b}_i) = \{j | D_j \in \mathcal{D}_i\}$ and $\bar{\mathbf{g}} = [\mathbf{g}_1, \ldots, \mathbf{g}_k]^T$. Let $\mathbf{B} = [\mathbf{b}_1^T, \mathbf{b}_2^T, \ldots, \mathbf{b}_m^T]^T$, which represents the encoding functions of all workers. Considering a scenario in which the non-stragglers are $\tilde{\mathcal{W}}_j$, the server seeks to find a row vector $\mathbf{a}_j \in \mathbb{R}^{1 \times m}$ satisfying $\mathbf{a}_j \mathbf{B} = [1, 1, \ldots, 1]$ such that

$$\mathbf{g}^T = h(\{\tilde{\mathbf{g}}_i\}_{i \in \tilde{\mathcal{W}}_j}) = \mathbf{a}_j[\tilde{\mathbf{g}}_1, \ldots, \tilde{\mathbf{g}}_k]^T = \mathbf{a}_j \mathbf{B} \bar{\mathbf{g}} = [1, 1, \ldots, 1]\bar{\mathbf{g}}, \tag{5.3}$$

where supp$(\mathbf{a}_j) = \{i | W_i \in \tilde{\mathcal{W}}_j\}$. Assuming that the number of scenarios with different non-stragglers is f and $\mathbf{A} = [\mathbf{a}_1^T, \ldots, \mathbf{a}_f^T]^T$ represents the decoding vectors for all scenarios, the decoding function for all scenarios can be written as

$$\mathbf{A}_{fm} \mathbf{B}_{mk} = \mathbf{1}_{fk}, \tag{5.4}$$

where each entry in the matrix $\mathbf{1}_{fk}$ is 1.

Recalling Example 5.1, the encoding matrix **B** and the decoding matrix **A** are

$$\mathbf{B}_{3\times 3} = \begin{bmatrix} \frac{1}{2} & 1 & 0 \\ 0 & 1 & -1 \\ \frac{1}{2} & 0 & 1 \end{bmatrix}, \qquad \mathbf{A}_{3\times 3} = \begin{bmatrix} 2 & -1 & 0 \\ 1 & 0 & 1 \\ 0 & 1 & 2 \end{bmatrix},$$

respectively. It is easy to check that **A** and **B** satisfy (5.4). Moreover, each row of **A** has only two non-zero entries, which indicates the tolerance to 1 stragglers.

5.3.2 Construction Encoding and Decoding Matrix

In this section, we elaborate the methods of designing the matrix **A** and **B** of gradient coding [284]. Gradient coding focuses on the cases where s stragglers are always tolerated. In these cases, the number of all combinations of non-stragglers is $f = \binom{m}{m-s} = \binom{m}{s}$. Also, it implies that the s entries of each row of **A** are 0. Under these constraints, to find the solutions for (5.4), we say that **B** has to satisfy the following condition:

LEMMA 5.1 (Condition 1 in [284])   *An encoding matrix* $\mathbf{B} = [\mathbf{b}_1^T, \mathbf{b}_2^T, \dots, \mathbf{b}_m^T]^T \in \mathbb{R}^{m\times k}$ *is robust to any s stragglers if and only if* **B** *satisfies the condition:*

Condition 1. *For every subset* $I \subseteq [m], |I| = m - s$, $\mathbf{1}_{1\times k} \in span\{\mathbf{b}_i | i \in I\}$ *where* $span\{\cdot\}$ *is the span of vectors.*

In fact, the condition C1 of Lemma 5.1 requires that any $m - s$ rows of the matrix **B** can be linearly combined into an all-one row vector $\mathbf{1}_{1\times k}$. Assuming we have gotten such a matrix **B**, the matrix **A** can be easily achieved by solving (5.4) under the condition of setting the different s entries of each row to be 0 in previous.

Example 5.2 Consider a machine learning system with 8 workers. Let 0 denotes the symbol of stragglers and $\star$ denotes the corresponding decoding value of non-stragglers. If the system tolerates 2 stragglers, then the support structure of the decoding matrix **A** is

$$\mathbf{A}_{28\times 8} = \begin{bmatrix} \star & \star & \star & \star & \star & \star & 0 & 0 \\ \star & \star & \star & \star & \star & 0 & \star & 0 \\ \cdots & & \cdots & & \cdots & & \cdots & \cdots \\ 0 & \star & 0 & \star & \star & \star & \star & \star \\ 0 & 0 & \star & \star & \star & \star & \star & \star \end{bmatrix}.$$

Intuitively, finding a feasible solution $(\mathbf{A}, \mathbf{B})$ is easy and can be done by just setting $\mathbf{B}_{m\times k} = \mathbf{1}_{m\times k}$. However, each worker has to compute all the gradients in this setting because the number of the non-zero entries has a linear positive correlation to the computing cost. We have to minimize the density of the matrix $\mathbf{B}$. Further, we have the following theorem to present the lower bound of the density.

THEOREM 5.1 (Theorem 1 in [284])   *Consider any coding matrix $(\mathbf{A}, \mathbf{B})$ robust to any s stragglers, given m workers (with $s < m$) and k partitions. Then, if all rows of $\mathbf{B}$ have the same number of non-zeros, we must have $\|\mathbf{b}_i\|_0 \geq \frac{k}{m}(s + 1)$ for any $i \in [m]$, where $\| \cdot \|_0$ denotes the l_0-norm.*

An intuitive understanding for the Theorem 5.1 is that each specific data partition D_i has to be made at least $s + 1$ copies for tolerating s stragglers. Since there are k specific data partitions, the total number of data partitions including copies is at least $k(s + 1)$ under the setting of tolerating s stragglers. Under the condition of all rows of $\mathbf{B}$ having the same number of non-zeros, as a consequence, each worker is allocated at least $\frac{k}{m}(s + 1)$ data partitions.

For the construction of $\mathbf{B}$, now, we introduce the Cyclic Repetition Scheme [284], which achieves the lower bound of density and satisfies Condition 1. The Cyclic Repetition Scheme consists of two stages: designing the support structure and filling values to solve the two objectives. In the Cyclic Repetition Scheme, the number of data partitions is the same as the number of workers – i.e., $k = m$ – and each worker is allocated the same number of data partitions. According to Theorem 5.1, to achieve the lowest bound of density, each row of the matrix $\mathbf{B}$ has $s + 1$ non-zero entries. In the first stage, the location of these non-zero entries is allocated in a cyclic manner that determines the support structure of the matrix $\mathbf{B}$. Specifically, the indexes of the non-zero entries in the ith row ranging from $(i - 1 \bmod m) + 1$ to $(i + s - 1 \bmod m) + 1$.

Example 5.3 Considering a machine learning system with 10 workers. Let $\star$ denote the location of non-zero entries. If the system tolerates 4 stragglers, then the support structure of $\mathbf{B}$ is

$$
\mathbf{B}_{m \times m} = \begin{bmatrix}
\star & \star & \star & \star & \star & 0 & 0 & 0 & 0 & 0 \\
0 & \star & \star & \cdots & \star & \star & 0 & \cdots & 0 & 0 \\
\vdots & \vdots & \vdots & \vdots & \vdots & \vdots & \ddots & \ddots & \vdots & \vdots \\
0 & 0 & 0 & 0 & 0 & \star & \star & \star & \star & \star \\
\star & 0 & 0 & 0 & 0 & 0 & \star & \star & \star & \star \\
\vdots & \vdots & \vdots & \vdots & \vdots & \vdots & \ddots & \ddots & \vdots & \vdots \\
\star & \star & \star & \star & 0 & 0 & 0 & 0 & 0 & \star
\end{bmatrix}.
$$

Given the support structure, we further solve the values of these non-zero entries to satisfy Condition 1. In particular, we seek to utilize the specific property of the support architecture of $\mathbf{B}$ of which any $m - s$ rows are linearly independent. Since Condition 1 is equivalent to the span of any $m - s$ rows of $\mathbf{B}$ containing all ones vector $\mathbf{1}$, to solve the values of these rows, we can solve the problem by directly designing a space S that equals to the span. Consequently, the rank of the space S should be $m - s$, and S should contain the all ones vector $\mathbf{1}$. Moreover, the space S also has to contain the vectors that have the same support structure as the rows of $\mathbf{B}$. The space is designed by referring to a matrix $H \in \mathbb{R}^{s \times m}$ as $S = \{x \in \mathbb{R}^m | Hx = 0\}$, where $H\mathbf{1} = 0$. Obviously, the space now contains the all ones vector $\mathbf{1}$. Further, the H is randomized to satisfy the condition that the rank of the space is $m - s$. Now, with the obtained space S, the matrix $\mathbf{B}$ can be constructed row by row, as illustrated in Algorithm 5.1.

Algorithm 5.1 Construct $\mathbf{B}$ in the Cylic Repetition Scheme

---

Input: m, s
Output: B $\in \mathbb{R}^{m \times m}$

1: Randomize $\mathbf{H}_{s \times m}$;
2: Sum 1st to mth column $\sigma = \sum_{i=1}^{m-1} \mathbf{H}(:,i)$;
3: Set mth column $\mathbf{H}(:,m) = \sigma$;
4: Initialize all entries of $\mathbf{B}$ to be 0;
5: **for** i from 1 to m **do**
6:     Set $j = [(i - 1 \bmod m) + 1, (i + s - 1 \bmod m) + 1]$;
7:     Set ith row $\mathbf{B}(i, j) = [1; -\mathbf{H}(:, j(2 : s + 1))^{-1}\mathbf{H}(:, j(1))]$;
8: **end for**

Besides, we have the following theorem shows that the matrix $\mathbf{B}$ constructed by the Algorithm 5.1 satisfies Condition 1.

THEOREM 5.2   *The matrix* $\mathbf{B}$ *constructed by Algorithm 5.1 has probability* 1 *to satisfy Condition 1.*

Example 5.4 Considering a machine learning system with 4 workers, please construct the coding matrix $(\mathbf{A}, \mathbf{B})$ that tolerates 2 stragglers.

Solution
Step 1. Divide the whole dataset into 4 parts, and design the support structure of $\mathbf{B}$ *as*

$$
\mathbf{B}_{4\times4} = \begin{bmatrix} \star & \star & \star & 0 \\ 0 & \star & \star & \star \\ \star & 0 & \star & \star \\ \star & \star & 0 & \star \end{bmatrix}.
$$

Step 2. Randomize the matrix $\mathbf{H}$:

$$
\mathbf{H}_{2\times4} = \begin{bmatrix} 0.1481 & -0.3979 & -0.3008 & 0.5505 \\ -0.1565 & -1.2398 & 0.8819 & 0.5144 \end{bmatrix}.
$$

Obtain each row of the $\mathbf{B}$ by solving $\mathbf{H}\mathbf{b}_i^T = \mathbf{0}$ to get

$$\mathbf{B}_{4\times4} = \begin{bmatrix} 1 & 0.1154 & 0.3397 & 0 \\ 0 & 1 & 0.7465 & 1.1305 \\ 3.9442 & 0 & 1 & -0.5147 \\ -1.9438 & 0.6602 & 0 & 1 \end{bmatrix}.$$

Step 3. *Obtain the matrix $\mathbf{A}$ by solving $\mathbf{A}\mathbf{B} = \mathbf{1}$:*

$$\mathbf{A}_{6\times4} = \begin{bmatrix} 1 & 0.8846 & 0 & 0 \\ \vdots & \ddots & \ddots & \vdots \\ 0 & 0 & 1 & 1.5147 \end{bmatrix}.$$

5.3.3 Construct B in the General Case

Although the Cyclic Repetition Scheme for constructing the encoding matrix $\mathbf{B}$ has enabled the tolerance of stragglers, its runtime efficiency relies on the key assumption that the computing capacity of all workers is the same. However, this assumption does not hold for the generally practical scenarios where the workers are usually heterogeneous – i.e., the computing capacities of different workers are different from each other. Considering this, in this section, we further introduce a method, the Heterogeneity-Aware Scheme, which allows the different number of data partitions in different workers [307].

Considering the heterogeneity of workers, the Heterogeneity-Aware Scheme first computes the number of data partitions allocated to each worker – i.e., the number of non-zero entries of each row $\mathbf{B}$, according to the principle of workload balance. Since the total number of data partitions is $k(s+1)$, denoting the computing capacity of worker i as c_i, the number of the data partitions allocated to worker i is then $n_i = k(s+1)\frac{c_i}{\sum_{j=1}^{m} c_j}$. It can be seen that $\sum_{i=1}^{m} n_i = k(s+1)$. Different from the Cyclic Repetition Scheme, the Heterogeneity-Aware Scheme does not rely on any particular support architecture of $\mathbf{B}$. Specifically, any support structure that has the following two properties is acceptable:

- (P1): The number of non-zero entries of each column is $s+1$.
- (P2): The number of non-zero entries of the ith row is n_i.

As an example, we here introduce a method that the support architecture designed by it has the two properties. The method is to decide the location of the non-zero entries of each row in a loop manner. The set of the column indexes of the ith row are $[(n_i'+1)\bmod k, (n_i'+2)\bmod k, \ldots, (n_i'+n_i)\bmod k]$, where $n_i' = \sum_{j=1}^{i-1} n_j$. It is straightforward to see that, for each data column, there are exactly $s+1$ non-zero entries.

Example 5.5 Consider a system with 5 workers. The normalized computing capacities of all workers are $[1,2,3,4,4]$. Under the setting of tolerating 1 straggler, please use the loop allocation method to design the support structure of $\mathbf{B}$.

Solution

According to computing capacities of all workers, we can divide the whole dataset into 7 parts, make 2 copies for each data partition, and then compute the number of data partitions of all workers as $[1,2,3,4,4]$. Subsequently, we decide the locations of the non-zero entries in a loop manner as

$$\mathbf{B}_{5\times 7} = \begin{bmatrix} \star & 0 & 0 & 0 & 0 & 0 & 0 \\ 0 & \star & \star & 0 & 0 & 0 & 0 \\ 0 & 0 & 0 & \star & \star & \star & 0 \\ \star & \star & \star & 0 & 0 & 0 & \star \\ 0 & 0 & 0 & \star & \star & \star & \star \end{bmatrix}.$$

Like the Cyclic Repetition Scheme, the Heterogeneity-Aware Scheme also requires an auxiliary matrix to solve the values of the non-zero entries in $\mathbf{B}$. To distinguish from the auxiliary matrix $\mathbf{H} \in \mathbb{R}^{s\times m}$ required by the Cyclic Repetition Scheme, here we denote the required auxiliary matrix as $\mathbf{C} \in \mathbb{R}^{(s+1)\times m}$. Specifically, we obtain the matrix $\mathbf{B}$ by solving $\mathbf{C}_{(s+1)\times m}\mathbf{B}_{m\times k} = \mathbf{1}_{(s+1)\times k}$. Moreover, the following lemma presents the properties that the auxiliary matrix $\mathbf{C}$ should have such that the obtained $\mathbf{B}$ can satisfy Condition 1.

LEMMA 5.2   *For a matrix $\mathbf{C}_{(s+1)\times m}$ satisfying the following two conditions:*

- *(C1): any $s+1$ columns of $\mathbf{C}$ are linearly independent.*
- *(C2): for any submatrix $\mathbf{C}'$ composed by s columns of $\mathbf{C}$, there exists some non-zero vector $\lambda = (\lambda_1,\dots,\lambda_{s+1}) \in \mathbb{R}^{s+1}$ such that $\lambda\mathbf{C}' = \mathbf{0}_{1\times s}$, $\sum_{i=1}^{s+1}\lambda_i \neq 0$,*

there exists a matrix $\mathbf{B}$ with its support structure having (P1) and (P2) properties such that $\mathbf{C}_{(s+1)\times m}\mathbf{B}_{m\times k} = \mathbf{1}_{(s+1)\times k}$ and $\mathbf{B}$ satisfies Condition 1.

The idea behind this lemma lies on two aspects. First, given the matrix satisfying the conditions (C1) and (C2), the $\mathbf{B}$ can be obtained column by column by solving $\mathbf{C}_{(s+1)\times m}\mathbf{B}_{m\times k} = \mathbf{1}_{(s+1)\times k}$. Considering $\mathbf{b}'_i \in \mathbb{R}^{m\times 1}$ to be the ith column of the matrix $\mathbf{B}$, it can be obtained by solving

$$\mathbf{Cb}'_i = \mathbf{1}. \tag{5.5}$$

Let $\mathbf{C}_i$ be the submatrix of $\mathbf{C}$ that is composed of all the jth columns where the jth element of the i-th column of $\mathbf{B}$ is not zero. Since any $s+1$ columns of $\mathbf{C}$ are linearly independent, $\mathbf{C}_i$ has an inverse matrix. As a consequence, the column $\mathbf{b}'_i$ in (5.5) can be obtained as

$$\mathbf{b}'_i = \mathbf{C}_i^{-1}\mathbf{1}. \tag{5.6}$$

Second, the obtained **B** satisfies the Condition 1 because $\mathbf{CB} = \mathbf{1}$ still holds when any s columns of **C** become zeros. To see this, we use the condition (C2) to construct a non-zero vector $\lambda = (\lambda_1, \ldots, \lambda_{s+1}) \in \mathbb{R}^{s+1}$. Then, we multiply it to the original matrix **C** to obtain $\frac{1}{\sum_{i=1}^{s+1} \lambda_i} \lambda \mathbf{C}$. Based on $\mathbf{CB} = \mathbf{1}$, we have

$$\left(\frac{1}{\sum_{i=1}^{s+1} \lambda_i} \lambda \mathbf{C}_{(s+1) \times m} \right) \mathbf{B}_{m \times k} = \frac{1}{\sum_{i=1}^{s+1} \lambda_i} \lambda (\mathbf{C}_{(s+1) \times m} \mathbf{B}_{m \times k}) = \mathbf{1}_{(s+1) \times k}.$$

Since s columns of $\lambda \mathbf{C}$ are zero, the span of the $m - s$ rows of **B** contains the **1** vector that satisfies the Condition 1.

In fact, such an auxiliary matrix **C** can also obtained by using a randomized method.

LEMMA 5.3   *For a matrix* $\mathbf{C} \in \mathbb{R}^{(s+1) \times m}$ *of which each entry is randomized independently, the matrix* **C** *satisfies both conditions of (C1) and (C2) with probability 1.*

The proof can be found in [307]. To summarize, we can now obtain the encoding matrix **B** according to the Lemma 5.2 and Lemma 5.3 and obtain the decoding matrix **A** by directly solving $\mathbf{AB} = \mathbf{1}$.

Example 5.6 Consider a 4-worker system with the normalized computing capacity as $[4, 3, 2, 1]$. Please construct the matrix $(\mathbf{A}, \mathbf{B})$ to tolerate 1 straggler.

Solution
Step 1. We divide the whole dataset into 5 parts and make 2 copies for each data partition. Based on the number of the total data partitions, we further decide the number of the data partitions of each worker to be $[4, 3, 2, 1]$. *By allocating these data partitions to workers in a loop manner, we achieve the support structure of* **B**:

$$\mathbf{B}_{4 \times 5} = \begin{bmatrix} \star & \star & \star & \star & 0 \\ \star & \star & 0 & 0 & \star \\ 0 & 0 & \star & \star & 0 \\ 0 & 0 & 0 & 0 & \star \end{bmatrix}.$$

Step 2. By randomizing an auxiliary matrix C

$$\mathbf{C}_{2 \times 4} = \begin{bmatrix} 0.3 & 0.04 & 0.94 & 0 \\ 0 & 0.65 & 0.71 & 0.78 \end{bmatrix},$$

and solving each column of the matrix **B** *according to (5.6), we obtain*

$$\mathbf{B}_{4 \times 5} = \begin{bmatrix} 3 & 3 & -1 & -1 & 0 \\ 1.5 & 1.5 & 0 & 0 & 24 \\ 0 & 0 & 1.4 & 1.4 & 0 \\ 0 & 0 & 0 & 0 & -19.5 \end{bmatrix}.$$

Step 3. *Finally, we get the matrix* **A** *by solving* **AB** = **1**:

$$\mathbf{A}_{4\times 4} = \begin{bmatrix} 0.3 & 0.04 & 0.94 & 0 \\ -0.94 & 2.53 & 0 & 3.17 \\ 0.32 & 0 & 0.95 & -0.05 \\ 0 & 0.65 & 0.71 & 0.78 \end{bmatrix}.$$

5.3.4   Recent Methods of Gradient Coding

As we have discussed, the coding scheme in distributed machine learning makes use of redundancy to guarantee the recovery of the full gradient with only a fraction of workers so that the impact of the stragglers can be minimized. The gradient-coding-based method was first proposed by Tandon et al. [284], as we have discussed in detail. Although this gradient-coding-based method performs well in circumstances with serious stragglers, the high performance also comes by increasing the computation cost. It is straightforward to see that such computation cost is caused by redundancy. To reduce the computing overhead, some methods propose that the gradient does not need to be exactly recovered. Based on this idea, the approximate coding methods are proposed [240], [33], where each worker computes much less data partitions than that of the accurate coding methods. Specifically, Netanel et al. [240] utilize the expander-graph-based technique to construct the encoding matrix **B**. They show that the computation achieves a theoretical reduction that breaks the constraint established in Theorem 5.1. Zachary et al. [33] present a mathematical formulation for the approximate coding methods. Further, they consider two distribution cases of the stragglers – i.e., uniformly random stragglers and Bernoulli random stragglers – and they propose the Fractional Repetition Scheme and Bernoulli Gradient Codes, respectively, for the two cases.

Considering that the approximate coding methods still have redundancy, some studies focus on designing the coding methods for the linear machine learning model. The initial work goes back to the large matrix multiplication, in which the matrix allocated to multiple workers is coded [152]. In [152], the erasure code is employed to construct the encoding matrix. They divide the data matrix into several submatrices, encode these submatrices, and allocate encoded submatrices to all workers. The decoding process in the master is similar to the gradient coding method, where the master node recovers the matrix multiplication results upon receiving the products of several workers. Beyond this idea, multiple studies have also been proposed for training the linear machine learning models [161], [224]. For the least-squares regression problem, Songze et al. [161] propose the Polynomial Coded Regression method. They encode the partial data stored at each worker, such that the computations at the workers can be viewed as evaluating a polynomial at distinct points. After that, the master computes the final gradient by interpolating this polynomial. For the linear regression models, Raj et al., in [191], propose encoding the second moment of data to reduce computational overhead of encoding raw data. Going beyond the traditional methods that only tolerate the stragglers, the method designed by Qian et al. [374] can also protect the privacy of the dataset based on the Lagrange Coded Scheme.

5.4 Improving the Inference Performance in the Edge Environment

Different from the training process of deep learning, inference refers to inferring things about new data via a trained model, which can be shown in Fig. 5.4. Inference cannot happen without training. That's how we gain and use our own knowledge to make a prediction (see the lower side of Fig. 5.4). Determining how to perform the computation to improve the inference performance – i.e., latency, accuracy and cost – plays an important role in edge learning.

5.4.1 Key Performance Indicators in Inference

Inference is the stage in which a trained model is used to infer/predict the testing samples and comprises a similar forward pass as training to predict the values. Unlike training, it does not include a backward pass to compute the error and to update weights of a neural network. It's usually the production phase in which you deploy your model to predict real-world data. There are some indicators to measure the performance of inferences:

- **Inference Accuracy**. When use the trained model to classify new data samples (i.e., inputs that were not seen before by the model), the limited availability of memory, computation, and energy on mobile and embedded platforms would pose a significant challenge to the adoption of the inference. These challenges cannot be ignored and can lead to reduction in model accuracy. Many researchers focus on compressing the trained model while maintaining a high accuracy ratio.

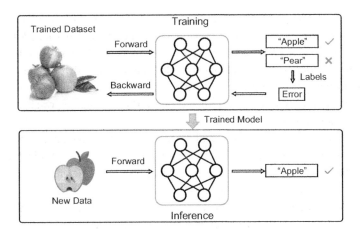

Figure 5.4 Illustration of the high-level deep learning workflow, which showing training and inference.

- **Latency**. Due to the ability of DNNs to perform highly accurate and reliable inference tasks, DNN has been the most commonly adopted machine learning technique and has become increasingly popular. However, as DNN-based applications typically require a tremendous amount of computation, they cannot be supported by today's mobile devices with reasonable latency. The execution time for inference becomes an important indicator in the current cloud-assisted frameworks.
- **Resource Consumption**. Compared to the training phase, the inference phase requires much fewer resources, which makes it possible to run the inference on mobile devices locally. Despite this possibility, running inference is still a resource-consuming task for mobile devices. Therefore, the model storage and computational costs are the main performance indicators in the inference phase.

5.4.2   Enabling Technologies for Inference

Inference in the edge has attracted much research attention, and diverse literature has contributed to improving inference performance. In this section, we review the related work for inference in the edge, which can be classified as the following aspects: reduced computational complexity, computational parallel, and computation offloading.

5.4.2.1   Reducing Computational Complexity

Because of the limited capability in edge devices, the scales of most of the conventional DNNs are also limited, which cannot achieve a high inference accuracy for various deep learning tasks. The most straightforward way to improve inference accuracy is to increase the scales of neural networks. However, large neural networks (e.g., DNNs) may lead to additional costs such as storage and computational costs. In order to address this problem, some researchers focus on reducing the computational complexity by compressing or removing redundant information in well-trained neural networks.

Wang et al. [319] provide an overview of current DNN model compression methods encompassing three aspects: (1) parameter pruning and sharing [94], [96] (i.e., Fig. 5.5); (2) low-rank factorization [54]; and (3) model distillation [106]. For example, in [21], the authors point out that most of the operations in the training process are precision-insensitive; quantization on these model parameters would not reduce the inference accuracy a lot. Moreover, they propose Range Batch Normalization, which can be compatible with the quantization strategies.

However, these methods cannot achieve higher compression quality. A novel lossy compression architecture based on error-bound evaluation and optimization on each layer of the neural network is developed in [134]. The efficiency of compressing sparse model weights in DNNs has been proven. To address the high time complexity occurring in this framework, they develop a dynamic algorithm to efficiently optimize the trade-off between each layer's error bound and overall accuracy ratio. Furthermore, a hybrid network that combines the leading structures and ternary quantization is proposed in [77]; for each inference, the process can be conducted by only a fraction

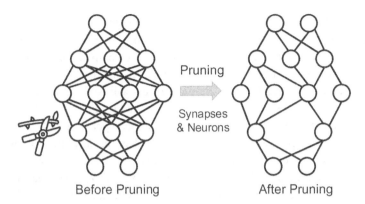

Figure 5.5 Pruning is removing connections that are less effective in computation of a neural network.

of model parameters and operations. Both the computation and the model footprint are decreased. Instead of compressing a single network, Chou et al. [44] focus on the goal of merging multiple networks simultaneously by finding and sharing the representative codes of weights. What's more, their method can restore the performance of the jointly compressed models by fine-tuning it with the training samples.

Another mainstream technique for computational complexity reduction is to modify the network structures. In contract to prior works, Chin et al. [43] explore the image down-sampling to reduce the computation needed for a standalone object detector, by adaptively selecting the scale of the input image, theory analysis shows that both the inference accuracy ratio and rate are improved. Specifically, they use the current frame to predict the optimal scale for the next frame. Experimental results on ImageNet VID and mini YouTube-BB datasets demonstrate 1.3 points and 2.7 points mAP improvement with 1.6 and 1.8 speedup, respectively. Authors in [53] propose an Efficient Multiple Instance learning (EMI-RNN) algorithm in RNN for sequential data classification, which is based on a multi-instance learning (MIL) formulation of the sequential data classification problem. Analysis of EMI-RNN shows that it outperforms baseline long and short-term memory (LSTM) while providing up to $70\times$ reduction in inference cost. To improve the inference performance of Deep CNN, a novel and comprehensive algebraic framework for incremental CNN inference are developed in [211]. For every re-inference request, they rewrite the queries to reuse the materialized views as much as possible and recompute only what is needed, thus avoiding computational redundancy. Zhang et al. [391] develop weight-centric streamlining to optimize data reuse in RNN-based deep learning models.

5.4.2.2   Computational Parallel

With the advent of mobile edge devices, it is now feasible to execute each neural network layer in different devices with diverse computation resources. More specifically, different parts of the model can be executed in parallel to obtain a better model inference performance. For example, unlike the current machine learning models that are trained on user-specific data center infrastructure, authors in [334] show that Facebook gains an improved performance in latency (inference time) and computation cost by bringing machine learning inference to the edge. The computation parallelism can be divided into two types: model parallelism and data parallelism.

For model parallelism, the deep learning models will be divided into pieces, a few consecutive layers will be placed at a single node, and its gradients will be calculated. In this way, the number of parameters in a single node gets reduced, and data could be used to train to get more accurate gradients. Kim et al. [140] propose μLayer, a multiprocessors-based inference architecture, which can significantly decrease the latency of NN-related tasks. More specifically, μLayer utilizes the unoccupied processors on the mobile devices to speed up the inference in each NN layer. Furthermore, quantization technology is combined in this paper, which improves the computation performance. Zhao et al. [399] use cross-kernel optimization to achieve model parallelism and improve resource utilization. They spatially parallelize and pipeline the computation graph in the data center. Experiments show that the performance of the proposed algorithm is able to achieve 10-20 times and 2 times improvement when compared with the GPU-based platform and the FPGA-based platform, respectively. Xu et al. [348] focus on addressing the limitations in existing DL programming models; that is, they cannot perform well in dynamic network conditions. In this case, they propose Cavs, an efficient runtime system that can have a good performance on dynamic neural networks.

The concept of data parallelism is to make the operation on data simultaneously by distributing the data to different nodes. To address the limited data parallelism in the small-dimensional of RNNs, Holmes et al. [109] propose GRNN, a GPU-based inference toolbox in RNN, which can significantly reduce the latency while improving the throughput and resource utilization by optimizing the number of global memory accesses and synchronization process. Dong et al. [58] investigate the effect of the sparsity of input data on inference performance. Based on it, an end-to-end optimization framework is proposed to generate programs for the inference with sparse input.

5.4.2.3   Computation Offloading

The exponential deployment of edge devices has put great pressure on the current network. Because the per-device computation ability is limited, offloading some of the computation tasks to other servers or even a data center becomes more feasible than executing on local devices.

With the emergence of edge computing, traditional centralized, cloud-based DNN offloading strategies are faced with several challenges – e.g., the limited communication bandwidth between edge servers, and delay-sensitive application in end users. There are some studies focusing on addressing these new challenges. For example, in [129], a DNN is divided into several parts, and each part can be offloaded to an edge server. When there is a need to make an inference, the fraction will be downloaded from edge servers one by one (Fig. 5.6). Guo et al. [85] explore the redundant computation in the process of inference, by cross-device approximate computation reuse, computation latency and energy consumption are both reduced. Canel et al.

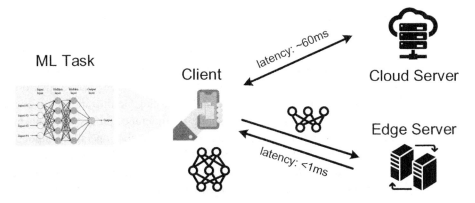

Figure 5.6 Example scenario of dividing a client's DNN model into several partitions and using remote servers to offload DNN partitions for image recognition.

[32] propose a combination framework to process the video of the camera. In this novel system, the large amount of camera data will be processed in the data center, while the relevant frames will be handled in lightweight edge filters.

5.5 Conclusion and Future Directions

In this chapter, we introduce the technologies enabling computation acceleration for edge learning. The chapter consists of three parts. First, we summarize and discuss the mainstream approaches to achieve computation-efficient and cost-effective edge learning, including low-rank factorization, quantization, network pruning, multiple computation primitive scheduling, hardware management, computation resource allocation, etc. Then, we point out that the training efficiency is seriously degraded by the stragglers in edge learning due to heterogeneous capabilities and sudden failure of the participants. We review the gradient-coding-based mechanisms for straggler tolerance in cooperative learning systems. We also introduce an example of decoding matrix and encoding matrix design according to our previous published work. Finally, we list the key performance indicators for inference in edge environments and summarize the technologies that improve inference performance in edge learning. The main approaches can be classified into three categories: reduction of the computation complexity, computation parallel, and computation offloading.

In the following, we point out some potential research directions in this field, covering the scope of software and hardware synergy and straggler tolerance, as well as large-scale model deployment and inference in the edge environment.

5.5.1 Jointly Optimize Learning Algorithm and Hardware Implementation in Edge Environments

Although NPUs specialize in the acceleration of matrix multiplication and convolution operation, the utilization of current hardware acceleration platforms is often low when serving operations between sparse vectors/matrices and multiplication between matrices with different precision. Moreover, on-chip memory constraints and inter-core communication bandwidth can significantly affect the performance of model training and inference. Therefore, it is important to design scheduling and resource allocation corresponding to the specific computation patterns among various platforms.

One critical problem is how to implement flexible operation on modern AI chips to improve training efficiency. Training and inference processes of machine learning models are essentially compositions of linear algebra operations among sparse and dense matrices. NPUs – e.g., TPU by Google, NVIDIA Deep Learning Accelerator (NVDLA) by Nvidia, and Ali-NPU by Alibaba – are microprocessors that specialize in handling such operations. Compared with CPU and GPU, they are efficient in linear algebra operations between large-dimension matrices but lack flexibility for computational logic. To tackle this issue, one promising research direction is designing and implementing a library to accelerate sophisticated operations on NPUs, including approximate computing for nonlinear, and matrix-matrix multiplication with distinct precision, which will be complementary to current accelerator platforms.

Moreover, parallelism schemes play an important role in the inference phase. The involved resource scheduling and allocation mechanisms directly affect efficiency and accuracy, which are crucial for intelligent applications. Through the decomposition of the calculation process and careful managing available resources, one approach is multi-level parallelism – i.e., gate-level parallelism, computation unit-level parallelism, and task-level parallelism. By estimating the time cost of inter-chip data communication, one can design optimization method to balance the resource allocation for different learning tasks with the constraints from on-chip memory.

5.5.2 Green and Sustainable Model Training among Heterogeneous Hardware Platforms

High energy consumption is still a challenging issue in state-of-the-art platforms. Current deep learning tasks are always implemented on various and heterogeneous hardware platforms (CPU, GPU, NPU, FPGA, etc.), which have different computation and energy consumption patterns. Also, different deep learning models have unique computation characteristics. It is therefore crucial to tackle energy consumption from the system level to match the power supply and consumption. The major challenge is balancing energy consumption, computation efficiency, and model accuracy.

Implementing deep learning tasks on heterogeneous hardware platforms requires extensive information exchange across these platforms. However, data communication between different hardware apparently will frequently increase energy consumption. Meanwhile, different layers of deep learning models have their own characteristics in terms of dependencies, interrelationships, and hardware compatibilities, which will also affect the data movement scheduling. A model-driven approach can significantly improve the training efficiency via optimizing the data movement scheduling strategy. In addition, in the machine learning systems, energy consumption can be greatly reduced by sharply lowering the chip's computational speed by attuning its main frequency. Therefore, one approach is to design an efficient computational resource allocation strategy that trade off between the learning time and the energy consumption – e.g., for delay-tolerant services is to delay the learning process by slowing the chip's speed, thus reducing the overall energy consumption.

5.5.3   Approximate Gradient Coding to Deal with Stragglers

In an edge learning system, the straggler phenomenon is common because some nodes suddenly fail/leave or the calculation speed is seriously backward, but this is difficult to predict in advance. Coding computations – i.e., generating redundant computation with coding technologies – are widely investigated to deal with stragglers. However, there are new challenges in the edge training process. First, previous coding computation schemes are aimed at linear systems – e.g., matrix multiplication and vector convolution – while popular learning models – such as neural networks – are nonlinear systems. Second, large-scale edge learning requires massive training dataset and model parameters. Traditional migration strategies are not directly suitable; they will incur unaffordable cost due to limited communication and energy.

To tackle this problem, one approach is approximate gradient coding schemes to deal with stragglers in edge learning. Since directly coding on training dataset leads to an incorrect model due to nonlinear property, gradient coding technology is widely used. In the synchronization process, a full gradient can be reconstructed even if some local gradients fail to be collect. Therefore, one important issue is to investigate the relationship between redundancy degree and resilience capability. In addition, gradient is not sensitive to noise – i.e., the approximate calculation of the full gradient is generally acceptable. Aiming at this kind of approximate calculation, it is important to characterize the impact of computational accuracy on the relationship between computational cost and straggler node tolerance, and then design an efficient coding method that accommodates different accuracy requirements. Moreover, the temporary calculation results on the backward nodes can still improve the accuracy due to the feature of iterative calculations, which is also a future research direction.

6 Efficient Training with Heterogeneous Data Distribution

6.1   Introduction to Federated Learning

In recent years, with the development of AI technologies and widespread applications, data privacy preservation has been given more and more attention. The collection of user data must be open and transparent between companies and institutions; data belonging to one user or company cannot be exchanged with others without user authorization. It brings new challenges to traditional machine learning technologies. If the data between organizations cannot be shared, and the amount of data in an organization is limited, only a small number of giant companies monopolize the large amount of data. It is difficult for small companies to obtain enough data, forming large and small "data islands." In this case, how can a joint model where there is no authority to obtain enough user data be trained?

The concept of federated learning was proposed to allow distributed worker nodes to collaboratively train a shared global model without exposing their private data. Federated learning is essentially a kind of distributed learning, but it still has several differences when compared to distributed learning. In Table 6.1, we compare the characteristics of federated learning and traditional distributed learning. First, in traditional distributed learning, we usually assume that the centralized server has full control over the all nodes and data. However, in federated learning, the worker nodes are usually unstable, and the data are controlled by owners. Furthermore, the local datasets are heterogeneous since the data is independently generated by the worker nodes. Beyond that, federated learning concerns more about the privacy and security. Federated learning can be regraded as a special case of edge learning, as the server and participants in federated learning can be not only the edge devices, but also the data center or isolated organizations. In federated learning, the eligible clients first register on the parameter server. Then, the parameter server proceeds federated learning synchronously in rounds. In each round, the selected clients first download the latest global model from the parameter server , train the model on their local datasets, and report their respective model updates to the parameter server for aggregation (Algorithm 6.1).

A typical architecture and training process of an federated learning system is shown in Fig. 6.1. In general, there are two main components in the federated learning system - i.e., the data owners (clients/workers) and model owner (federated learning server). We define $\mathcal{M} = \{1, \ldots, K\}$ as the set of K clients, each of which has a private

Table 6.1. Comparison of distributed learning and federated learning.

Characteristics	Distributed Learning	Federated Learning
The server has full control over the devices and data	✓	×
Worker nodes are unstable	×	✓
Local datasets are heterogenous	×	✓
Concerns about the privacy and security	×	✓

Algorithm 6.1 Federated Averaging. The K clients are indexed by k; B is the local mini-batch size, E is the number of local epochs, and η is the learning rate

---

1: **procedure** SERVER EXECUTES:
2:      initial w_0
3:      **for** each round $t = 1, 2, \dots$ **do**
4:          $m \leftarrow \max(C \cdot K, 1)$
5:          $S_t \leftarrow$ (random set of m clients)
6:          **for** each client $k \in S_t$ **in parallel do**
7:              $w_{t+1}^k \leftarrow$ ClientUpdate(k, w_t)
8:          **end for**
9:          $w_{t+1} \leftarrow \sum_{k=1}^K \frac{n_k}{n} w_{t+1}^k$
10:      **end for**
11: **end procedure**
12:
13: **procedure** CLIENTUPDATE(k, w) :   ▷ Run on client k
14:      $\mathcal{B} \leftarrow$ (split $\mathcal{P}_k$ into batches of size B)
15:      **for** each local epoch i from 1 to E **do**
16:          **for** batch $b \in \mathcal{B}$ **do**
17:              $w \leftarrow w - \eta \nabla \ell(w; b)$
18:          **end for**
19:      **end for**
20:      **return** w to server
21: **end procedure**

---

dataset $\mathcal{D}_k$, $k \in \mathcal{M}$. The number of samples in $\mathcal{D}_k$ are n_k, and $n = \sum_{k=1}^K n_k$. The data sample in dataset $\mathcal{D}_k$ can be denoted by (x_i, y_i), where x_i is the the input/feature vector for sample $i \in \mathcal{D}_k$, and y_i is the corresponding label. Each client will train a local model with parameters $\mathbf{w}_k$ by using its own dataset $\mathcal{D}_k$ and send only the local model parameters rather than the raw data to the federated learning server. Then, all collected local models are aggregated $w = \cup_{k \in \mathcal{M}} w_k$ to generate a global model w. This is different from the traditional centralized training, which uses the whole data $\mathbf{D} = \cup_{k \in \mathcal{M}} \mathcal{D}_k$ to train a model - i.e., data from each individual source is aggregated and processed centrally. For each sample i, we denote the loss function as $f(x_i, y_i; w)$, which is also written as $f_i(w)$ in short. In this system, the data owners serve as the

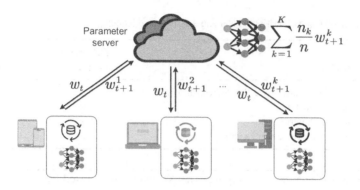

Figure 6.1 An illustration of federated learning.

federated learning participants that collaboratively train a machine learning model required by an aggregate server. More specifically, the training process of federated learning can be summarized into three steps: initialization, local model training and update, and global aggregation. It should be noted that the local model refers to the model trained locally at each participating client, and global model refers to the model aggregated by federated learning server.

Step 1: Initialize. The federated learning server first decides the training task, such as the target application and the corresponding data requirements. The server also initializes the hyper-parameters of the global model randomly or by pretraining with public data - i.e., the learning rate. Then, the server distributes the initialized parameters w_0 of the global model to selected clients.

Step 2: Local model training and update. Based on the global model parameter w_t where t denotes the current iteration index, each selected client updates the local model parameters w_t^k using their local data and uploads the updated model parameters to the server. The goal of client k in $t-$ iteration is to minimize the empirical loss $F(w_t^k)$ based on the local training dataset, i.e.,

$$w_t^{k*} = \arg\min_{w_t^k} F\left(w_t^k\right) \tag{6.1}$$

$$F(w_t^k) = \frac{1}{n_k} \sum_{i \in \mathcal{D}_k} f(x_i, y_i; w_t^k). \tag{6.2}$$

The update process in each client can be achieved by performing SGD with mini-batches sampled from its local dataset:

$$w_{t+1}^k = w_t^k - \eta \nabla F(w_t^k), \tag{6.3}$$

where $\nabla F(w_t^k)$ represents the gradient of loss function and η is the learning rate. After that, the updated local model parameters will be sent to federated learning server.

Step 3: Global Aggregation. In this step, the server aggregates the local updated parameters from client, replaces the global model with the average model, and then sends the updated global model parameters w_{t+1} back to the data owners. In particular, the aim is to minimize the global loss function value, i.e.,

$$F(w_t) = \sum_{k=1}^{K} \frac{n_k}{n} F(w_t^k), k \in 1, 2, ..., K. \qquad (6.4)$$

The preceding steps are repeated until a targeted accuracy is achieved. As compared to traditional machine learning model training approaches, the implementation of federated learning for model training has the following advantages:

- *Lower latency:* With federated learning, each client can consistently train and update a local machine learning model. The updated model can be used to make predictions on the user's device. Therefore, the latency is much lower than that when decisions are made in the centralized server.
- *Privacy Preservation:* Since the raw data of users need not be sent to the server, this guarantees user privacy. In fact, with guaranteed privacy, more users will be willing to take part in collaborative model training, and so better inference models are built.
- *Highly efficient use of network resources:* In the federated learning training process, only the updates are required to transmitted to the federated learning server, which reduces the total communication overhead. Besides, the computation resource can be highly used in multiple local updates. As a result, both the computation and communication resources can be efficiently used in federated learning.

In federated learning, the data are generated and stored in end users' own devices such as mobile phones and personal computers, which causes data heterogeneity. In the next section, data heterogeneity and related training frameworks will be introduced.

6.2   Training with Non-IID Data

Most machine learning algorithms assume that the training data is independently and identically distributed (IID). For example, SVM, backward propagation for neural networks, and many other common algorithms implicitly make this assumption as part of their derivation. Nevertheless, this assumption is commonly violated in many real-life problems where subgroups of samples exhibit a high degree of correlation among both features and labels. In edge learning, due to the decentralized architecture, the data is independently generated by the multiple node devices. The data from different devices have different distribution characteristics - namely, the training data is non-IID on each device, which decreases the efficiency of the training process as it heavily relies on SGD [49, 73, 141]. Without the strong assumption that the local data are IID, it is hard to provide an guarantee to the convergence rate. Therefore, improving the learning efficiency on non-IID data is of great significance for edge learning.

6.2.1   What Does Non-IID Mean?

Informally, identically distributed means the distribution does not fluctuate, and all items in the sample are taken from the same probability distribution. Independent means that the sample items are all independent events. In other words, they are not able to connect to each other in any way. A more technical definition of an IID statistics is

- Each $x^{(i)} \sim Q$ (Identically Distributed)
- $\forall i \neq j, p(x^{(i)}, x^{(j)}) = P(x^{(i)})P(x^{(j)})$ (Independently Distributed).

A statistical model for edge learning involves two levels of sampling: accessing a data point requires first sampling a client $i \sim \mathcal{D}$, the distribution over available clients, and then drawing an example $(x, y) \sim \mathcal{P}_i(x, y)$ from that client's local data distribution, where x is the features and y is the label. Non-IID data in edge learning typically means the difference between $\mathcal{P}_i$ and $\mathcal{P}_j$ for different clients i and j.

The IID sampling of the training data is important to ensure that the stochastic gradient is an unbiased estimate of the full gradient. Namely, having IID data at the clients means that each mini-batch of data used for a client's local update is statistically identical to a uniformly drawn sample (with replacement) from the entire training dataset, which is the union of all local datasets at the clients. In practice, it is unrealistic to assume that the local data on each edge device is always IID. More specifically, the data in real-life applications usually has the following characteristics:

- *Violations of Independence*: If the data are processed in an insufficiently random order. (e.g., if ordered by collection of devices and/or by time, then independence is violated. Moreover, devices within the same geo-location are likely to have correlated data.
- *Violations of Identicalness*: Because devices are tied to particular geo-regions, the distribution of labels varies across partitions. Besides, different devices (partitions) can hold vastly different amounts of data.

Thus, data distributed among federated learning clients have the following properties:

- Data on each node are generated by a distinct distribution $x_t \sim \mathcal{P}_t$.
- The number of data points on each node, n_t, may also vary significantly.
- There may be an underlying structure present that captures the relationship among nodes and their associated distributions.

Most empirical work on synthetic non-IID datasets have focused on label distribution skew, where a non-IID dataset is formed by partitioning an existing dataset based on the labels.

6.2.2   Enabling Technologies for Training Non-IID Data

Due to the non-IID data in edge learning, many of the methods have been designed to improve the performance of edge learning from different research perspectives.

Existing solutions can be categorized into three types: data sharing, robust aggregation methods, and other optimized methods.

6.2.2.1 Data Sharing

The most straightforward idea to solve non-IID data is to share a small IID sub-dataset containing a uniform distribution over classes from the server to the clients. For example, Zhao et al. [397] propose that the skewness of data distribution can be roughly interpreted as the distance between the data distribution on each client and the population distribution. The distance is termed as weight divergence, and it can be computed by the following equation:

$$weight\_divergence = \left\| w^{FedAvg} - w^{SGD} \right\| / \left\| w^{SGD} \right\|. \tag{6.5}$$

More specifically, they assume there are K clients in edge learning, w_t^c denotes the weight after the tth update in the centralized setting, and w_t^f denotes the weight calculated after the tth synchronization. As shown in Fig. 6.2, when data is IID, for each client k, the divergence between $w_t^{(k)}$ and $w_t^{(c)}$ is small, and after the tth synchronization, $w_t^{(f)}$ is still close to $w_t^{(c)}$. When data is non-IID, for each client k, due to the distance between the data distribution, the divergence between $w_t^{(k)}$ and $w_t^{(c)}$ becomes much larger and accumulates very fast, which makes the divergence between $w_T^{(f)}$ and $w_T^{(c)}$ much larger. In addition, this distance can be evaluated with the earth mover's distance (EMD) between distributions. Because the globally shared data can reduce EMD for the clients, the test accuracy is expected to improve.

They propose a data-sharing strategy in the federated learning setting, as illustrated in Fig. 6.2. A globally shared dataset G that consists of a uniform distribution over classes is centralized in the cloud. At the initialization stage of $FedAvg$, the warmup model trained on G and a random α portion of G are distributed to each client. The local model of each client is trained on the shared data from G together with the private data from each client. The cloud then aggregates the local models from the clients to train a global model with $FedAvg$.

While this approach can help create more accurate models, it still has several shortcomings: the most crucial one is that we generally cannot ensure the availability of such a public dataset. Even if a public data set were to exist, sending shared public dataset would increase the communication overhead, which imposes burdens

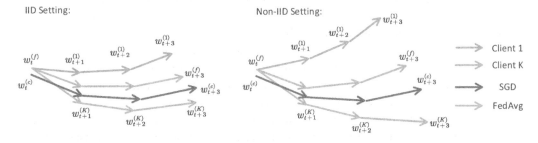

Figure 6.2 Illustration of the weight divergence for federated learning with IID and non-IID data.

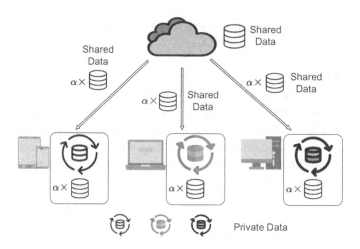

Figure 6.3 Illustration of the data-sharing strategy.

on network bandwidth. Furthermore, if all clients share (part of) the same public data set, overfitting to this shared data can become a serious issue. This effect will be particularly severe in highly distributed settings where the number of data points on every client is small. For these reasons, we believe that the data-sharing strategy proposed by [397] is an insufficient workaround to the fundamental problem of federated averaging having convergence issues on non-IID data [250].

Jeong et al. [128] combine the generative model with federated learning to construct an IID dataset. In their proposed federated augmentation (FAug) framework, each device collectively trains a GAN model and reproduces the data samples of all devices in local. In this case, the trained GAN augments its local data toward yielding an IID dataset. Instead of direct data sample exchanges, which may increase the communication overhead, FAug first trains a generative model in the server by uploading some seed samples of the labels lacking in each device. The server oversamples the uploaded seed data samples - e.g., via Google's image search for visual data, so as to train a conditional GAN [204]. Finally, each client download the trained generator component of GAN to replenish the missing data samples until an IID training dataset is reached, which significantly reduces the additional communication overhead, especially with a large number of devices. However, sending local data or related information (missing labels) to the server violates the key privacy assumptions of federated learning.

6.2.2.2 Robust Aggregation Methods

Due to the existence of non-IID data, there maybe huge differences between the models on different clients after the process of local update. There are several works focusing on estimating the contribution of each update according to the data distribution or local model performance on clients [19, 186, 223].

Only the relevant updates and valuable clients are selected in each aggregation phase. Gaia [112] measures the significance of a local update from one data center by the update's magnitude relative to the current parameter, i.e. - $\frac{\|local\_update\|}{\|model\|}$, where $\| \cdot \|$ means the Euclidean norm. Any local update satisfies $\frac{\|local\_update\|}{\|model\|} <$ threshold is considered insignificant and will be excluded in the aggregation phase. Wang et al. [186] notice that this identification is made based only on the local update, without accounting for the federation of all clients. As the global model is the federation of a large number of clients, whether a local update is useful in model optimization cannot be simply measured by its magnitude. Moreover, the update's magnitude will decreases exponentially when the training approaches convergence. It is hard to tune the threshold used in identifying updates' significance. To address these limitations, Wang et al. propose a novel measurement to estimate the effectiveness of the local update. More specifically, they compare the two updates - local and global - parameter-wise. The number of parameters of the same sign in the two updates is computed, and the result is normalized by the total number of parameters. This gives the percentage of same-sign parameters in the two updates, which are used to measure the relevance of a local update. The relevance of a local update can be expressed by

$$e(\mathbf{u}, \bar{\mathbf{u}}) = \frac{1}{N} \sum_{n=1}^{N} I(sgn(u_n) = sgn(\bar{u}_n)), \tag{6.6}$$

where $\mathbf{u} =< u_1, u_2, ..., u_N >$ denotes a local update over N model parameters. $\bar{\mathbf{u}}$ is similarly defined for the (estimated) global update. $I(sgn(u_n) = sgn(\bar{u}_n)) = 1$ if and only if u_n and $\bar{u}_n$ are of same sign, and 0 otherwise. This method can not only eliminate the impact of non-IID data, but also reduce the communication overhead.

Another method considers designing a robust averaging mechanism. Yeganeh et al. [361] propose a robust aggregation method at the server side. The weighting coefficients are adaptively determined by the statistical properties of the model parameters. They aim to train global model with a low variance given the high-variance local models that are robust to non-IID and unbalanced data. The averaging process can be expressed as follows

$$w_t^g = \sum_{k=1}^{K} \alpha_k \cdot w_{t-1}^k, \tag{6.7}$$

where α_k is the weighting coefficient for client k, w_t^g and w_{t-1}^k are global model parameters in tth round and local model parameters of client k, respectively. In [361], Inverse Distance Aggregation (IDA) is defined to calculate the coefficient α_k, which is based on the inverse distance of each client parameters to the average model of all clients, i.e.,

$$\alpha = \frac{1}{Z} \left\| \omega_{t-1}^{Avg} - \omega_{t-1}^k \right\|^{-1}, \tag{6.8}$$

where $Z = \sum_{k=1}^{K} \| \omega_{t-1}^{Avg} - \omega_{t-1}^k \|^{-1}$ is a normalization factor. Note that $\alpha_k = 1$ when clients' parameters are equivalent to the average one, and $\alpha_k = n_k$ is equivalent to the $FedAvg$.

6.2.2.3 Other Optimization Method to Tackle Non-IID Data

In addition, some solutions make a small modification on the $FedAvg$ method to help deal with non-IID data and even ensure convergence, both theoretically and in practice. The objective function in $FedAvg$ is

$$\min_{w} f(w) = \sum_{k=1}^{K} p_k F_k(w). \tag{6.9}$$

Recent works have proposed modified modeling approaches that aim to reduce the variance of the model performance across devices. For example, FedProx [162] proposes a proximal term to minimize the distance between the local and global models. A key insight behind developing FedProx is that an interplay exists between systems and data heterogeneity in federated learning. Indeed, both dropping stragglers (as in *FedAvg*) and naively incorporating partial information from stragglers (as in Fed-Prox with the proximal term set to 0) implicitly increase data heterogeneity and can adversely impact convergence behavior. The added proximal term to the objective can help increase the stability of the method. While tolerating nonuniform amounts of local updates to be performed across devices can help alleviate negative impacts of systems heterogeneity, too many local updates may still cause the methods to diverge due to the underlying heterogeneous data. So they propose to add a proximal term to the local sub-problem to effectively limit the impact of variable local updates, e.g.,

$$\min_{w} h_k (w; w_t) = F_k(w) + \frac{\mu}{2} \|w - w_t\|^2. \tag{6.10}$$

$F_k(w)$ is the original local loss function, and w_t is the global model parameters in tth round. The proximal term is beneficial in two aspects: (1) It addresses the issue of data heterogeneity by restricting the local updates to be closer to the initial (global) model without any need to manually set the number of local epochs. (2) It allows for safely incorporating variable amounts of local work resulting from system heterogeneity. It should be noticed that μ is an important parameters in this method, which affects the convergence speed in the training process. The setting of the μ has a big influence on the whole model training. Similarly, Shoham et al. [265] add a penalty term to the loss function in the multitask federated learning framework.

Huang et al. [118] consider further optimizing the local models with a high cross-entropy loss before model averaging on the server. Since they focus on a health dataset that the data labels are either 0 (survival) or 1 (expired), binary cross-entropy loss is adopted as the error measure of model-fitting, such as

$$-\sum_{i=1}^{N} \left[y_i \log f(x_i) + (1 - y_i) \log (1 - f(x_i)) \right], \tag{6.11}$$

where N denotes the number of samples. x_i was the input drug feature vector, y was the binary mortality label, and f was the federated learning model. The objective function of each client model is to minimize Equation (6.11), which measured goodness of fit: the lower the loss was, the better a model was fitted. The proposed method utilizes the median cross-entropy loss L_{t-1}^{median} of clients who participated in the training in round $t - 1$ as the threshold to measure whether current client need boost or not. Based on this idea, each client can perform a varied number of local updates based on local loss. Furthermore, Sattler et al. [249] propose clustering loss terms and using cosine similarity to overcome the divergence problem when clients have different data distributions.

When modeling non-IID data, it is also important to consider issues beyond accuracy, such as fairness. Simply solving an aggregate loss function of each local model may implicitly advantage or disadvantage some of the devices, as the learned model may become biased towards devices with larger amounts of data, or to commonly occurring groups of devices. Other more principled approaches to addressing these issues include agnostic federated learning [207], which optimizes the centralized model for any target distribution formed by a mixture of the client distributions via a minimax optimization scheme. Another more general approach is taken by Li et al. [163], which proposes an objective called q-FFL in which devices with higher loss are given higher relative weight to encourage less variance in the final accuracy distribution. The modified objective can be represented by

$$\min_{w} f_q(w) = \sum_{k=1}^{K} \frac{p_k}{q+1} F_k^{q+1}(w), \tag{6.12}$$

where $F_k^{q+1}(\cdot)$ denotes $F_k(\cdot)$ to the power of $(q+1)$. Here, q is a parameter that tunes the amount of fairness we wish to impose. Setting $q = 0$ does not encourage fairness beyond the classical federated learning objective 6.9. A larger value of q means that we emphasize devices with higher local empirical losses, $F_k(w)$, thus imposing more uniformity to the training accuracy distribution and potentially inducing fairness.

6.3 Conclusion and Future Directions

Federated learning has been proposed as a promising solution for future AI applications with strong privacy protection. Its basic idea is to let mobile devices train local models using their own data, and then upload the local models, instead of raw data, to a logically centralized parameter server that synthesizes a global model. Since its inception undertaken by Google, federated learning has been extensively studied, however, under an unrealistic assumption that the devices involved in the learning process are homogeneous, i.e., their training data are IID. The preceding assumptions are invalid in many real-life applications.

In this chapter, we comprehensively introduce the federated learning under a practical heterogeneous setting that mobile devices hold non-IID data. Then, we list important related work about efficient training with heterogeneous data distribution. However, existing solutions still have limitations. The optimization theories involved in machine learning algorithms are always oblivious to the resource-constrained computing environment. On the one hand, existing related studies in hyper-parameter settings in federated learning (e.g., batch size, learning rate, and aggregation frequency) mainly focus on analyzing convergence properties with homogeneous communication and computation capabilities, failing to take the resource heterogeneity and dynamics into consideration. On the other hand, current resource allocation and computation offloading approaches for MEC have not considered the unique features of federated learning tasks - e.g., iterative computation and the additional costs for data encryption. Therefore, it is essential to conduct a systematical investigation on federated learning in order to tackle the limitations in existing studies. More work needs to be done to improve the training efficiency of federated learning for the rapidly proliferating machine learning applications. In this section, we discuss three possible future directions on efficient training mechanism for federated learning, with respect to non-IID data over resource-constrained mobile edge networks.

6.3.1   Tackle the Non-IID Data via Learning-based Data Selection

Existing work dealing with non-IID data is either to construct an IID sub-dataset by carefully choosing parts from all raw data or to simply optimize the aggregation phase. However, both of them are suboptimal and even cost additional resources. For example, the data-sharing mechanisms are far from solving an acceptable solution due to two defects. First, they rely on the acquisition of the data distribution, which is difficult to recognize or to obtain in practice. Moreover, the distributions of raw data from some complex learning tasks, such as machine translation, are often difficult to represent. Second, the influence of non-IID data has been investigated only for some simple machine learning algorithms - e.g., logistic regression - whose objective functions are convex. However, many machine learning algorithms - e.g., neural networks - pursue nonconvex objective functions, which are difficult to handle, and their state-of-the-art form has not been thoroughly studied.

As shown in Fig. 6.4, we can address the challenges from non-IID data by designing a reinforcement-learning -based data selection mechanism to deal with the

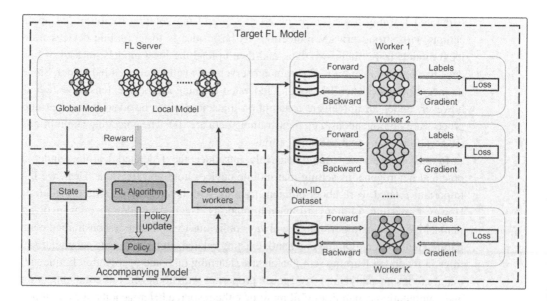

Figure 6.4 Accompanying model for training data selection.

aforementioned weaknesses. A new convergence theory for the general problem will be revisited and established since the most popular neural network models in federated learning are nonconvex. This fundamental theory will provide basic constraints and guidelines for data selection. Then we can construct a set of training data using learning techniques, instead of assuming a known data distribution like that in most existing literature. An overview of our design is shown in Fig. 6.4. We design an accompanying model (the bottom left corner of Fig. 6.4) working with the given target federated learning model (the top left corner of Fig. 6.4). The accompanying model adopts a data feature encoder to assess the data quality, and then trains a reinforcement learning agent by the training loss returned from the target federated learning model, and finally chooses proper subset of data samples and workers. The target model is supposed to conduct SGD-based training, in which each worker randomly samples a batch over the chosen subset.

6.3.2   Adaptive Parameter Setting for Non-IID Data

Hyper-parameters of a model (e.g., batch size, aggregation frequency, compression rate) have significant impact on the training process. The optimal hyper-parameter settings of a model are difficult to be obtained, especially in federated learning scenarios where the available training resources are limited and heterogeneous. We can design a reinforcement-learning-based model which takes these resource properties into consideration and adjusts the hyper-parameters to accelerate the loss descent efficiency. We can first estimate resource costs for hyper-parameters. Then, we can mine features of the resource state of workers. Finally, we can design a reinforcement learning model to set hyper-parameters based on resource features of workers and estimated resource cost.

Our *policy network* takes the state - i.e., resource feature vectors - as inputs and makes decisions of hyper-parameter values based on the corresponding estimated/stored resource cost. In particular, the policy network research covers the following contents.

(1)   Joint optimization for multiple factors. The performance of federated learning is affected by efficient resource allocation and proper hyper-parameter selection. The batch size affects the computation cost and training time overhead of a single iteration. It will further affect the gradient aggregation cycle/frequency. The uploading cycle is determined based on the computation speed and the communication capacity. Meanwhile, hyper-parameters impact both the accuracy and convergence rate. We will jointly consider these hyper-parameters and optimization targets in one model.

(2)   RNN-based encoding for dynamic resource. The resources of each worker are dynamic. Long-term profit of hyper-parameters selection should be considered for the whole training process. However, the values of hyper-parameters for future training cycles are determined by the past resource states. We need to find the pattern of resource variations and accordingly adjust the hyper-parameters.

Our hyper-parameter selection model will take a list of past resource feature vectors as inputs to capture the variation pattern by an RNN to decide values of hyper-parameters using a reinforcement learning model.

(3)   Multi-agent framework for interactive workers. Because of the competitive usage on shared resources and the interaction between workers, hyper-parameter selections of workers will interfere with each other. Thus, we apply a multi-agent training framework to train the policy network. Workers are regarded as different agents using a common shared policy. The policy network makes decisions for each worker and aggregates the experiences of different agents.

6.3.3   Straggler-Tolerant Federated Learning Algorithms

The straggler phenomenon is common in federated learning over the mobile edge environment due to sudden failure/leave of unreliable devices. Coded computation and gradient coding technologies - i.e., generating redundant computation with coding technologies - have been investigated to deal with the straggler problem. Solid theories and feasible algorithms are proposed in such areas. However, they are not applicable for federated learning in the mobile edge environment. On one hand, previous coding computation schemes are designed for addition or multiplication computation - e.g., matrix multiplication and vector convolution - while computation in training common learning models such as neural network is more complicated. On the other hand, the gradient coding scheme requires aggregating the training dataset and centralized control for dataset distribution, which goes against the non-sharable data principle in federated learning.

We can design the federated learning algorithm with adaptive gradient aggregation policy, in which each individual device pulls the global model from the server after one or several local epochs. The process of adaptive parameter setting in federated learning with non-IID data is illustrated in Fig. 6.5. Each device adaptively selects its own transmission frequency with the parameter server based on its current computation capacity and link status. In other words, the workers who do not download

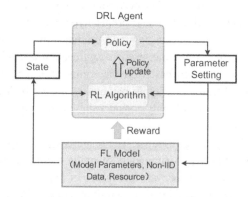

Figure 6.5 Adaptive parameter setting for non-IID data in federated learning.

the global model from the server can utilize their local updated model for the next step computation. In this way, though some tiny faults occur, the federated learning algorithm could still converge efficiently. Moreover, because mobile devices share the wireless spectrum resource, balancing the number of workers in multiple cellular base stations and scheduling the transmission efficiently will further accelerate federated learning training process.

7 Security and Privacy Issues in Edge Learning Systems

Conventional distributed machine learning manages the training data in a centralized mode without considering the privacy and security problem during training or inference. With the rapid development of AI technology these days, privacy protection has gained more and more attention. The European Union proposed the General Data Protection Regulation (GDPR), the first data privacy protection bill, which introduces some stipulations against data privacy protection. In 2017, China also implemented the "Cyber Security Law of the People's Republic of China" and "General Principles of the Civil Law of the People's Republic of China", which state that "network operators must not disclose, tamper with, or destroy the personally collected information, and when conducting data transactions with third parties, it is necessary to ensure that the proposed contract stipulates the scope of the proposed transaction data and data protection obligations." According to this legislation, all enterprises and organizations need to collect user data openly and transparently. Additionally, data can be exchanged only under users' authorization. This brings the challenge to edge learning that when companies possess user data without sharing it, data islands will eventually result. Moreover, edge learning participants usually are small devices (e.g. smartphones, sensors) that have weak abilities for defense and can be easily compromised under possible attacks. In this chapter, we first introduce a security guarantee mechanism in edge learning, including the defense methods for data-oriented attacks and model-oriented attacks. Then we summarize the mainstream methods of privacy protection, including differential privacy, secure multiparty computation, and homomorphic encryption. Finally, we discuss future directions in this field.

7.1 Security Guarantee

When training models using distributed machine learning in an edge environment, at first, the server sends the global model to all clients and clients train it with local data; then clients send the new model or model update back; and finally, the server aggregates these models to update the global model. During the training process, the update of the global model completely depends on the information clients sent. Nevertheless, clients on edge are mainly using mobile devices like smartphones, which have limited defense abilities and face a high risk of being compromised under potential attacks. Furthermore, since the server cannot directly access clients' data, the server cannot verify the model updates sent by the clients. Therefore, in this case, a malicious participant or a participant controlled by an outside attacker may send corrupted information to the server to contaminate the model. The summary of various data-oriented and model-oriented defense methods in Table 7.1 provides more information for a clearer understanding.

7.1.1 Data-Oriented Attacks

Data-oriented attacks, also known as data poisoning attacks, tend to tamper with the training data or inject false data such as samples with wrong labels into the training set. In this way, even though the model can fit the training set, it won't perform well in practical use. One example of this type of attack is called adversarial examples (AE). AE adds small perturbations to the input signal. These perturbations can be hardly perceived by humans but enough to cause significant changes to the output of the model. Experiments have shown that when facing AE attacks, the performance of DNN deteriorates rapidly and drastically. In recent years, research has been conducted to study data poisoning attacks and corresponding defense methods. And these works can be roughly classified into optimization-based attacks and decision-based attacks.

7.1.1.1 Optimization-Based Attacks

Optimization-based attacks are usually deployed when the attacker has all the configuration information about the target model such as network structure and loss function. Since machine learning model training can be viewed as an optimization problem that tries to minimize the model loss by adjusting model parameters, by contrast, an adversary can construct an inverse optimization problem that maximizes the loss function by adjusting training data. Optimization-based attacks can generate attacking points by solving this optimization problem and injecting these them into the training set to fulfill the attack.

Jagielski et al. use this approach and designed an attacking algorithm against linear regression models [187]. They maintain a set of poisoning points and optimize the points by updating their feature vectors using gradient ascent. Eventually, the poisoning set achieves max loss on the training set or validation set and thus decreases the model's accuracy.

Steinhardt et al. adopt a similar idea and attempted to generate a poisoning attack on specific defense algorithm [274]. A defense algorithm examines the full dataset and tries to remove outliers residing outside a feasible set and then minimizes a margin-based loss on the remaining data. For a defense method, the proposed attacking algorithm first chooses the point with the largest loss value from the feasible set, add the point into the training set, then update the model using the poisoned set. After a certain iteration, the attacking algorithm generates a poisoning set, achieving optimal attacking effect, and gets the corresponding upper bound on the loss of the model using a defense algorithm.

He et al. demonstrate that an optimization-based attack also performs well against defense methods that only consider the vicinity around an input such as region

Table 7.1. Summary of data-oriented and model-oriented defense methods

Defense Oriented	Basic Approach	Literature	Suitable Models	Specific Ideas
Data	Optimization based	[189]	DNN	Optimize a saddle point formulation
		[351]	DNN	Integrate an adversarial perturbation-based regularizer to the loss function
		[227]	DNN	Minimize the reverse cross-entropy(RCE)
	Model Pruning	[87]	DNN	Increase model sparsity
		[56]	DNN	Randomly prune the activation function
		[290]	DNN	Enhance activation values of critical neurons and weaken the others
	Remove poisoned data	[274]	ANY	Remove points far away from class centroids
	Train with subset	[187]	Linear regression, CNN	Initiate the model by randomly chosen subset and train with subsets having the lowest loss each round
		[258]		
	Others	[292]	Linear regression	Model a multi-learner Stackelberg game
		[31]	DNN	Discretize the model inputs
		[403]	DNN	Model hidden layer's distribution under true inputs and false inputs
		[358]	DNN	Randomly drop some pixels of inputs and reconstruct them using matrix estimation
		[293]	DNN	Train the model with adversarial example to increase the model's robustness against attack
Model	Attack detection	[26]	Multi-layer perception	Find the $(n - f)$-nearest gradients every round
		[11]	Convex	Exclude updates that statistically exceed certain bound
		[340]	Nonconvex	Score and rank the updates, use the Top-k updates to update the global model
	Mean or median	[41]	Linear regression	Use gradients' geometric median to update model
		[363]	Logistic regression, CNN	Use coordinate-wise median or coordinate-wise trimmed mean to update model
	Other	[364]	Non-convex	Add perturbation to gradient to defend saddle attacks

classification [102]. Region classification makes the prediction of an input based on predictions of points around the input instead of the single input point. It first samples several perturbations uniformly from a hypercube around the input and generates slightly perturbed versions of the input. Then the model makes predictions

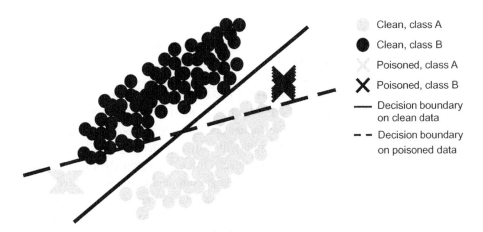

Clean, class A

Clean, class B

Poisoned, class A

Poisoned, class B

Decision boundary
on clean data

Decision boundary
on poisoned data

Figure 7.1 One example of data poisoning attacks. The gray and black dots represent two classes of the clean dataset; the gray and black crosses represent the poisoned data. The decision boundary on clean data (black solid line) is shifted after the poisoning attack (black dotted line).

on all the new points, and the prediction of the input is decided by the majority of the predictions. The attacking method against region classification uses another loss function that increases when the model makes the right prediction to generate an attacking point. Moreover, it uses 20 classifiers in the attack's ensemble to make it likely for a random perturbation. An example of an optimization-based attack is shown in Fig. 7.1.

7.1.1.2 Decision-Based Attacks

Optimization-based attacks, a.k.a. white-box attacks, can be very effective when we know the model configuration; however, in most situations, it's difficult to access the model's detailed information. Thus, optimization-based attacks are hard to implement in real scenarios. Decision-based attacks, or black-box attacks, which solely rely on the final decision of the model, are found very useful in causing damage to models with only a little information about them. The main idea of decision-based attacks is to first study the distribution of the training data and then generate samples outside the distribution to poison the training set. Intuitively, if an attacking point is further from the model's output, it causes more changes to the model. Jagielski et al. observe that the most effective attacking points are usually distributed around the corners of the input space, and they proposed a decision-based attacking algorithm [187]. It samples from a multivariate normal distribution with the mean and covariance estimated from the training data, then rounds the feature values of the points to the corners, and finally selects the response variable's value at the boundary to maximize the loss.

It has been shown that the stochastic multi-armed bandit can be easily manipulated through decision-based attacks [178]. The multi-armed bandit problem is a classic reinforcement learning problem that exemplifies the exploration–exploitation trade-off dilemma. In this problem, a gambler plays a bandit with multiple arms. When one arm is pulled, the bandit returns a random reward from a probability distribution specific to the arm. The objective of the gambler is to maximize the total reward after a series of pulls. The crucial trade-off the gambler faces at each trial is between "exploitation" of the machine that has the highest expected payoff and "exploration" to get more information about the expected payoffs of the other arms. The multi-armed bandit problem has multiple solutions like ϵ-greedy, UCB (upper confidence bound), and Thompson sampling. The framework Liu et al. proposed generates efficient attacks against the multi-armed bandit with only knowledge of which arm is pulled and the corresponding reward. These attacks force the bandit algorithm to pull a target arm by increasing the rewards of the target arm and reducing the rewards of other arms. Experimental results demonstrate that attacks manage to force the bandit to pull a target arm with a 100% success rate against all three strategies aforementioned.

p-tampering $(0 < p < 1)$ attacks tamper p fraction of training set to interfere with the model's performance. Mahloujifar et al. studied p-tampering attacks in a distributed setting in which clients send data to the server for centralized training [190]. They introduced (k, p)-poisoning attacks, which corrupt k clients among total m clients and tamper p fraction of the data of the corrupt party. They also showed that in *anym*-party learning protocol, there exist a (k, p)-poisoning adversary that causes the model to fail on a particular target instance.

Brendel et al. apply another decision-based attack called Boundary Attack to complex deep learning models and achieved a good attacking effect [29], even against some defense algorithms. Boundary Attack initializes an adversarial instance (instance model fails to categorize correctly) and then performs walks closer to the target instance while staying adversarial. Using Boundary Attack, Brendel et al. generated images that very closely resemble the target images but can't be classified by the model.

7.1.2   Defense Technologies for Data-Oriented Attacks

7.1.2.1   Optimization-Based Defense

Based on a similar idea to optimization-based attacks, optimization-based defense algorithms handle a specific attack by constructing an optimization problem and solving it. Madry et al. tried to improve neural network's robustness against perturbations by optimizing a saddle point problem (a composition of an inner maximization problem and an outer minimization problem) that first maximizes the loss of the perturbed training data and then minimizes the risk of loss function by adjusting model parameters [189]. The inner maximization problem tries to find an adversarial version of an instance that computes a high loss, and the outer minimization problem aims to minimize the loss with adversarial examples in the training set. Experiments show that models trained using this method can still perform well facing a wide range of attacks.

Yan et al. attempt to reduce the influence of adversarial attacks by giving a perturbation-based regularization to the original objective function [351]. The regularization function increases when the model classifies the sample correctly and reduces otherwise. In this way, the training will prefer model parameters that can resist perturbations.

Pang et al. design a new objective function called reverse cross-entropy to improve the robustness of DNN classifiers [227]. Through minimizing the reverse cross-entropy, a deep learning model can learn latent representations that better distinguishes adversarial examples from normal ones.

7.1.2.2 Model Pruning

Model pruning removes a certain amount of neurons of a neural network or sparsifies model parameter matrices to reduce the model size or overcome the over-fitting problem. So model pruning can be applied to poisoning defense because, intuitively, data attacks can be considered as model over-fitting the attacking points. Guo et al. observed the intrinsic relationship between the model's sparsity and the robustness of the classifier to white-box adversarial attacks; a proper higher model sparsity implies better robustness of DNNs [87].

Dhillon et al. design a defense method for DNNs against data poisoning attacks called Stochastic Activation Pruning (SAP) [56]. During every forward pass of training, SAP randomly prunes a subset of activations with smaller magnitude and scales up the remaining activations to compensate. Through random pruning, the model becomes more stochastic and has more freedom to deceive the adversary. Experiments show that SAP improves the model's robustness against adversarial examples while maintaining model accuracy.

Tao et al. propose a novel adversarial example defense method for face recognition based on the interpretability of DNN models [290]. They featured a bidirectional correspondence inference between input attributes and hidden neurons to distinguish neurons of the greatest importance for individual attributes. Then they enhanced the activation value of the important neurons to increase the influence of the reasoning part of the model, and the values of other neurons were reduced to suppress the uninterpretable part. By doing this, the model classifies samples based more on the features perceptible to humans and can resist perturbations imperceptible to humans.

7.1.2.3 Remove Poisoned Data

Since data-oriented attacks inject false data into the training set, an intuitive counterpart solution is to remove them. This method scans the whole dataset and tries to remove as many poisoned samples as possible. For example, in classification tasks, we can filter out samples far away from the center of its class. Steinhardt et al. design two filtering methods on the training set [274], the sphere filter and the slab filter. The sphere filter removes data points outside a spherical center of their label class, and the slab filter removes points that far away from the class center in horizontal distance. Experiments demonstrate that these two methods have a good defensive ability for cluster-structure data (e.g., images) but fail to resist the poisoning attack on linear-structure data (e.g. text, speech). Moreover, these two approaches perform well only when the real center of the class is known. Without this premise, the defenses have to compute a center using the poisoned dataset, and the defensive ability is significantly reduced. In edge learning, servers usually don't have direct access to the original data, so it's inefficient and unrealistic to defend potential data attacks by operating the dataset directly.

7.1.2.4   Train with Subsets

Another interesting and novel defense idea against data poisoning does not attempt to remove the attacking points but trains the model with the poisoned dataset and tries to obtain an unaffected or less affected model. Jagielski et al. proposed a training algorithm named TRIM. TRIM doesn't use the full dataset to train models [187]; instead it uses subsets of the data. During every iteration, TRIM first computes losses of all training samples using current model parameters; then it selects a set of samples with the lowest losses and uses the subsets to update the model. TRIM uses the majority of the data to train the model and shows good performance on regression models under data poisoning attacks. Intuitively, this method draws a random line at the beginning and modifies this line each round until it fits the majority distribution. Shen et al. adopted the same idea to train deep learning models using poisoned datasets and obtained good performance on defending CNN and GAN [258]. However, this approach can work well only when the attacking points take small parts of the dataset. When the amount of attacking points increases, the defensive effect will drop because, in this case, attacking points have a greater probability of being chosen into the subsets and thus damaging the model.

7.1.2.5   Other Defense Machanisms

Tong et al. study the defense approaches for linear regression problems and modeled a Stackelberg game between multiple learners and one attacker [292]. All learners train their models from data, and the attacker tampers with features of test data to achieve a target output. The Stackelberg game can be solved using the Multi-Learner Stackelberg equilibrium, and experiments show that the equilibrium is much more robust against attacks than standard regularization approaches.

Buckman et al. observe that the loss function of some neural networks tends to be highly linear with respect to its inputs, and this linearity implies that even imperceptibly small perturbations can have a large effect on the model's predictions [31], making the model vulnerable to adversarial attacks. Therefore, they tried to reduce this linearity by preprocessing the input with an extremely nonlinear function such as quantization or discretization. Through the preprocessing, the model gains more robustness against the strongest known white-box attack.

Zheng et al. design an adversarial sample detecting method by modeling the intrinsic properties of deep learning networks [403]. When a deep learning classifier assigns an adversarial sample to an incorrect class, the states of the hidden layers are quite different from those when assigning a natural data of the same class. Based on this observation, they construct the distribution of hidden layers when training on a clean dataset to detect adversarial examples and achieved good performance against black-box attacks. Nevertheless, this approach needs a clean training set in advance, which is difficult to realize in an actual scenario.

Yang et al. propose a defense method for image tasks that randomly drops pixels of an input image and reconstructs it using matrix estimation [358]. Pixel dropping destroys the structure of adversarial perturbation added to the input and can improve the model's robustness against both black-box and white-box attacks.

Tramèr et al. found that adversarial training (an approach that increases model robustness by training model with poisoned data) [293], although effective to white-box attacks, is still vulnerable to certain black-box attacks. They solve this problem by training models with adversarial examples transferred from other undefended models.

7.1.3   Model-Oriented Attacks

During an iteration of training in edge learning, the server receives model updates from clients and aggregates them to update the global model. Since the server can't verify the validity of updates and most aggregation strategies just simply take the average of all updates, changes to even one update will have a great influence on the global model. Therefore, another way of attacking is directly tampering with the updates sent by clients. This kind of attack strategy is usually called a model-oriented attack or model poisoning. An example of a model-oriented attack is shown in Fig. 7.2.

Bhagoji et al. propose a model poisoning attack initiated by a single, non-colluding malicious client where the adversarial objective is to cause the model to misclassify multiple target inputs with high possibility [24]. The malicious client computes updates by optimizing an adversarial objective that minimizes the loss values when the target samples are classified to the target classes and the generated malicious update is scaled up to reduce the combined effect of the benign ones.

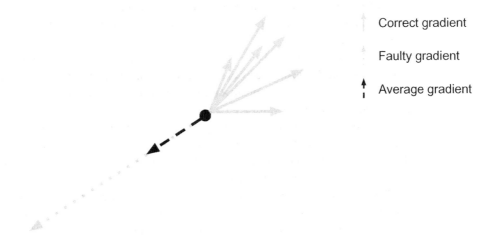

Figure 7.2 An example of model attacks. The gray solid arrow lines represent the direction of the correct gradients; the gray dotted arrow line represent the faulty gradient. The black dotted arrow line represents the direction of the global gradient after aggregation. We can see that one false gradient can cause the global model to update in the wrong direction.

Then the stealth of the malicious update is optimized to deal with potential performance checks and statistic checks by the server. They improved the classification accuracy of nontargeted inputs and minimized the range of distance between malicious updates and others to avoid being flagged as anomalous. The evaluation demonstrates that this attack enables an adversary controlling a single malicious agent to achieve targeted misclassification at the global model with 100% confidence while ensuring convergence of the global model.

7.1.4   Defense Technologies for Model-Oriented Attacks

Studies for model poisoning defenses often use a Byzantine setting where a subset of machines in a distributed computing system behaves completely arbitrarily and the objective of Byzantine fault tolerance is to be able to defend against failures of system components. A malicious client in an edge learning system can be considered as a failed machine in a Byzantine setting. Blanchard et al. propose the first provably Byzantine-resilient algorithm called Krum to defend potential attacks for distributed machine learning [26]. Krum examines all the updates and chooses updates that are statistically closer to other neighbors. Assuming a system consists of n workers among which are at most f Byzantine machines, Krum chooses the updates that minimize the sum of squared distances to its $n - f$ neighbors and aggregates the chosen updates. Since most Byzantine updates are very different from normal ones in both scale and distribution because in this way attacks will cause more damages, Krum can filter out most of these Byzantine attacks, and the surviving attacks won't have much effect on model.

Alistarh et al. propose another method to filter potential Byzantine updates called Byzantine Stochastic Gradient Descent (BSGD) [11]. BSGD constructs an upper bound based on gradients and the derivative of the loss function. A client's update is considered Byzantine if it exceeds the upper bound and will be discarded during current iteration.

Xie et al. present an update ranking and selection mechanism called Zeno [340]. Zeno ranks a candidate update by examining its magnitude and comparing its direction with the estimated direction of the current model (the direction model moves at the last iteration). An update with a direction opposite to the estimated direction and an update with a step longer than other updates will both be ranked low scores. During every iteration, Zeno first ranks all the updates received and chooses k updates with the highest score to aggregate the model. Experiments show that Zeno can tolerate more than a half of Byzantine faults.

Chen et al. design a Byzantine-resilient aggregation algorithm that will learn the true model despite the existing Byzantine updates [41]. They first partition all the updates received from clients into k groups and compute the mean of each group; then they compute the geometric median of the k means; and, finally, they perform a gradient descent step with the geometric mean. This algorithm uses geometric mean to mitigate the influence of Byzantine attacks and therefore gains good model performance without examining every update.

Yin et al. adopt a similar idea and used the coordinate-wise median and coordinate-wise trimmed mean of the updates to update the global model [363]. Experiments demonstrate that both aggregation methods achieve 10% and increased accuracy on logistic regression and CNN models under Byzantine settings. They then study defending saddle point attacks in Byzantine settings [364]. The saddle point is a stationary point with a gradient that equals zero but is far away from any local minimum, and the gradient descent stops when it arrives at a saddle point that leads to a poor performance model. Observing that some Byzantine machines can create a fake local minimum near a saddle point and tempt the model to go to the saddle point, they design a defense algorithm called Byzantine Perturbed Gradient Descent (ByzantinePGD), which can escape a saddle point efficiently. The key idea of ByzantineSGD is that it invokes a so-called Escape algorithm when it detects potential saddle points. The escape algorithm continuously adds a random perturbation to the model parameters and performs gradient descent until the discrepancy of parameters exceeds a threshold, which means the parameters move a sufficiently large distance in the parameter space. Intuitively, ByzantineSGD pushes the model when hitting a saddle point until it falls off the saddle and proceeds to descent.

7.2   Privacy Protection

One of the main objectives of edge learning is to provide a certain degree of privacy. In edge learning, clients send model updates instead of sending raw data to the server. Although this method keeps the server from accessing the sensitive data directly and avoids greater risk of data leaking, the private data of users is not completely secure. The exchanging model updates, which mostly are model parameters or gradients during the training, can still cause information leaks because parameters and gradients are directly relevant to input samples and thus can carry information about user data. A malicious participant can infer critical features of user data from model parameters and gradients. For example, in linear regression classification tasks, the weight of the model implies the importance of the corresponding feature to correctly classify the sample, so the adversary can infer features of input from subtle changes in weights. Therefore, we still need to pay attention to data privacy in edge learning. This section discusses potential privacy attacks and approaches of protection.

7.2.1   Introduction to Privacy Attacks in Edge Learning

Hitaj et al. use GANs to estimate information in collaborative deep learning architectures [107]. A GAN consists of a generative network and a discriminative network. Typically, the generative network learns to map from a latent space to a data distribution of interest, while the discriminative network distinguishes candidates produced by the generator from the true data distribution. For example, a GAN trained on photographs can generate new photographs that look at least superficially authentic to human observers, having many realistic characteristics. In Hitaj's design, a malicious server or client can train a GAN that generates prototypical samples of target training data of other clients using only the parameters transferred between the server and the clients during the training.

In edge learning, the server controls the whole training process, including criteria, and sends out programming code to clients at the beginning of training. Song et al. propose an attacking method initiated by a malicious central server who tampers with the training code and encodes sensitive information into model parameters [270]. After adding a regularizer to the loss function, the training algorithm forces the parameters to be highly correlated with the sensitive information and encodes it into the signs of parameters. Then the server can extract privacy information by decoding the parameters sent by clients.

Based on the observation that each data sample will leave a distinguishable footprint on the gradients of loss function subject to model parameters during the gradient descent process, Nasr et al. propose an attack approach utilizing deep learning [215]. They train an attacking model using gradients of the target model as the main feature to inference the membership probability of a target data point. Experiments show that under this inference attack, even well-generalized models can leak a huge amount of private information.

Melis et al. design a similar inference attacking algorithm against deep learning models and obtained information about input features that are irrelevant to the learning objective [201]. For example, models trained to classify genders or races may leak information about whether a person wears glasses, which is a feature uncorrelated with the main objective.

Shokri et al. propose a membership inference attack in a black-box setting where the attacker only knows inputs and outputs of the target model [266]. The attacking algorithm trains an inference model to recognize differences in the target model's predictions on the inputs it trained on versus the inputs that it did not train on. In this way, given a data sample, the algorithm will be able to tell if it belongs to the training dataset.

7.2.2   Enabling Technologies for Private Edge Learning

7.2.2.1   Differential Privacy

Differential privacy (DP) is a privacy-protecting approach that allows the public sharing of information by describing the patterns of groups within the dataset while withholding information about individuals in the dataset. Generally, an algorithm is differentially private if an observer seeing its output cannot tell if a particular individual's information was used in the computation. For example, differentially private algorithms are used by some government agencies to publish demographic information or other statistical aggregates while ensuring the confidentiality of survey responses, and by companies to collect information about user behavior while controlling what is visible even to internal analysts.

Adjacent datasets, a commonly used term used in DP, refers to datasets that differ by only one element. By comparing two adjacent datasets, adversaries can infer the information of the different elements. DP avoids this kind of information leak by adding perturbation or noise. The perturbed adjacent datasets look similar enough to eliminate the difference and therefore ensure the privacy of a particular individual's information.

DP has recently gained attention for the ability to protect privacy with a theoretical guarantee. Let ϵ be a positive real number and $\mathcal{A}$ be a randomized algorithm that takes a dataset as input (representing the actions of the trusted party holding the data). Let im$\mathcal{A}$ denote the image of $\mathcal{A}$. The algorithm $\mathcal{A}$ is said to provide ϵ-differential privacy if, for adjacent datasets D_1 and D_2 and all subsets S of im$\mathcal{A}$:

$$Pr[\mathcal{A}(D_1) \in S] \leq exp(\epsilon) \cdot Pr[\mathcal{A}(D_2) \in S].$$

However, employing DP in edge learning faces the problem that too little noise has more chances of privacy leaking while too much noise harms the model performance. Recently, many studies have been conducted to investigate the methods to protect privacy using DP without losing accuracy.

Wang et al. derive the upper bounds of the optimization and utility of empirical risk minimization (ERM) when applying DP to protect privacy [306]. Then they design optimization algorithms with less gradient complexity that reach the upper utility bound. Wang et al. then extend their work to nonconvex loss functions and presented a DP algorithm called DP-GLD [304]. They prove that the excess empirical risk of DP-GLD can be upper bounded and discovered a connection between DP and saddle points escaping based on the observation that the DP algorithm can find a local minimum under some condition. They also explain the possibility of using the Bernstein polynomial approximation to realize a non-interactive DP algorithm that can complete the training in one round of data exchange [305].

Ge et al. study principal component analysis (PCA) under DP constraints and proposed a distributed privacy-preserving PCA algorithm that can generate a minimax-optimal sparse PCA estimator to solve the corresponding PCA problems [71]. Jain et al. present the first provable joint DP algorithm for the user-level privacy protection collaborative filtering problems [125]. Neel et al. address the bias problem in models gathering data adaptively like bandit algorithm and demonstrated that gathering data in a DP way in stochastic bandit algorithms can mitigate the bias problem [216]. Yu et al. apply DP in neural network models, proposing an algorithm called concentrated differential privacy (CDP) to optimize the privacy loss and implementing a dynamic privacy budget allocator during the training process to improve model accuracy [372]. Schein et al. propose an approach for private Bayesian inference satisfying local privacy, which is a strong variant of DP under which the sensitive data is privatized (or perturbed) via a randomized response method before inference [251].

Most research studying DP follow the same pattern that first set up the expected privacy requirement and attempt to improve the model performance as much as possible under the privacy constraints. Ligett et al. consider the problem from another perspective and tried to maximize the privacy level subject to an accuracy requirement [173]. Based on this idea, they design a noise reduction framework that computes a high-level private hypothesis in the beginning and reduces the noise gradually until the accuracy reaches the requirements.

Most distributed machine learning mechanisms need to access the same dataset multiple times and repeatedly exchange data between server and clients; such repetitive operations cause a significant amount of communication overhead and, more importantly, increased risk of information leaking. Due to this problem, much research has been done in a distributed DP setting to study the design of a non-interactive training method that collaborate training only involving much fewer or even just one data exchange [269], [400]. In the algorithm proposed by Smith et al. [269], clients don't send model parameters or gradients to the server; instead, they send a binary tree and a corresponding entry vector from which latent features of data can be extracted to the server. In this way, the server only needs one data transmission and uses the data repeatedly every iteration.

Other works study the price – i.e. the loss of accuracy, when achieving DP. Agarwal et al. propose an algorithm to implement DP in online learning and discovered that ϵ-DP can be guaranteed without any loss in accuracy in the full-information setting where the algorithm has access to the loss vector every round [8]. McMahan et al. study the implementation of DP in large recurrent language models and demonstrated that the performance cost of achieving user-level DP guarantees can be remedied by increasing computation [200]. Therefore, given a dataset with a sufficiently large number of users, achieving DP only causes negligible accuracy loss.

7.2.2.2   Secure Multi-Party Computation

Secure multi-party computation (MPC) is a subfield of cryptography that creates methods for parties to jointly compute a function over their inputs while keeping those inputs private. Unlike traditional cryptographic tasks, where cryptography assures security and integrity of communication or storage and the adversary is outside the system of participants (an eavesdropper on the sender and receiver), the cryptography in this model protects participants' privacy from other participants.

Mohassel propose a secure and efficient two-party computation (2PC) protocol to preserve privacy during the training of linear regression, logistic regression, and neural networks [234]. The method applies a non-colluding two-server system in which clients transfer their sensitive data randomly to two servers; they train models collaboratively without disclosing private data to each other. 2PC uses two important methods to protect privacy: oblivious transfer (OT) and gargled circuit (GC). An OT protocol is a type of protocol in which a sender transfers one of the potentially many pieces of information to a receiver but remains oblivious to what piece has been transferred. A simple example of OT is 1-2 OT, in which, the sender has two messages, m_0 and m_1, and the receiver has a bit b. The receiver wishes to receive m_b without the sender learning b, while the sender wants to ensure that the receiver receives only one of the two messages. OT is considered one of the critical problems in the field because of the importance of the applications that can be built based on it. GC is a cryptographic protocol that enables two-party secure computation in which two mistrusting parties can jointly evaluate a function over their private inputs without the presence of a trusted third party. In the GC protocol, the underlying function is described as a Boolean circuit with 2-input gates. The two parties involved in the computation take turns to garble (encrypt) the circuit with their input and obtain the encrypted outputs without knowing each other's private data.

Bonawitz et al. construct an MPC protocol among servers and clients to aggregate the model updates from the individual client without revealing private data to any party, including the server [28]. Mohassel et al. design a secure three-party computation (3PC) protocol allowing three machines to jointly train models [206]. In the 3PC protocol, an encrypted private value x is randomly sampled to three values, x_1, x_2, x_3, so that $x = x_1 + x_2 + x_3$ and shared as pairs$\{(x_1, x_2), (x_2, x_3), (x_3, x_1)\}$ to three parties where party i holds pair i. Any random two pairs of values can be sufficient to reconstruct the actual value, so a 3PC protocol can stand single-point failure and have more robustness than a 2PC protocol.

Heikkila et al. combine MPC with DP to study methods of reducing DP noise level while maintaining the level of privacy [104]. In each round, every client partitions its data into M pieces and sends them with perturbation to M computing nodes. Each message is just a random noise inidividually, but once combining all the messages will get the actual data. They reduce the Gaussian noise added in the DP process to improve the model accuracy and add another M random noises, which sum up to zero, to messages to maintain the privacy level. In this way, a single message can stay private because of the extra noise, and these noises can be canceled out when all results are added up, thus causing no extra damage to model accuracy. Jayaraman et al. use MPC in a DP distributed learning setting to reduce the noise level of both gradient perturbation and output perturbation [126]. Based on MPC, instead of adding perturbation to each output or gradient, they added perturbation to the mean of output or gradient of m clients and reduced the noise level by a factor of $\sqrt{m}$. Experiments demonstrate that this method guarantees the privacy level and achieves accuracy close to the naive method without any noise added.

Zheng et al. design a system that allows multiple machines to collaboratively train a linear model without disclosing any private data [402]. They use the Alternating Direction Method of Multipliers (ADMM) as the optimizer instead of SGD to train models on cryptographic data, and experimental results demonstrate great improvement in performance compared to SGD. Jia et al. use Oblivious Evaluation of Multivariate Polynomial (OMPE), an MPC protocol that computes the multivariate polynomial privately, to protect the privacy of the learned SVM model and test dataset [130].

7.2.2.3 Homomorphic Encryption

Homomorphic encryption (HE) is a type of encryption allowing calculations on encrypted data without decrypting it first, generating an encrypted result that, when decrypted, matches the result of the operations as if they had been performed on the raw data. HE can be used for privacy-preserving outsourced storage and computation. This allows data to be encrypted and outsourced to commercial cloud environments for processing, all while being encrypted. In highly regulated industries, such as

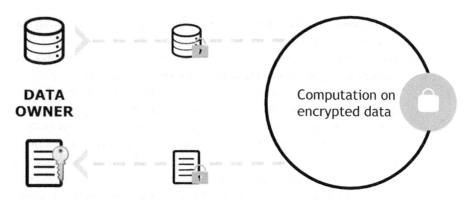

Figure 7.3 An illustration of HE. The data owner encrypts his/her data and sends to the server; the server computes functions on the encrypted data and sends it back; and finally, data owner decrypts the encrypted data to obtain the result. Since the server performs computation on encrypted data, the privacy of data owner is protected.

healthcare, HE can be used to enable new services by removing privacy barriers that inhibit data sharing. HE includes multiple types of encryption schemes that can perform different classes of computations over encrypted data. Some common types of HE are partially homomorphic, somewhat homomorphic, leveled fully homomorphic, and fully HE. The computations are represented as either Boolean or arithmetic circuits. Partially HE encompasses schemes that support the evaluation of circuits consisting of only one type of gate – e.g., addition or multiplication. Somewhat HE schemes can evaluate two types of gates, but only for a subset of circuits. Leveled fully HE supports the evaluation of arbitrary circuits of bounded (predetermined) depth. Fully homomorphic encryption allows the evaluation of arbitrary circuits of unbounded depth and is the strongest notion of HE. For the majority of HE schemes, the multiplicative depth of circuits is the main practical limitation in performing computations over encrypted data. In edge learning, a server can aggregate encrypted data from clients and return the result without decrypting the data. Therefore, using HE allows us to train models in a distributed manner while protecting users' privacy. Fig. 7.3 gives an illustration of HE.

Hall et al. apply HE during the training of linear regression and ridge regression models in an edge learning setting where each client holds its training data [244]. During one round of training, a client encrypts its data and sends it to the next client. The receiver client encrypts its data and sends both the received data and local data to the next client until the last client gets all the encrypted data. Then the last client adds up the encrypted data using HE operations and decrypts it to get a covariance matrix, which leads to the calculation of the regression coefficient vector.

Giacomelli et al. propose a two-server system in a similar scenario to address the privacy problems in regression learning [75]. The system consists of multiple clients and two servers with different functions: a machine learning engine (MLE) to operate the training algorithm of linear regression models on an encrypted dataset and a crypto service provider (CSP) server responsible for managing cryptographic keys and decrypting data. The system operates in the following way:

1. The CSP generates two keys: a public key to encrypt data and a secret key to decrypt data; the CSP sends the public key to all the clients.
2. Clients encrypt training data using the public key and send the encrypted data to the MLE.
3. The MLE performs aggregation on the encrypted data and sends the encrypted result to the CSP.
4. The CSP decrypts the result and sends back to the MLE.
5. Finally, the MLE updates the model using the result.

The defect of this system is obvious: once CSP is compromised, the privacy guarantee disappears.

One disadvantage of HE is that most HE algorithms can only support one or two specific functions, such as addition or multiplication, while most complex models like neural networks need many nonlinear calculations, thus preventing HE's application in more areas. Yuan et al. address this problem in the backward propagation neural network (BPNN) and decompose most of the sub-algorithms of BPNN into simple operations such as addition, multiplication, and scalar product [375]. And they adopt multiple HE algorithms to support these operations. Zhang et al. and Hesamifard et al. follow the same idea and approximate the activation functions to low-degree polynomials that can be computed by an HE algorithm. Experiment results demonstrate that approximation has very little effect on the model accuracy [394],[105]. Brutzkus et al. apply HE to neural networks and propose a novel and efficient training algorithm [30]. Instead of encrypting the raw training data, the algorithm encrypts the deep representation of the data (the data is converted by a standard network to create a deep representation), resulting in great optimization and improvement on the inference speed, while keeping the privacy level.

7.2.2.4   Other Privacy-Preserving Approaches

Papernot et al. demonstrate an approach to provide privacy guarantees for training data named by Private Aggregation of Teacher Ensembles (PATE) [228]. PATE is a multiple-teacher–one-student model where multiple teacher models train with disjoint datasets first and a student model learns to predict an output using teachers' output voting without accessing teachers' parameters or data. However, this method operates under the assumption that teacher models can't be accessed by an adversary, which is hard to realize in practice. Nasr et al. protect membership privacy (ensuring the prediction on different data are distinguishable) by modeling the optimization problem as a minimax privacy game between the defense algorithm and the inference attack [214]. They add the gain of the inference attack as a regularizer to the classifier and minimize it along with the classification loss. Park et al. protect privacy by training models with synthetic data instead of the original data [232]. This approach uses GAN to synthesize fake data that are statistically similar to the original data. Experiments show that it can achieve similar accuracy while protecting privacy. Epasto et al. introduce an on-device public–private model for data mining and machine learning, which ensures that any computation based on private information and contacts must be performed on local devices [64]. This model allows the user to employ all the information available on his/her device, as well as social contacts, without sharing them with the central server. Park et al. protected private data in edge nodes by isolating the private data and its computations in a trusted execution environment on the edge [230]. The data will be processed in a trusted computing base, and every execution on the private data will be verified. Table 7.2 demonstrates all the privacy-preserving methods and corresponding models they can be applied to.

7.3   Conclusion and Future Directions

Edge learning should guarantee the privacy and security of training data and machine learning models as required. Compared with the traditional cloud-centric model, edge learning strikes a good balance between learning accuracy and data privacy by establishing privacy policies that allow the full exploitation of data while guaranteeing the security and privacy of different data as required. In what follows, we discuss new challenges and potential research directions in this field.

7.3.1   Multi-level Privacy-Protection for Efficient Edge Learning

Privacy protection is quite important in the edge environment because the data on edge usually involves the interests and safety of users – e.g., the family photos stored in smart furniture. To protect the data privacy of users, existing training methods usually impose complex protection schemes on the learning process. Though they could protect privacy well, they have poor training performance for the cloud-edge environment due to the following reasons. The first reason is that they require strict synchronization in the training process. This incurs dramatic performance reduction for heterogeneous and complex edge environments. Another reason is that they only consider data privacy to be a single level. In the cloud-edge environment, data privacy is de facto in a multi-level format; e.g., some users want to share their data with the public, but the others do not. This limitation is a great hinderance to performance improvement. Hence, a scheme that could protect privacy while keeping efficiency needs to be elaborately designed.

7.3.2   Hierarchical Outlier Detection for Security Guarantee

Compared to the cloud, the edge environment is not secure. Malicious attackers could easily control edge devices and poison training data. Because of this, the learning process suffers two risks – i.e., data poison and Byzantine error. Data poison is when the training data is poisoned by bad data. Attackers could easily implement this by interfering with the process of data collection steps. A model trained from poisoned data could not be in a security guarantee. Byzantine error occurs when the learning

Table 7.2. Summary of privacy-preserving methods

Approach	Literature	Suitable Models	Specific Idea
Differential Privacy	[306]	Convex	Optimize the utility of ERM in DP settings
	[304]	Nonconvex	
	[71]	PCA	Generate a sparse PCA estimator under DP constraints
	[125]	Collaboratively Filtering	Consistently estimate the underlying preference matrix
	[216]	Bandits problem	Employing DP in bandits problem can mitigate bias
	[372]	DNN	Dynamically allocate privacy to improve accuracy
	[251]	Bayesian inference	Enable local DP in Bayesian inference for Poisson factorization
	[173]	Regression	Maxmize the privacy given a fixed accuracy requirement
	[305]	Convex	Design non-interactive DP algorithms
	[269]		
	[400]		
	[8]	Online learning	Study the price of achieving DP
	[200]	RNN	
Secure Multi-Party Computation	[104]	Bayesian model	Combine MPC and DP
	[126]	Regression	
	[234]	ANY	Privately comupute the objective function using MPC protocols and methods
	[28]		
	[130]		
	[206]	ANY	Sample the value to three pairs distributed to three parties
	[402]	Linear models	Use ADMM instead of SGD to train models on encrypted data
Homomorphic Encryption	[244]	Linear models	All parties send encrypted data to one party who computes the result using HE
	[75]	Linear models	Use a two-server model: a machine learning engine server and a crypto provider server
	[375]	DNN	Approximate activation functions to low-degree polynomials that can be computed by HE
	[394]		
	[105]		
	[30]	DNN	Encrypt the deep representation of the data
Others	[228]	ANY	Train multiple models and choose the majority of the results
	[214]	DNN	Model a minimax privacy game between attacks and defenses
	[232]	ANY	Use synthetic data to train models, achieving similar accuracy as the raw data
	[230]	ANY	Isolate private data and its computation to a trusted execution environment

nodes are controlled by malicious attackers. In the training process, the Byzantine nodes could generate arbitrary training updates to the attack model. As a result, security guarantee schemes should be proposed for both the two risks. The essence of the poisoned data risk is that the bad data follow a different distribution from good data, and the essence of the Byzantine error risk is that the Byzantine updates deviate from normal updates. Consequently, the two risks have the same attack principle that attacks the learning process by adding outliers to good training data or updates. Considering this, a two-layer hierarchical outlier detection could be a promising approach. The first layer of the scheme is running in each learning node to detect the poisoned data. The scheme in this layer can adaptively choose various outlier detection methods according to the requirement of accuracy and computing latency. After detecting poisoned data in learning nodes, the outlier detection run in the coordinators to detect the Byzantine updates with the second layer. It is particularly worthwhile to note that the outlier detection methods in the learning nodes and in the coordinators need not be the same. They can be designed separately to maximize the detection efficiency.

7.3.3 Attack Detection in Communication-Compressed Training

One popular line of thought of defending model attacks is trying to detect false updates by examining the parameters or gradients matrix. The updates with longer steps or larger deviation in direction than the majority will be excluded from aggregation. However, many algorithms send the compressed updates (e.g., quantized or sparse gradient vectors) instead of the whole matrix to reduce communication overhead and avoid overfitting. Without the whole knowledge of model updates, attack detection loses its performance significantly. A more robust defense method needs to be investigated for compressed models.

7.3.4 Computation Offloading for Encrypted Data Training

Computation offloading technologies are widely used in MEC to save resource consumption of the mobile device and speed up the process of computation. However, previous approaches to computation offloading are not directly suitable for edge learning due to the non-sharable feature of training data. One feasible scheme of computation offloading in edge learning is migrating encrypted training data or intermediate results to a mobile edge server. By employing HE, the mobile edge server conducts computation on encrypted data and transmits the encrypted result to the data owner. However, decisions for such computation offloading should be carefully designed due to the additional costs for data encryption and transmission.

8   Edge Learning Architecture Design for System Scalability

With the growth of model complexity and computational overhead, modern edge learning applications are usually handled by the distributed systems, where the training procedure is conducted in parallel. Basically, the datasets and models are partitioned to different workers in data parallelism and model parallelism, respectively. In this chapter, we present the details of these two schemes. Moreover, considering some of the latest research that handles distributed training via multiple primitives, we also discuss the extension of training parallelism - i.e., learning frameworks and efficient synchronization mechanisms over the hierarchical architecture.

8.1   Introduction to the Learning Architecture

8.1.1   Parallelism Schemes: Data Parallelism and Model Parallelism

In order to design a high-performance distributed machine learning system, we need to determine how to divide the primary large task into several small subtasks. The consideration factors contain the dataset, neural network model, and available hardware resources. In this section, we will discuss how to handle the training parallelism mainly in two categories: (1) *model parallelism* [153], [69], [98] and (2) *data parallelism* [389], [37], [155], [339], [297], [132]. Basically, the datasets and models are partitioned to different workers in data parallelism and model parallelism, respectively. The following sections will present the details of these two schemes. Moreover, considering some latest researches that handle distributed training via multiple primitives, we also discuss the extension of training parallelism at the end of this section.

8.1.1.1   Data Parallelism

In commodity clusters built in the data center networks, the machine may not be able to share their memory via the remote procedure calling because these nodes are often organized in the geo-distributed manner [113]. Besides, with the rise of edge intelligence, plenty of machine learning applications are deployed in the edge-to-cloud environment [47], [261], where the machine's processing speed is bound by the scarce

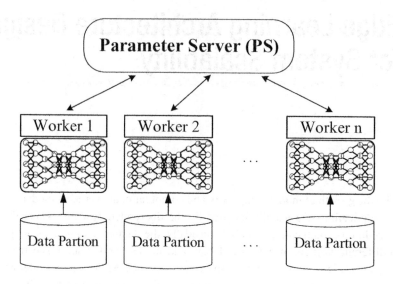

Figure 8.1 Data parallelism.

on-device memory, especially for the mobile and IoT devices [65], [72], [195]. In this condition, loading the network model or the whole data to a single machine is not feasible in practice. We need to partition the workload into several subtasks and handle the job via distributed processing, so as to alleviate the huge computation pressure and resource demands. It is a natural way to handle the parallel processing based on data division scheme, which is often called the data parallelism.

We use Fig. 8.1 to illustrate the rationale of data parallelism, where the entire dataset is partitioned into several pieces, and each machine is allocated with a part of these data. With its own dataset, each machine can conduct the model training and update the local model independently. According to partition dimension of the training data, there are two branches in data parallelism: (1) sample-level partition [51], [202] and (2) feature-level partition [124].

Sample-Level Partition. The sample-level partition is the most straightforward way to implement data parallelism. We can employ the data shuffling [202] algorithms to reorganize the global dataset. Then it is feasible to use the random sampling [51] techniques to select subsets and assign them to different workers.

Basically, the key in random sampling is to use the bootstrapping methods to make the subset allocation procedure, during which the factors of machine memory footprint and available storage will yield significant impact on the division efficiency. One of the most critical issues is to ensure the IID [145] assumption of the data partition that the distribution of each local datasets should be consistent with the global dataset as much as possible. A large difference between each worker's data distribution will lead to the degradation of training efficiency and even make the model not converge. By employing the random sampling, we can obtain a linear or sub-linear convergence rate in theory [199], [27], which is sufficient enough for model training. It is worth noting that there are also some restrictions in random sampling. As the random sampling is a time-consuming procedure, it may not be suitable for the large-scale dataset environment. Also, the amount of each local subset is far smaller than the original full dataset; the local model is trained by using a small part of entire dataset. As a great amount of data is unused during the sampling, the local model may become over-fitting easily.

As to limitations of random sampling, an effective way to address this problem is to conduct the data shuffling at first. The gist is to shuffle the global data and make the data partition match the worker numbers. Each worker owns a specific part of the entire dataset, with no overlap with other workers. In an iteration of the training process, the workers conduct local model training independently, and the local data is reshuffled after several iterations [155]. Moreover, we can repartition the global dataset and make the assignment to each worker when a certain epochs is done [389]. This shuffling procedure can satisfy the IID assumption of parameter optimization. Thus, the model convergence efficiency of distributed training is guaranteed. Overall, data shuffling holds the advantages of lower computational overhead and higher data utilization [339], [297], [132]. Consequently, using data shuffling is a promising way to handle distributed model training in real-world machine learning applications.

Feature-Level Partition. As the data features in model training are usually in a high dimension, it is natural to resolve the dataset from the perspective of feature dimensions. We refer to this scheme as the feature-level partition, which can better captures the network characteristics and match the theory of parameter optimization. Here, we will discuss two major branches of feature-level partition: tree-based optimization [139] and linear model training [120].

In the tree-based methods, the global dataset will be partitioned based on different feature dimensions. A worker will figure out the information gain of all the features and select the dimension corresponding to the highest information gain. The final results are obtained by aggregating all the dimension of each worker. Consequently, this dimension-aware partition can be used in the decision tree tasks. Meanwhile, in the linear model training, the feature dimension usually matches the model parameters, where the global model can be partitioned into sub-models fit the dimension division scheme, which is called the model parallelism. We will discuss the details in the next section.

To sum up, data parallelism is one of the most common ways to handle the large-scale distributed machine learning training, including linear regression [219], logistic regression [110], and SVM [46].

8.1.1.2 Model Parallelism

In the edge intelligence or mobile learning applications, the devices are usually in a resource-constraint environment, where the available on-device memory is quite scarce. In this condition, we need to resolve the large model into several small parts to alleviate the memory pressure, as shown in figure 8.2. Each worker only handles a sub-model and updates the parameters contained inside. According to the model

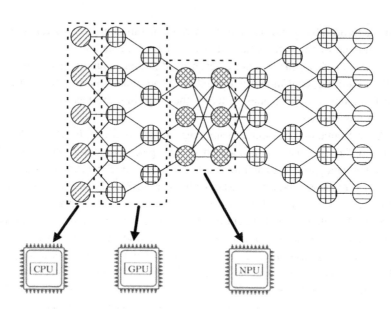

Figure 8.2 Model parallelism.

structures, we mainly discuss two branches - i.e., the linear models [110], [219] and nonlinear neural networks [101], [343].

Linear Models. As the parameter amount in linear models is strongly dependent on the number of data dimensions, it is natural to uniformly partition the entire model, and each worker is allocated with a part of the global model. In this condition, the *Coordinate Descent* [218] approach is a promising way to handle the searching of the optimized parameters. Also, considering the linear separability of the optimization objective, it is possible to update each dimension of the parameters by calculating the data of the objective function in the corresponding dimension, while the data in other dimension will not yield interference. As a result, we can merge the training results of all the workers from the perspective of dimension-level data aggregation, rather than exchanging the entire model.

Nonlinear Neural Networks. Modern neural networks are usually designed in a nonlinear structure, where each layer's weights and activations are dependent in sequence. Therefore, dividing the global model requires us to consider the factors of network structures, neuron amounts, and block functions. Basically, we can resolve this problem in three directions.

The first is the horizontal layer-wise partition [213], which stands in the perspective of layer depth. Each worker conducts the matrix calculations according to the layers assigned to it. All the workers collaborate in a sequential order, from the shallowest layer to the deepest layer.

Another common direction is the vertical cross-layer partition [68], which is often used in the wide-layer models. The key difference from the horizontal layer-wise partition is that the neurons of a layer can be allocated to different machines - i.e., following the neuron-level partition. Therefore, the workers can update the parameter to a single neuron. However, as the neurons often hold the computation dependency according to the network structure, intermediate data need to be exchanged during model training. As a result, heavy communication traffic will be generated. This is the key challenge limiting the effectiveness of vertical cross-layer partition.

Moreover, considering the parameter redundancy of neural networks, it is possible to use a simpler small model to mimic the function of the complex large model. A promising manner is to use the model random partition methods [280], [97], which aims at extracting a "backbone" structure of the original model by assembling the training results from different workers. This procedure can be designed from both horizontal and vertical directions. Therefore, random partition has become a hot topic in model parallelism, with a promising improvement space.

8.1.1.3 Hybrid Parallelism

Hybrid parallelism can be employed when the model size exceeds the local memory capacity of a worker. It is a combination of data parallelism and model parallelism. As shown in Fig. 8.3, the neural network model is partitioned into several sub-models and each worker updates the parameters of the assigned sub-model. HetPipe is a typical system applying hybrid parallelism [231]. In the HetPipe system, each virtual worker uses pipelining to concurrently process N_m mini-batches that depend on memory requirements. Let local staleness be the maximum tolerable missing updates from the most recent updates, and let the local staleness threshold be $S_{local} = N_m - 1$. The weight of the mini-batch p used for training is w_p. Assuming w_0, the initial weights are given to the virtual worker. Then, the first N_m mini-batches are executed with $w_0 = w_1 = \ldots = w_{N_m}$. When the executing of mini-batch p completes, the local

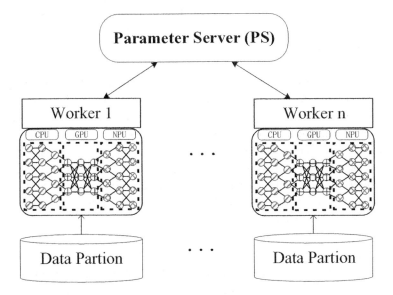

Figure 8.3 Illustration of hybrid parallelism.

weights are updated with $w_{local} = w_{local} + u_p$, where u_p is the computed gradients of processing mini-batch p. The processing of mini-batch p will use the latest w_{local}, which is updated by mini-batch $(p - S_{local} - 1)$.

The data parallelism of HetPipe can be illustrated as follows. HetPipe uses a parameter server to maintain the global weight - that is, the gradient results calculated by each virtual worker are uploaded to update the global weight. At this time, heterogeneous virtual workers will lead to the inefficiency of synchronous data parallelism mode across virtual workers. Therefore, in HetPipe, a method similar to SSP is used to improve the efficiency - that is, each virtual worker does not have to wait for the gradient calculation results of all virtual workers every time. Each virtual worker maintains a local clock c_{local}, and the global clock c_{global} is saved by the parameter server. The two clocks are 0, initially. A wave means sequential mini-batches that are executed concurrently in a virtual worker. When a virtual worker completes all the mini-batches in wave c, the virtual worker aggregates updates from mini-batch $c * (s_{local} + 1) + 1$ to mini-batch $(c + 1) * (s_{local} + 1)$ and pushes the updates to the parameter server . Let D represents the distance between the fastest and slowest of c_{local}. When $D = 0$, the global weights across virtual workers are synchronized, because each virtual worker must ensure the processing of mini-batches in the same order wave.

8.1.1.4 Extension of Training Parallelism

Apart from the data and model parallelism, recent research also has focused on the distributed training by using multiple primitives, which is closely related to the computational resource sharing. In this case, all workers share a same area of the memory, where the training data and model parameters are stored. Similar to multiple threads on a single machine, datasets and models do not need to be partitioned among workers. As all the workers can access the shared memory and global dataset, each worker can independently conduct the optimization algorithm in parallel to accelerate the distributed DL training.

Besides, as to the stochastic optimization algorithm used in this scheme, two assumptions usually hold when generating the training data: (1) online data generation [62] and (2) offline data generation [35]. The online generation assumes that the real-time training data accessed by any worker can be generated based on the real distribution. In contrast, the offline generation uses the real distribution to yield an offline dataset, and each worker employs bootstrapping (i.e., random sampling with replacement [148]) on this dataset to form the corresponding training data, following the uniform distribution. Generally, the online generation is useful to the theoretical analysis of computation-parallel algorithms while the offline generation is widely used in real-world training scenarios.

8.1.1.5 Summary

Overall, training parallelism is a key part for the implementation of high-performance distributed machine learning systems. In practice, data parallelism and model parallelism are the most widely used schemes, from the perspective of data scale and model complexity. In addition, the extension of parallelism based on multiple computation primitives is also a promising way to handle the distributed training. Basically, the research of training parallelism is still a hot topic because we need a more efficient training paradigm for the emerging edge intelligence and the TinyML application on micro IoT devices.

8.1.2 Large-Scale Model Training Architecture

The architecture design is a fundamental factor impacting the performance of distributed machine learning systems. In this section, we will discuss two major system architectures for large-scale model training: the parameter server [155] and decentralized P2P scheme. Employing these architectures in real-world scenarios requires the careful consideration of application-level job characteristics, communication-level flow patterns, algorithm-level optimization theory, and topology-level network construction.

8.1.2.1 Parameter Server

The parameter server [155] architecture is one of the most widely used distributed training paradigms, which follows a server - worker structure. The servers and workers directly connect to each other. This scheme decouples the data processing and model update on the workers and servers, respectively. As each worker owns a copy or a part of the global model, the workers can train their local models based on local datasets. The latest model parameters will be fetched from the servers at the beginning of the training. With these parameters, the workers can yield the predicted labels and figure out current loss. The gradients are calculated by each worker to minimize the loss function. The workers will send their local gradient to the server for global model update. Meanwhile, the servers collect all the local gradients and merge them into the global gradients, which are usually calculated by the average operation. With this global gradient, the servers can update the global model parameters under the control of the hyper-parameter called learning rate. The number of servers used in the parameter server cluster can be adjusted to match the transmission requirements. It is worth noting that workers do not communicate with each other. All the data are exchanged between servers and workers.

As the training procedure is compromised by a series of iterations we intend to discuss the distributed processing details within an iteration. Generally, each worker will be initialized by using the latest model parameter fetched from the server side at the beginning of each round. This parameter fetching is usually handled by the pull interface. After the model parameters is set, all the workers will conduct their local training by using the local datasets. Then, each worker will calculate the gradients to optimize the values of loss function. These gradients will be sent to the servers via the push interface. The server will aggregate all the gradients and update the global model parameters. Finally, the current iteration is ended, and the next iteration will start.

Regarding the implementation of distributed parameter synchronization, the BSP [389], [320], [192] scheme is the most straightforward choice for many systems, where all the workers are synchronized by a barrier at the end of each iteration. Under this strongly consistent control, the synchronization error will be bound and the system can holds a sublinear convergence rate.

8.1.2.2   Decentralized P2P Scheme

In spite of the implementation convenience of parameter server architecture, the frequent data exchange between workers and servers will yield a large volume of network traffic, especially in a large-scale cluster [335], [376]. This communication pattern will become the performance bottleneck of the distributed machine learning systems because the data transmission time will dominate the time consumption in each iteration.

Consequently, it is natural to study how to handle the distributed machine learning training in a decentralized scheme. Existing decentralized training approaches often achieve this target by employing the P2P communication techniques [263], [262]. The rationale of decentralized training is to make each worker communicate with its adjacent neighbours. Therefore, all the workers collaborate together in a P2P mode and the centralized servers can be removed.

Among existing decentralized algorithms, the Gossip collaboration scheme [172], [285] is widely used in many studies due to its ease-of-use. In the Gossip scheme, each worker calculates its own local gradients based on the local data and just exchange these gradients with other workers who are directly connected to it. As the data volume for gradient exchange is significantly reduced, the Gossip scheme can fundamentally alleviate the communication pressure and bring the training speedup over the parameter server paradigm. Additionally, all the workers are equally treated in the Gossip scheme without the control of the servers. The bandwidth bottleneck of large-scale clusters can be addressed. Therefore, the training cluster based on Gossip scheme holds a highly elastic scalability and can provide robust fault tolerance of link connections. Moreover, the corresponding optimization algorithms need to be carefully designed to match the Gossip scheme. A promising way to handle the P2P parameter synchronization is to use the *decentralized parallel stochastic gradient descent* (D-PSGD) algorithms [208]. Related researches on this topic have shown that the D-PSGD requires less gradient aggregation and yields less network traffic. Basically, the decentralized P2P scheme can provide a better training convergence efficiency while not degrading the final model quality.

8.1.2.3   Collective Communication-Based AllReduce

The Message Passing Interface (MPI) [3] is a widely used collective communication framework in distributed process, which can also be adopted for machine learning training. Different from the centralized parameter server architecture, the AllReduce programming interface is a highly efficient method that handles decentralized parameter and gradient exchange among the workers - e.g., the Baidu Ring-AllReduce [1] and Uber Horovod [255]. The AllReduce method can be used to synchronize any kinds of information via the distributed operation, including calculating the average, minimum, maximum, and sum. As the model aggregation in distributed machine

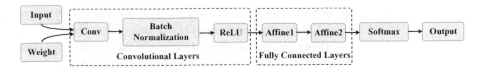

Figure 8.4 The dataflow of training MNIST via Keras.

learning applications is mainly calculating the sum of the local gradients and the corresponding average, the AllReduce method is feasible for the processing logic of these operations. The Allreduce method is an abstract programming interface, which can be implemented via different kinds of algorithm and supports various network topologies, including the Fat-Tree [10] and BCube [84] networks. Note that the communication overhead of the AllReduce method depends on the topology of underlying network topology.

8.1.2.4 Dataflow-Based Graph

Another method of deploying distributed machine learning procedure is to deploy the functions to different workers. The dataflow of a machine learning task can be described as a *Directed Acyclic Graph*, where each vertex is a worker or an operation, and the edge between two vertices represents the dataflow (the logic dependency) of different stages. Also, if two functions are deployed on two workers, these two workers need to communicate to each other for information exchange. Fig. 8.4 shows the dataflow of training MNIST [151] via Keras [2]. We can observe that there are two kinds of flows between the vertices (rectangles), the operation logic flow and the intermediate result flow. The operation logic flows control the execution logic of the entire program, and the intermediate result flows transfer the computational information between different stages. Actually, the dataflow-based graph can also be employed to the three previously mentioned scenarios. A pertinent case in industry is the Google TensorFlow [4] framework.

8.2 Edge Learning Frameworks over the Hierarchical Architecture

Edge learning is a promising machine learning paradigm to cooperatively train a global model with highly distributed data located on mobile devices. In this section, we consider a scenario where a global model is cooperatively trained among large-scale distributed mobile edge devices - e.g., smartphones. The cooperative learning system is formed over a hierarchical learning architecture, which consists of a macro base station (MBS), a number of small base stations (SBSs), and a number of mobile edge devices. Each SBS is associated with a mobile edge server that can provide storage and computation resources. Therefore, every MU can connect to the MBS directly but can only connect to its nearby MESs.

During the learning process, based on the widely used SGD-based algorithm, each mobile device iteratively computes local gradient separately according to its local dataset and then uploads the gradient to a logically centralized parameter server, where all updates are aggregated to obtain a new global model for the next-step computation. Generally, communications between the mobile edge devices and the centralized server dominate the training process, especially when training large machine learning model over bandwidth-constrained wireless environment. To tackle this problem, in this section we present an efficient synchronization scheme named community-based synchronization parallel. By exploiting the broadcast characteristic of SBSs, models and gradients are transmitted simultaneously and aggregated at SBSs, resulting in traffic reduction.

In the community-based synchronization parallel with high communication efficiency, the synchronization procedure is totally different with BSP in the traditional parameter server architecture. Thus, to guarantee the efficiency of the entire training process, we prove that the community-based synchronization parallel has the same convergence rate as the sequential synchronization approaches via rigorous analysis. To further accelerate the training process, we also employ compression technologies in the community-based synchronization parallel and show its convergence properties.

8.2.1 Introduction to the Hierarchical Architecture

8.2.1.1 Background and Motivation

Modern mobile edge devices like smartphones are usually equipped with GB level memory and powerful chips including CPUs and GPUs, which have the capabilities to train machine learning models using their own resources. In addition, the recent advances of MEC make the edge learning system over mobile edge devices easily to be implemented in reality. In this scenario, system scalablity is of great importance in edge learning. System scalability is meaningful in edge learning from the following two aspects. First, a scalable architecture enables a large number of mobile edge devices to participate in the edge learning. With a large amount of data, the machine learning model would show good performance in terms of accuracy and generalization. Second, a scalable architecture enriches the available resources for training - including computation, communication, and storage resource - which show great potential to efficiently train large models in the edge environment.

However, training efficiency of a large-scale edge learning system depends on participating training nodes being efficiently organized and cooperative. In the traditional parameter server architecture, communication efficiency is of great importance in edge learning due to the dynamic and resource-limited wireless environment. To improve communication efficiency, previous work usually focused on reducing the total transmission bits - e.g., gradient sparcification and quantization. Despite these efforts, communication overhead still becomes the major bottleneck of the training due to the bandwidth constraint of the parameter server.

We except that the training speed could linearly accelerate with the increase of participating mobile edge devices (here we assume the resource statuses are homogeneous among mobile edge devices). To achieve this objective, we should improve the utilization of wireless resources based on the communication and computation

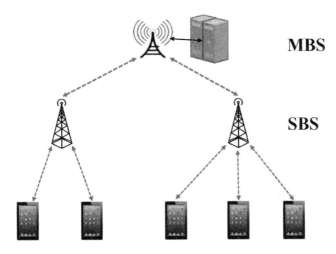

Figure 8.5 An illustration of the hierarchical architecture.

features of edge learning. In the current edge environment, SBSs - e.g., femto base stations and pico base stations - have been widely deployed in the network edge. Such SBSs can enable high-frequency reuse or high-density spatial reuse of cellular spectrum and provide high data rates, low loss ratios and small delays for data trans-missions. Generally, the MBS has a large communication range but a low transmission rate, while each SBS has a limited communication range but a high transmission rate. Each mobile device can connect to its nearby MESs via a high-performance link. Therefore, by carefully designing the communication scheduling and aggregation strategy involved in the training process, the training efficiency can be significantly improved.

In this section, we introduce a novel hierarchical architecture for edge learning and show how to accelerate edge learning over this architecture with the assistance of SBSs. The hierarchical architecture is shown in Fig. 8.5. An MBS is associated with a mobile edge server that has the responsibility to aggregate local gradients generated by mobile edge devices and to update the global parameter in each iteration. We design a community-based synchronization parallel scheme to accelerate edge learning over the two-tier network. Different from the sequential synchronization approaches such as BSP, global parameter and local gradients are transmitted simultaneously to the SBSs in this synchronization approach. Each SBS broadcasts the combination of local gradients and global parameters to both the MBS and mobile devices.

Under these transmission processes, the MBS can decode the aggregation of gra-dients from all the mobile edge devices, which is used to update the global model parameter for the next step computation. The mobile edge devices covered by an SBS form a community. To simplify the problem, we assume that each mobile edge device only connects to the nearest SBS such that there is no overlap between communities. Under this assumption, each mobile edge device receives the combination of local gradients calculated by mobile edge devices in the same community and the global parameter from the MBS. We refer to this combination as a local parameter for each community. Consequently, in the next iteration, each mobile edge device calculates the gradient with respect to the local parameter, which can be seen as a partial synchronization including all mobile edge devices from community it belongs to. The gradients are immediately updated to the local parameter in current iteration, but the effect of these gradients will spread to other communities in the next iteration through the aggregation on MBS. By breaking the traditional transmission-order constraint, the number of transmissions in each iteration is reduced.

However, there exists a trade-off between communication improvement and aggregation loss, since partial gradients are aggregated in the group of MDs covered by an SBS while these updates will spread to the whole network in the next iteration. Compared to BSP, the distinction caused by aggregation loss may possibly affect the convergence.

8.2.1.2   System Model

In this section, we first introduce the basic optimization problem of training over hierarchical architecture. Then, we briefly describe the wireless communication model and present the algorithm of transmission scheduling for the community-based synchronization parallel.

Similar to the basic optimization problem mentioned in Chapter 2, the main objective of machine learning is to solve the sum optimization problem. Consider a dataset that consists of D training samples denoted by $\xi_1, \xi_2, \ldots, \xi_D$. For a model parameter vector ω, we use $f(\omega, \xi_i)$ to represent the loss of model ω fitting the sample ξ_i. Then the machine learning problem is to find a model such that the total fitting loss of all samples in the whole dataset is minimized - i.e.,

$$\arg \min_{\omega} F(\omega) = \frac{1}{D} \sum_{i=1}^{D} f(\omega, \xi_i). \tag{8.1}$$

To solve this problem, we use a mini-batch SGD approach - i.e., selecting a random mini-batch instead of the whole dataset to compute the local gradient. Let $\mathcal{M}$ be the set of mobile edge devices, and let ξ_t^i be the random samples selected by mobile edge device i in tth iteration. Then, under the BSP scheme, the model parameter changes in each iteration according to the following formula:

$$\omega_{t+1} = \omega_t - \frac{\eta_t}{M} \sum_{i \in \mathcal{M}} g_{\xi_t^i}(\omega_t), \tag{8.2}$$

where M is the number of mobile edge devices, and $g_{\xi_t^i}(\omega_t)$ is the local gradient computed with respect to the random mini-batch ξ_t^i and model ω_t.

Then we present the network topology and the wireless transmission model. In this hierarchical architecture, the edge network is organized in a two-tier topology, which consists of an MBS, a set of SBSs, and a number of mobile edge devices. The MBS is associated with a mobile edge server that has the responsibility of aggregating all local gradients generated by mobile edge devices and updating the global parameter in each iteration. The set of the SBSs is denoted as $\mathcal{N} = \{1, 2, \ldots, N\}$. Generally, SBSs have a smaller communication range compared to MBS, but they can provide a larger transmission rate to associated mobile edge devices. The set of the mobile edge devices is denoted as $\mathcal{M} = \{1, 2, \ldots, M\}$. Under the assumption that each mobile edge devices connects to one SBS that can provide the best communication performance, mobile edge devices are divided into N groups $\mathcal{M}_1, \ldots, \mathcal{M}_N$, where $\mathcal{M}_j$ denote the set of mobile edge devices associated with SBS j. Let $|\mathcal{M}_j| = M_j$; then we have $\sum_{j=1}^{N} \mathcal{M}_j = M$.

One of the most widely used transmission scheduling mechanisms in the wireless environment is OFDMA (orthogonal frequency division multiple access). Here, we consider the scenario that MBS and SBSs in the edge learning system share the prescribed frequency band. Specifically, the whole frequency band is equally divided into multiple subcarriers that are bonded in a group to form a set of sub-channels. The time is partitioned into multiple slots. The transmission scheduling, usually conducted by MBS, is determined among two-dimensional resources to allocation slots and sub-channels to MBS and SBSs. Since interference analysis and the fading are complicated in practical applications, we apply the assumption that MBS collected the channel state information (CSI) periodically in each iteration, and the link rate is constant in each iteration.

8.2.2 Community-Based Synchronization Parallel over the Hierarchical Architecture

Based on the training model and the two-tier network model, we introduce the main principle of the community-based synchronization parallel and discuss the corresponding scheduling algorithm in this hierarchical architecture.

First, we discuss the global model update rule and the local model update rule under the community-based synchronization parallel. In each iteration, each mobile edge device computes a one-step gradient based on the local parameter and then waits for the update of the parameter. On the whole, the updating policy of global model is similar to BSP, since the MBS can collect gradients from all mobile edge devices and derive the new global model parameter at the end of each iteration. However, to improve the training efficiency, the mobile edge devices do not have to received the updated global model and they calculate the gradients with respect to the local model received form associated SBSs.

We present the details of the community-based synchronization parallel as follows. In the first iteration, the MBS initializes a global parameter ω_1 and deliver it to all mobile edge devices. At this time, the local parameter for MDs in any group j are the same - i.e., $\omega_1^j = \omega_1$. In the tth iteration ($t \geq 1$), the global parameter maintained by MBS is denoted by ω_t. For each mobile edge device associated with SBS $j, j \in \mathcal{N}$, the local parameter is denoted by ω_t^j. Each mobile edge device calculates the stochastic gradient on the local parameter and transmits the update to the adjacent SBS. Meanwhile, the MBS broadcasts the global parameter to all SBS. After SBS

j received the global parameter and all gradients of its community, a combination $\omega_t - \eta_t \frac{1}{M_j} \sum_{i \in \mathcal{M}_j} g_{\xi^i}(\omega_t^j)$ is broadcast to mobile edge devices and the MBS. We assume that the MBS maintains the value of η_t and M_j for all iterations t and SBS j. With the global parameter ω_t always cached, MBS can decode the summation of local gradients and update the global parameter for the next iteration. Consequently, by fully exploiting the opportunity of broadcast, the communication time can be reduced.

According to the preceding description, the updating policies of global model parameter and the local model parameter in the $(t + 1)$th iteration can be formally written as

$$\omega_{t+1} = \omega_t - \eta_t \frac{1}{M} \sum_{n \in \mathcal{N}} \sum_{i \in \mathcal{M}_n} g_{\xi^i}(\omega_t^n) \tag{8.3}$$

$$\omega_{t+1}^j = \omega_t - \eta_t \frac{1}{M_j} \sum_{i \in \mathcal{M}_j} g_{\xi^i}(\omega_t^j), \forall j \in \mathcal{N}. \tag{8.4}$$

In previous literature, efficient scheduling schemes in the OFDMA-based cellular network have been extensively studied. One of the main approaches is to allocate time slots and frequency bands to MBS and SBS, with the consideration of a trade-off between the throughput and the fairness over the whole system. However, these solutions are not suitable for edge learning over the hierarchical architecture due to the special properties of the learning procedure - e.g., iterative transmission due to the SGD algorithm as well as the order dependence caused by gradient aggregation and model synchronization. In other words, the communication process in the community-based synchronization parallel still has precedence constraints - i.e., an SBS cannot calculate and broadcast local parameter before it receives gradients from mobile edge devices and global parameters from the MBS. Moreover, from the perspective of training efficiency, fairness among mobile edge devices is less important. The critical problem is how to allocate the sub-channels to improve the utilization of bandwidth resources.

A simple but efficient sub-channel allocation scheme is presented as follows. To simplify the problem, the basic principle is that each sub-channel is occupied until the transmission of parameter or gradient is finished. In each iteration, the objective is to minimize the transmission time under the constraint of available sub-channels. Under the assumption that each sub-channel can be allocated to only one transmission link due to the interference, we can formulate this problem as a minimum makespan on the unrelated machine, considering that the links between mobile edge devices and SBS (also links between SBSs and MBSs) have different link rates in different sub-channels. This problem is known as NP-hard and the greedy algorithm scheduling the transmission can solve this problem with the approximation ratio of 2. In the community-based synchronization parallel, mobile edge devices and MBS transmit gradients and parameters to SBS simultaneously, and then SBS broadcasts the combination. Thus, the communication time can be saved, as illustrated before.

In this section, we focus on the architecture design for a scalable edge learning system. Since the community-based synchronization parallel can significantly save the transmitted bits compared to sequential mechanism, we believe that it also has better performance under other complicated, slotted-based scheduling algorithms. Although sophisticated wireless scheduling algorithms could further improve the training efficiency of edge learning, it is difficult to exactly model the wireless environment in real world. Considering the fading and the interference of wireless link, the problem is too complicated to solve. Thus, we refer to this as the future direction and discuss the convergence rate of the community-based synchronization parallel in the following subsection.

8.2.3 Convergence Rate of Community-Based Synchronization Parallel

Although the community-based synchronization parallel has great advantage in communication efficiency, the synchronization is slightly scarified, which may negatively impact on the convergence rate of training. In other words, there exists a tiny gap among the local model parameters of communities and global parameter parameter under the community-based synchronization parallel. Consider mobile edge devices in a community j; all gradients computed by mobile edge devices in community j are updated with respect to the local parameter in the current iteration, while gradients computed by other communities will be updated in the next iteration. Therefore, whether the community-based synchronization parallel can improve the training efficiency over the hierarchical architecture depends on the convergence rate, to a significant degree.

To analyze the convergence rate of the community-based synchronization parallel, we apply the assumptions introduced in Chapter 2, including L-smooth function, bounded scaler, unbiased gradient, and bounded variance gradient. Similarly, we use L to denote the Lipschitz constant, use δ^2 to denote the upper bound of the gradient variance, and we use $\|\cdot\|$ to denote the L_2 norm for a vector. Without loss of generality, we consider the function F as a nonconvex function.

First, we introduce the core ideas in proving the convergence rate of the community-based synchronization parallel. In each iteration, each mobile edge device calculates the local gradient with respect to the local model parameter of its belonging community, but the global model parameter is updated according to gradients collected from all mobile devices. Thus, we should first derive bound of the difference of the global model parameters between two consecutive iterations, and then establish the upper bound of the gap between the local model parameter and global model parameter.

Note that the global model parameters are updated based on the average stochastic gradient of all mobile devices. According to the update policy formulated in (8.3), the bound of the difference of the global model parameters between two consecutive iterations can be written as

$$\|\omega_{t+1} - \omega_t\|^2 = \left\| \eta_t \frac{1}{M} \sum_{n \in \mathcal{N}} \sum_{i \in \mathcal{M}_n} g_{\xi_{t+1}^i}(\omega_t^n) \right\|^2$$

$$= \frac{\eta_t^2}{M^2} \left\| \sum_{n \in \mathcal{N}} \sum_{i \in \mathcal{M}_n} [g_{\xi_{t+1}^i}(\omega_t^n) - \nabla F(\omega_t^n)] + \sum_{n \in \mathcal{N}} \sum_{i \in \mathcal{M}_n} \nabla F(\omega_t^n) \right\|^2$$

$$= \frac{\eta_t^2}{M^2} \left\| \sum_{n \in \mathcal{N}} \sum_{i \in \mathcal{M}_n} [g_{\xi_{t+1}^i}(\omega_t^n) - \nabla F(\omega_t^n)] \right\|^2 + \frac{\eta_t^2}{M^2} \left\| \sum_{n \in \mathcal{N}} [M_n \nabla F(\omega_t^n)] \right\|^2,$$

(8.5)

where $\nabla F(\omega_t^n)$ denotes the gradient calculated on all training samples with respect to the local model parameter ω_t^n of community n in iteration t, and $g_{\xi_{t+1}^i}$ denotes the stochastic gradient calculated with respect to the local model parameter ω_t^n and the random samples ξ_{t+1}^i in mobile device i. By taking the expectation of both sides, we can obtain

$$\mathbb{E}_{\xi_{t+1}^i} [\|\omega_{t+1} - \omega_t\|^2]$$

$$= \mathbb{E}_{\xi_{t+1}^i} \left[\frac{\eta_t^2}{M^2} \left\| \sum_{n \in \mathcal{N}} \sum_{i \in \mathcal{M}_n} [g_{\xi_{t+1}^i}(\omega_t^n) - \nabla F(\omega_t^n)] \right\|^2 \right] + \frac{\eta_t^2}{M^2} \left\| \sum_{n \in \mathcal{N}} [M_n \nabla F(\omega_t^n)] \right\|^2$$

$$\leq \frac{\eta_t^2 \sigma^2}{M} + \frac{\eta_t^2}{M^2} \left\| \sum_{n \in \mathcal{N}} [M_n \nabla F(\omega_t^n)] \right\|^2,$$

(8.6)

where the inequality follows according to the variance bound of stochastic gradient.

One approach to deriving the convergence rate of gradient-based algorithm for nonconvex optimization is to bound the average squared L_2 norm of the gradient in any T iterations. When refer to SGD, the essential component of the proof is represented the upper bound of $\frac{1}{T} \sum_{t=1}^{T} \mathbb{E} \|\nabla F(\omega_t)\|^2$ by a formula decreasing with T. The expectation is respect to the random training samples selected in iteration 1 to T, and the gradient is respect to the global model parameter in each iteration. According to (8.6), the bound of the $\mathbb{E}_{\xi_{t+1}^i} [\|\omega_{t+1} - \omega_t\|^2]$ can be represented as a formula with $\nabla F(\omega_t^n)$ - i.e., the gradient with respect to the local model parameter. Therefore, to derive the convergence rate of the community-based synchronization parallel, we should first reformulate the difference between the local model parameter and the global model parameter. More specially, we intend to bound the $\mathbb{E}[\|\nabla F(\omega_t) - \nabla F(\omega_t^j)\|^2]$.

According to updating policies of the local model parameter (8.4) and the global model parameter (8.3), we have

$$\omega_t - \omega_t^j = \eta_t \frac{1}{M_j} \sum_{i \in \mathcal{M}_j} g_{\xi_t^i}(\omega_{t-1}^j) - \eta_t \frac{1}{M} \sum_{n \in \mathcal{N}} \sum_{i \in \mathcal{M}_n} g_{\xi_t^i}(\omega_{t-1}^n)$$

Since function F is L-smooth, we have $\|\nabla F(\omega_1) - \nabla F(\omega_1)\| \leq L\|\omega_1 - \omega_2\|$ for any ω_1 and ω_2 with the same dimension. Therefore, we can obtain the following inequality

$$\mathbb{E}[\|\nabla F(\omega_t) - \nabla F(\omega_t^j)\|^2]$$

$$\leq L^2 \mathbb{E}[\|\omega_t - \omega_t^j\|^2]$$

$$= L^2 \mathbb{E}\left[\left\|\eta_t \frac{1}{M_j} \sum_{i \in \mathcal{M}_j} g_{\xi_t^i}(\omega_{t-1}^j) - \eta_t \frac{1}{M} \sum_{n \in \mathcal{N}} \sum_{i \in \mathcal{M}_n} g_{\xi_t^i}(\omega_{t-1}^j)\right\|^2\right]$$

$$= L^2 \eta_t^2 \mathbb{E}\left[\left\|\frac{1}{M_j} \sum_{i \in \mathcal{M}_j} g_{\xi_t^i}(\omega_{t-1}^j) - \nabla F(\omega_{t-1}^j) + \nabla F(\omega_{t-1}^j)\right.\right.$$

$$\left.\left. - \frac{1}{M} \sum_{n \in \mathcal{N}} \sum_{i \in \mathcal{M}_n} g_{\xi_t^i}(\omega_{t-1}^j)\right\|^2\right]$$

$$\leq 2L^2 \eta_t^2 \mathbb{E}\left[\left\|\frac{1}{M_j} \sum_{i \in \mathcal{M}_j} g_{\xi_t^i}(\omega_{t-1}^j) - \nabla F(\omega_{t-1}^j)\right\|^2\right]$$

$$+ 2L^2 \eta_t^2 \mathbb{E}\left[\left\|\nabla F(\omega_{t-1}^j) - \frac{1}{M} \sum_{n \in \mathcal{N}} \sum_{i \in \mathcal{M}_n} g_{\xi_t^i}(\omega_{t-1}^j)\right\|^2\right], \tag{8.7}$$

where the expectation is taken with respect to $\{\xi_t^i\}$ and the last inequality holds according to the fact that $\|a + b\|^2 \leq 2\|a\|^2 + 2\|b\|^2$.

Then, according to the assumption of bounded gradient variance, let δ^2 be the upper bound of stochastic gradient. Then for any t and j, we have

$$\|\nabla F(\omega_{t-1}^j) - g_{\xi_t^i}(\omega_{t-1}^j)\|^2 \leq \delta^2. \tag{8.8}$$

Thus, we can reformulate the (8.7) as follows:

$$\mathbb{E}[\|\nabla F(\omega_t) - \nabla F(\omega_t^j)\|^2] \leq 2L^2 \eta_t^2 \frac{1}{M_j^2} M_j \sigma^2 + 2L^2 \eta_t^2 \frac{1}{M^2} M \sigma^2$$

$$= \frac{2L^2 \eta_t^2 \sigma^2 (M + M_j)}{M M_j}, \tag{8.9}$$

Here, the convergence rate means the decreasing speed of the loss value under the SGD method. We can bound the difference of loss values between two consecutive iterations using the stochastic gradients of all mobile edge devices:

$$\mathbb{E}[F(\omega_{t+1}) - F(\omega_t)]$$

$$\overset{(a)}{\leq} \mathbb{E}[\nabla F(\omega_t)^T (\omega_{t+1} - \omega_t) + \frac{L}{2} \|\omega_{t+1} - \omega_t\|^2]$$

$$= -\frac{\eta_t}{M} \mathbb{E}[\nabla F(\omega_t)^T \sum_{n \in \mathcal{N}} \sum_{i \in \mathcal{M}_n} g_{\xi_{t+1}^i}(\omega_t^n)] + \frac{L}{2} \mathbb{E}\|\omega_{t+1} - \omega_t\|^2$$

$$\stackrel{(b)}{=} -\frac{\eta_t}{M} \sum_{n\in\mathcal{N}} \sum_{i\in\mathcal{M}_n} \mathbb{E}[\nabla F(\omega_t)^T \nabla F(\omega_t^n)] + \frac{L}{2}\mathbb{E}\|\omega_{t+1} - \omega_t\|^2$$

$$= -\frac{\eta_t}{M} \sum_{n\in\mathcal{N}} \mathbb{E}[M_n \nabla F(\omega_t)^T \nabla F(\omega_t^n)] + \frac{L}{2}\mathbb{E}\|\omega_{t+1} - \omega_t\|^2$$

$$\stackrel{(c)}{=} -\frac{\eta_t}{2M} \sum_{n\in\mathcal{N}} \mathbb{E}[M_n(\|\nabla F(\omega_t)\|^2 + \|\nabla F(\omega_t^n)\|^2 - \|\nabla F(\omega_t) - \nabla F(\omega_t^n)\|^2)]$$

$$+ \frac{L}{2}\mathbb{E}\|\omega_{t+1} - \omega_t\|^2$$

$$= -\frac{\eta_t}{2}\mathbb{E}\|\nabla F(\omega_t)\|^2 - \frac{\eta_t}{2M} \sum_{n\in\mathcal{N}} \mathbb{E}[M_n\|\nabla F(\omega_t^n)\|^2] + \frac{L}{2}\mathbb{E}\|\omega_{t+1} - \omega_t\|^2$$

$$+ \frac{\eta_t}{2M} \sum_{n\in\mathcal{N}} \mathbb{E}[M_n\|\nabla F(\omega_t) - \nabla F(\omega_t^n)\|^2], \tag{8.10}$$

where the inequality (a) holds according to the definition of gradient, (b) comes after the assumption of unbiased stochastic gradient and the fact that ξ_{t+1}^i are IID for any t, i, and (c) follows according to the definition of inner product. Based on the result of (8.6) and (8.9), we can reformulate (8.10) as follows:

$$\mathbb{E}[F(\omega_{t+1})] - \mathbb{E}[F(\omega_t)]$$

$$\leq -\frac{\eta_t}{2}\mathbb{E}[\|\nabla F(\omega_t)\|^2] - \frac{\eta_t}{2M}\mathbb{E}\left[\sum_{n\in\mathcal{N}}[M_n\|\nabla F(\omega_t^n)\|^2]\right]$$

$$+ \frac{\eta_t}{2M} \sum_{n\in\mathcal{N}} \frac{2L^2\eta_t^2\sigma^2(M + M_n)}{M}$$

$$+ \frac{L\eta_t^2\sigma^2}{2M} + \frac{L\eta_t^2}{2M^2}\mathbb{E}\left[\left\|\sum_{n\in\mathcal{N}}[M_n\nabla F(\omega_t^n)]\right\|^2\right]. \tag{8.11}$$

We can relax the right side of the above inequality to eliminate the term $\mathbb{E}[\sum_{n\in\mathcal{N}}\|\nabla F(\omega_t^n)\|^2]$ in the following two steps.

Step 1: Obviously, for any community n in the edge training, the number of mobile edge devices satisfies the constrain $1 \leq M_n \leq M$. Thus, we obtain

$$\mathbb{E}[F(\omega_{t+1})] - \mathbb{E}[F(\omega_t)]$$

$$\leq -\frac{\eta_t}{2}\mathbb{E}[\|\nabla F(\omega_t)\|^2] - \frac{\eta_t}{2M}\mathbb{E}\left[\sum_{n\in\mathcal{N}}\|\nabla F(\omega_t^n)\|^2\right] + \frac{L\eta_t^2 N}{2}\mathbb{E}\left[\sum_{n\in\mathcal{N}}\|\nabla F(\omega_t^n)\|^2\right]$$

$$+ \frac{L\eta_t^2\sigma^2(2L\eta_t N + 2L\eta_t + 1)}{2M}. \tag{8.12}$$

Step 2: By introducing a constraint on learning rate, we can finally eliminate the local model parameter in the formula. If we set the learning rate as $\frac{\eta_t}{2M} \geq \frac{L\eta_t^2 N}{2}$, i.e., $\eta_t \leq \frac{1}{LMN}$, we have

$$\mathbb{E}[F(\omega_{t+1})] - \mathbb{E}[F(\omega_t)] \leq -\frac{\eta_t}{2}\mathbb{E}[\|\nabla F(\omega_t)\|^2] + \frac{L\eta_t^2\sigma^2(2L\eta_t N + 2L\eta_t + 1)}{2M}.$$

(8.13)

We can establish the relationship between the loss value decreasing and the gradient with respect to the global model parameter by taking the summation on both side of (8.13) for $t = 1$ to T and get the following inequality:

$$\mathbb{E}[F(\omega_{T+1})] - \mathbb{E}[F(\omega_1)] \leq \sum_{t=1}^{T}\left[-\frac{\eta_t}{2}\mathbb{E}[\|\nabla F(\omega_t)\|^2]\right]$$
$$+ \frac{TL\eta_t^2\sigma^2(2L\eta_t N + 2L\eta_t + 1)}{2M}.$$

(8.14)

When the loss function is nonconvex, we give the convergence rate of the community-based synchronization parallel in the following theorem.

THEOREM 8.1 (Convergence Rate of Community-Based Synchronization Parallel) *Given that $F(\cdot)$ is nonconvex, there exists a fixed learning rate η such that for sufficient large iteration times T, the community-based synchronization parallel has a convergence learning rate $O(1/\sqrt{TM})$, where M is the number of mobile edge devices.*

Thus, the community-based synchronization parallel has the following properties on the convergence rate:

- *The community-based synchronization parallel has a sublinear convergence rate.*
- *It shows linear speedup with respect to the number of mobile edge devices.*

Proof Let $\eta_t = \eta$ in all iterations of the training process. By dividing by T and rearranging (8.14), we obtain the following inequality:

$$\frac{1}{T}\sum_{t=1}^{T}\mathbb{E}[\|\nabla F(\omega_t)\|^2] \leq \frac{2[F(\omega_1) - F(\omega^*)]}{\eta T} + \frac{L\eta\sigma^2}{M} + \frac{2L^2\eta^2\sigma^2}{M} + \frac{2L^2\eta^2\sigma^2 N}{M},$$

(8.15)

where ω^* is the optimal solution to the optimization problem, such that $F(\omega^*)$ is less than or equal to $F(\omega_t)$ for any positive integer number t.

When η is sub-linearly decreasing with respect to T - e.g., $\eta \sim O(\frac{1}{\sqrt{T}})$ - the right side of (8.15) will converge to 0 with the increasing of T, which means the community-based synchronization parallel can converge. More specifically, the first part and the second part of the right side of (8.15) mainly determine the convergence rate. By ignoring other parts of the right side, when the first term equals the second term, the right side of (8.15) achieves the minimum. Therefore, by setting

$$\eta = \sqrt{\frac{[F(\omega_1) - F(\omega^*)]M}{L\sigma^2 T}},$$

(8.16)

We have

$$\frac{1}{T}\sum_{t=1}^{T}\mathbb{E}[\|\nabla F(\omega_t)\|^2] \leq 4\sqrt{\frac{[F(\omega_1) - F(\omega_{inf})]\sigma^2 L}{MT}} + O\left(\frac{1}{T}\right). \qquad (8.17)$$

Note that the inequality in (8.15) holds only when $\eta \leq \frac{1}{LMN}$. Therefore, for sufficiently large T such that

$$T \geq \frac{LM^3N^2[F(\omega_1) - F(\omega^*)]}{\sigma^2}, \qquad (8.18)$$

the convergence rate of the community-based synchronization parallel with an order less than or equal to $O\left(\frac{1}{\sqrt{TM}}\right)$, where T is the number of the iterations and M is the number of mobile devices. The proof is completed. $\qquad\square$

Theorem 8.1 indicates that the community-based synchronization parallel essentially admits the same convergence rate as sequential distributed SGD since it has the asymptotical convergence rate $O\left(\frac{1}{\sqrt{T}}\right)$. More specifically, the community-based synchronization parallel runs with the convergence rate $O\left(\frac{1}{\sqrt{TM}}\right)$, which means it has the linear speedup property with respect to the number of mobile edge devices. The theoretical results show that PSP is efficient in large-scale distributed learning.

8.3   Extension of Community-Based Synchronization Parallel

In the previous section, we introduced the community-based synchronization parallel. The intercommunity and intracommunity synchronization schemes are in BSP mode, such that the synchronizations are conducted at SBSs and MBSs in each iteration. Although the community-based aggregation can reduce the communication cost, the fast training nodes should wait for the slow training nodes when the participants are heterogeneous in communication and computation capabilities. To further improve the training efficiency, we introduce two extensions of the community-based synchronization parallel. The first is the community-based hybrid synchronization mechanism over the hierarchical architecture, and the second is the community-based synchronization with gradient compression.

8.3.1   A Hybrid Synchronization Mechanism over the Hierarchical Architecture

In the previous section, we presented that communities are organized based on the coverage of SBSs. The major disadvantage of this is that communities require different amounts of time to aggregate the gradients from their covered mobile edge devices. To better explain the reason behind grouping training workers, we introduce a more flexible synchronization mechanism where the training workers inside a community are very similar in computation capacity, network condition, and task-level iteration significance. This grouping policy is applicable in edge server or distributed cloud environments. Then we devise a hybrid community-based synchronization mechanism, which conducts parameter synchronization in a server-community structure, and the basic scheduling unit is a community. This hybrid synchronization scheme exchanges parameters among workers via intracommunity and intercommunity synchronization. The former uses BSP policy to guarantee the strong consistency of parameter aggregation with a synchronization barrier, and the latter uses ASP policy to exploit the advantage of iteration acceleration with a delay-bounded staleness threshold.

8.3.2   Abstract of Community and Communication-Aware Parameter Servers

Here we explain the organization and management of communities. We consider a scenario where the training is conducted in a edge server or a distributed cloud. A community is a collection containing a number of workers. To eliminate the influence from the heterogeneous environment, our proposal is to divide workers in the parameter server cluster into several communities for more efficient synchronization and communication. The partition of the community follows three principles:

- High cohesion: Inside a community, high intracluster similarity exists on each worker, with three aspects of computation capacity, network condition and iteration significance.
- Low coupling: Among different communities, the inter-cluster similarity should be low.
- Flexibility: Division standard should be applicable and dynamical in the heterogeneous environment.

The architecture follows a server-worker structure. During an iteration, workers pull the latest parameters from servers, then locally train the models, and finally push the pruned parameters to the server. The server aggregates all the results and updates the global parameters for future iterations.

Different from existing parameter server systems that manage the synchronization in the fine-grained granularity based on each worker, we handle the cluster in the coarse-grained granularity that a community is a basic scheduling unit. Assuming that workers have been divided into a number of communities, the synchronization of gradients can be formulated as the coordination of these communities. Specifically, we introduce a hybrid community-based synchronization parallel to handle this procedure. We rearrange the parameter server cluster as the server-community structure, in which the similar workers are grouped together. Each community owns a master worker and several slave workers. Inside a community, the master worker acts as a community-server to aggregate gradients computed by slave workers and form the local model of this community. The interaction between the master worker and slave workers are operated by gather and scatter methods in a synchronous mode. Across communities, the logical central server coordinates all communities and maintains the global model. Each community pushes the local model to the server and pulls the latest global model from the server. The communities communicate with server via the asynchronous send and receive methods. In brief, the intracommunity synchronization of the hybrid community-based synchronization parallel follows BSP, while its inter-community synchronization can be handled by ASP with a staleness threshold configured at the community level.

8.3.3   Convergence Result of Hybrid Community-Based Synchronization Parallel

In this section, we establish theories for the convergence rate of CSP for nonconvex objective. For the convenience of theoretical analysis, we use the following notations in the rest of this section.

- $\omega \in \mathbb{R}^d$ denotes model parameter vectors.
- $F(\cdot)$ denotes the loss function.
- $\nabla F(\omega)$ denotes the full gradient of a function $F(\cdot)$.
- $\mathbf{g}(\omega; \xi)$ denotes the stochastic gradient respect to a mini-batch ξ.
- ω^* denotes the optimal solution.
- η denotes the learning rate.
- $\| \cdot \|$ denotes the L_2 norm for vectors.

Let C_t be the community that updates the gradient to the server in iteration t and $C_t = |C_t|$, for any $t > 0$. Then, the model parameter is updated in iteration t as follows:

$$\omega_{t+1} = \omega_t - \eta \frac{1}{C_t} \sum_{i \in C_t} g(\omega_{t-\tau_t}, \xi_{t,i}), \tag{8.19}$$

where τ_t denotes the staleness of C_t in iteration t and $\xi_{t,i}$ denotes the mini-batch selected by ith worker of C_t in iteration t. Based on the L-smooth assumption and the update policy of model parameter (8.19), we have

$$F(\omega_{t+1}) - F(\omega_t)$$

$$\leq \langle \nabla F(\omega_1), \omega_2 - \omega_1 \rangle + \frac{L}{2} \| \omega_{t+1} - \omega_t \|^2$$

$$= \left\langle \nabla F(\omega_t), -\frac{\eta}{C_t} \sum_{i \in C_t} g(\omega_{t-\tau_t}, \xi_{t,i}) \right\rangle + \frac{L}{2} \| -\frac{\eta}{C_t} \sum_{i \in C_t} g(\omega_{t-\tau_t}, \xi_{t,i}) \|^2$$

$$= -\frac{\eta}{C_t} \sum_{i \in C_t} \langle \nabla F(\omega_t), g(\omega_{t-\tau_t}, \xi_{t,i}) \rangle + \frac{L\eta^2}{2C_t^2} \left\| \sum_{i \in C_t} g(\omega_{t-\tau_t}, \xi_{t,i}) \right\|^2. \tag{8.20}$$

Based on the ASP policy among communities, the training workers use the stale parameter to calculate the gradient. Therefore, to establish the convergence rate of the hybrid community-based synchronization parallel, the major challenge is to derive the relationship between the bound of the difference of loss values between two consecutive iteration and the gradient with respect to fresh parameter. That is to say we have to eliminate the terms of the gradient with respect to the staleness parameter. For the first part of (8.20), by taking the expectation with respect to $\xi_{t,i}$, we obtain

$$\mathbb{E}\left[-\frac{\eta}{C_t}\sum_{i\in C_t}\langle\nabla F(\omega_t),g(\omega_{t-\tau_t},\xi_{t,i})\rangle\right]$$

$$=-\frac{\eta}{C_t}\sum_{i\in C_t}\langle\nabla F(\omega_t),\nabla F(\omega_{t-\tau_t})\rangle$$

$$=-\frac{\eta}{2C_t}\sum_{i\in C_t}[\|\nabla F(\omega_t)\|^2+\|\nabla F(\omega_{t-\tau_t})\|^2-\|\nabla F(\omega_t)-\nabla F(\omega_{t-\tau_t})\|^2]$$

$$=-\frac{\eta}{2}\|\nabla F(\omega_t)\|^2-\frac{\eta}{2}\|\nabla F(\omega_{t-\tau_t})\|^2+\frac{\eta}{2}\|\nabla F(\omega_t)-\nabla F(\omega_{t-\tau_t})\|^2,\quad(8.21)$$

where the first equality comes after that all $\xi_{t,i}$ are IID and the unbiased gradient assumption, and the second equality holds according to $\langle a,b\rangle=\frac{1}{2}(\|a\|^2+\|b\|^2-\|a-b\|^2)$. Then we have to obtain the upper bound of $\|\nabla F(\omega_t)-\nabla F(\omega_{t-\tau_t})\|^2$.

The following equation always holds for any iteration:

$$\omega_t=\omega_{t-1}-\eta\frac{1}{C_{t-1}}\sum_{i\in C_{t-1}}g(\omega_{t-1-\tau_{t-1}},\xi_{t-1,i})$$

$$=\omega_{t-\tau_t}-\sum_{k=1}^{\tau_t}\eta\frac{1}{C_{t-k}}\sum_{i\in C_{t-k}}g(\omega_{t-k-\tau_{t-k}},\xi_{t-k,i}).\qquad(8.22)$$

We obtain that

$$\|\nabla F(\omega_t)-\nabla F(\omega_{t-\tau_t})\|^2\le L^2\|\omega_t-\omega_{t-\tau_t}\|^2$$

$$=L^2\eta^2\left\|\sum_{k=1}^{\tau_t}\frac{1}{C_{t-k}}\sum_{i\in C_{t-k}}g(\omega_{t-k-\tau_{t-k}},\xi_{t-k,i})\right\|^2$$

$$\le L^2\eta^2\tau_t\sum_{k=1}^{\tau_t}\frac{1}{C_{t-k}^2}\left\|\sum_{i\in C_{t-k}}g(\omega_{t-k-\tau_{t-k}},\xi_{t-k,i})\right\|^2$$

$$\le L^2\eta^2\tau_t\sum_{k=1}^{\tau_t}\frac{1}{C_{t-k}}\sum_{i\in C_{t-k}}\|g(\omega_{t-k-\tau_{t-k}},\xi_{t-k,i})\|^2$$

$$=L^2\eta^2\tau_t\sum_{k=1}^{\tau_t}\frac{1}{C_{t-k}}\sum_{i\in C_{t-k}}\|g(\omega_{t-k-\tau_{t-k}},\xi_{t-k,i})$$

$$-\nabla F(\omega_{t-k-\tau_{t-k}})+\nabla F(\omega_{t-k-\tau_{t-k}})\|^2$$

$$\le 2L^2\eta^2\tau_t\sum_{k=1}^{\tau_t}\frac{1}{C_{t-k}}\sum_{i\in C_{t-k}}\big[\|g(\omega_{t-k-\tau_{t-k}},\xi_{t-k,i})$$

$$-\nabla F(\omega_{t-k-\tau_{t-k}})\|^2+\|\nabla F(\omega_{t-k-\tau_{t-k}})\|^2\big]$$

$$\le 2L^2\eta^2\tau_t\sum_{k=1}^{\tau_t}\frac{1}{C_{t-k}}\sum_{i\in C_{t-k}}\big[\delta^2+\|\nabla F(\omega_{t-k-\tau_{t-k}})\|^2\big]$$

$$=2L^2\eta^2\tau_t^2\delta^2+2L^2\eta^2\tau_t\sum_{k=1}^{\tau_t}\|\nabla F(\omega_{t-k-\tau_{t-k}})\|^2,\quad(8.23)$$

where the first inequality comes after L-smooth assumption, and the last inequality holds based on the bounded variance assumption. Combining (8.21) and (8.23), we bound the first part of (8.20) as

$$\mathbb{E}\left[-\frac{\eta}{C_t}\sum_{i\in C_t}\langle \nabla F(\omega_t), g(\omega_{t-\tau_t},\xi_{t,i})\rangle\right] = -\frac{\eta}{2}\|\nabla F(\omega_t)\|^2 - \frac{\eta}{2}\|\nabla F(\omega_{t-\tau_t})\|^2$$

$$+L^2\eta^3\tau_t\sum_{k=1}^{\tau_t}\|\nabla F(\omega_{t-k-\tau_{t-k}})\|^2 + L^2\eta^3\tau_t^2\delta^2.$$

(8.24)

For the second part of (8.20), we have

$$\frac{L\eta^2}{2C_t^2}\left\|\sum_{i\in C_t} g(\omega_{t-\tau_t},\xi_{t,i})\right\|^2$$

$$\le \frac{L\eta^2}{2C_t}\sum_{i\in C_t}\|g(\omega_{t-\tau_t},\xi_{t,i})\|^2$$

$$\le \frac{L\eta^2}{C_t}\sum_{i\in C_t}\|g(\omega_{t-\tau_t},\xi_{t,i}) - \nabla F(\omega_{t-\tau_t})\|^2 + \frac{L\eta^2}{C_t}\sum_{i\in C_t}\|\nabla F(\omega_{t-\tau_t})\|^2$$

$$\le L\eta^2\delta^2 + L\eta^2\|\nabla F(\omega_{t-\tau_t})\|^2.$$

(8.25)

Based on these preliminary results, the following theorem gives the convergence rate of the hybrid community-based synchronization parallel.

THEOREM 8.2 (Convergence Rate of the Hybrid Synchronization Parallel)   *When the objective function $F(\cdot)$ is nonconvex and the hybrid community-based synchronization parallel is running with fixed learning rate η for all iterations and satisfying $2L^2\eta^3\tau^2 + 2L\eta^2 - \eta \le 0$, where τ is the threshold of staleness, the expected average-squared gradients satisfies the following inequality for all $T \in \mathbb{N}$:*

$$\frac{1}{T}\sum_{t=1}^{T}\|\nabla F(\omega_t)\|^2 \le \frac{2[F(\omega_1) - F(\omega^*)]}{\eta T} + 2L\eta\delta^2 + 2L^2\eta^2\tau^2\delta^2.$$

(8.26)

Proof   Replacing the first part and the second part of (8.20) with the bounds obtained in (8.24) and (8.25) immediately yields

$$\mathbb{E}\left[F(\omega_{t+1}) - F(\omega_t)\right]$$

$$\le -\frac{\eta}{2}\|\nabla F(\omega_t)\|^2 + \frac{2L\eta^2 - \eta}{2}\|\nabla F(\omega_{t-\tau_t})\|^2 + L^2\eta^3\tau_t\sum_{k=1}^{\tau_t}\|\nabla F(\omega_{t-k-\tau_{t-k}})\|^2$$

$$+ L\eta^2\delta^2 + L^2\eta^3\tau_t^2\delta^2.$$

(8.27)

By summing the both sides of (8.29) from $t = 1$ to T, we obtain

$$\mathbb{E}\left[F(\omega_{T+1})\right] - F(\omega_1) \leq -\frac{\eta}{2}\sum_{t=1}^{T}\|\nabla F(\omega_t)\|^2 + \frac{2L\eta^2 - \eta}{2}\sum_{t=1}^{T}\|\nabla F(\omega_{t-\tau_t})\|^2$$

$$+ L^2\eta^3\sum_{t=1}^{T}\tau_t\sum_{k=1}^{\tau_t}\|\nabla F(\omega_{t-k-\tau_{t-k}})\|^2$$

$$+ L\eta^2\delta^2 T + \sum_{t=1}^{T}L^2\eta^3\tau_t^2\delta^2. \tag{8.28}$$

The inequality $\tau \geq \tau_t$ holds for any t. Combined with the fact that for any $t = 1$ to T, the term $\|\nabla F(\omega_{t-\tau_t})\|^2$ appears at most τ times in $L^2\eta^3\tau\sum_{t=1}^{T}\sum_{k=1}^{\tau}\|\nabla F(\omega_{t-k-\tau_{t-k}})\|^2$, we obtain the following result:

$$\mathbb{E}\left[F(\omega_{T+1})\right] - F(\omega_1)$$

$$\leq -\frac{\eta}{2}\sum_{t=1}^{T}\|\nabla F(\omega_t)\|^2 + \frac{2L\eta^2 - \eta}{2}\sum_{t=1}^{T}\|\nabla F(\omega_{t-\tau_t})\|^2$$

$$+ L^2\eta^3\tau\sum_{t=1}^{T}\sum_{k=1}^{\tau}\|\nabla F(\omega_{t-k-\tau_{t-k}})\|^2 + L\eta^2\delta^2 T + L^2\eta^3\tau^2\delta^2 T$$

$$\leq -\frac{\eta}{2}\sum_{t=1}^{T}\|\nabla F(\omega_t)\|^2 + \frac{2L\eta^2 - \eta}{2}\sum_{t=1}^{T}\|\nabla F(\omega_{t-\tau_t})\|^2$$

$$+ L^2\eta^3\tau^2\sum_{t=1}^{T}\|\nabla F(\omega_{t-\tau_t})\|^2 + L\eta^2\delta^2 T + L^2\eta^3\tau^2\delta^2 T$$

$$= -\frac{\eta}{2}\sum_{t=1}^{T}\|\nabla F(\omega_t)\|^2 + \frac{2L^2\eta^3\tau^2 + 2L\eta^2 - \eta}{2}\sum_{t=1}^{T}\|\nabla F(\omega_{t-\tau_t})\|^2$$

$$+ L\eta^2\delta^2 T + L^2\eta^3\tau^2\delta^2 T. \tag{8.29}$$

where the second inequality holds due to $\tau \geq \tau_t$ for any t, and the third inequality comes after the fact that for any $t = 1$ to T, the term $\|\nabla F(\omega_{t-\tau_t})\|^2$ appears at most τ times in $L^2\eta^3\tau\sum_{t=1}^{T}\sum_{k=1}^{\tau}\|\nabla F(\omega_{t-k-\tau_{t-k}})\|^2$.

Let $2L^2\eta^3\tau^2 + 2L\eta^2 - \eta \leq 0$. By rearranging and dividing both sides of (8.29) by T, we have

$$\frac{1}{T}\sum_{t=1}^{T}\|\nabla F(\omega_t)\|^2 \leq \frac{2\left[F(\omega_1) - F(\omega_{T+1})\right]}{\eta T} + 2L\eta\delta^2 + 2L^2\eta^2\tau^2\delta^2$$

$$\leq \frac{2\left[F(\omega_1) - F(\omega^*)\right]}{\eta T} + 2L\eta\delta^2 + 2L^2\eta^2\tau^2\delta^2, \tag{8.30}$$

which completes the proof. ◻

Based on Theorem 8.2, by setting the learning rate as diminishing with iteration number T - i.e., $\eta = \sqrt{\frac{F(\omega_1)-F(\omega^*)}{L\delta^2 T}}$, for sufficiently large T that satisfying the learning rate constrain $2L^2\eta^3\tau^2 + 2L\eta^2 - \eta \leq 0$ - we have

$$\frac{1}{T}\sum_{t=1}^{T}\|\nabla F(\omega_t)\|^2 \leq 4\sqrt{[F(\omega_1) - F(\omega^*)]L\delta^2}\frac{1}{\sqrt{T}} + 2L\tau^2[F(\omega_1) - F(\omega^*)]\frac{1}{T},$$

(8.31)

which indicates that the hybrid community-based synchronization parallel admits a sublinear convergence rate as $O(\frac{1}{\sqrt{T}} + \frac{1}{T})$ where the dominant term is $O(\frac{1}{\sqrt{T}})$. Note that τ only affects the term with $\frac{1}{T}$. When $\tau = 0$, the result is consistent with the convergence rate of BSP. Moreover, the iteration number is increased by 1 when any community updates the gradient; thus, the hybrid community-based synchronization parallel has a linear speedup property with respect to the number of community.

8.3.3.1 Community-Based Synchronization with Gradient Compression

Gradient compression can reduce the communication cost and improve the training efficiency, as proven in Chapter 4. In this section, we show how to apply compression technology in the edge learning over the hierarchical architecture. By integrating the community-based synchronization parallel and the gradient compression technologies, the training efficiency can be further improved.

We give an example of community-based synchronization with gradient compression. For the convenience of analysis, we consider unbiased and error-bounded compression methods such as random quantization like QSGD and random sparsification. For any gradient g, let $C(g)$ be the compressed gradient. Then we have $\mathbb{E}[C(g)] = g$, which indicates the property of unbiasedness. The magnitude of the quantization error is bounded for any parameter ω and mini-batch ξ; i.e.,

$$\mathbb{E}[\|C(g_\xi(\omega)) - g_\xi(\omega)\|] \leq \epsilon\|g_\xi(\omega)\|.$$

(8.32)

Then, we show the convergence rate of the community-based synchronization with gradient compression is in the same order of distributed sequential SGD without compression over traditional single-layer parameter server architecture - i.e., $O(1/\sqrt{MT})$.

THEOREM 8.3   *Let*

$$\eta = \sqrt{\frac{[F(\omega_1) - F(\omega^*)]M}{2L(1 + \epsilon^2)\sigma^2 T}};$$

(8.33)

then for sufficiently large T, the community-based synchronization with gradient compression satisfies the ergodic convergence rate

$$\frac{1}{T}\sum_{t=1}^{T}\mathbb{E}\|\nabla F(\omega_t)\|_2^2 \leq O\left(\frac{1}{\sqrt{MT}}\right).$$

(8.34)

To prove this theorem, the main idea is to bound the L_2 norm of the difference between compressed stochastic gradient with respect to random samples and the gradient with respect to the whole dataset. Based on the definition, the following inequality holds for any ω and ξ:

$$\|C(g_\xi(\omega)) - \nabla F(\omega)\|^2 \leq 2\|C(g_\xi(\omega)) - g_\xi(\omega)\|^2 + 2\|g_\xi(\omega) - \nabla F(\omega)\|^2$$
$$\leq 2\epsilon^2\|g_\xi(\omega) - \nabla F(\omega) + \nabla F(\omega)\|^2 + 2\sigma^2$$
$$= 2(1 + \epsilon^2)\sigma^2 + 2\epsilon^2\|\nabla F(\omega)\|^2 \tag{8.35}$$

With the similar proof framework of Theorem 8.1, the convergence rate of the community-based synchronization with gradient compression can be easily derived.

8.4   Conclusion and Future Directions

In the scenario of big data analytics, operating large-scale machine learning applications often resorts to distributed processing and parallel computing, where handling the collaboration between edge nodes, especially in the heterogeneous environment, has become a promising research direction for both algorithm design and system implementation. We intend to elaborate an efficient and scalable edge learning platform, which is compatible with the heterogeneous environment and fully exploits the capacity of edge devices when conducting machine learning applications. To achieve this goal, one critical question is how to build a high-performance architecture for large-scale edge learning systems.

Different from existing distributed machine learning frameworks, handling the applications among heterogeneous edge devices requires more complicated insight of architecture design. Traditional approaches often concentrate on the optimization of communication overhead or computation efficiency while lacking the co-design of these two aspects. Moreover, they ignore the impact of physical network topology and logical cluster management.

Architecture design plays an important role in edge learning as a fundamental infrastructure that provides essential supports to upper modules. Most machine learning applications follow the iteration-based scheme, where partitioning the data and the machine learning model to distributed nodes is the first crucial issue that needs to be considered. The key to solving this issue is to properly determine the parallelism scheme, which significantly impacts the training efficiency.

In this chapter, we first summarized the existing architecture and parallelism mechanisms for edge learning. Then we introduced a community-based synchronization parallelism scheme to improve the training efficiency and the system scalability. The key idea is to properly determine the parallelism scheme, which significantly impacts the training efficiency. Then, we extended the community-based synchronization parallel from two aspects - i.e., (1) a hybrid ASP and BSP mechanism for flexible intra-community and intercommunity synchronization and (2) community-based synchronization with gradient compression. Now we list some future direction in this field.

One direction is integrating the server and serverless connection paradigms for flexible collaboration. On top of an appropriate partition of data and model, the intermediate results of different edge devices need to be shared and exchanged among the clusters. The connection paradigm impacts the transmission efficiency and consistency between physical network topology and logical cluster management are important. The physical network topology represents the link pattern of edges devices, including edge servers, switches, and routers. Additionally, in terms of logical cluster management, how to support the server, serverless, and hybrid management in the architecture is a critical problem. The server management adopts a central node to store and share parameters, so as to ensure consistency control across the cluster. The parameter server paradigm follows this manner. By contrast, serverless management is implemented based on the peer-to-peer connection that does not require a central node. Another direction is hybrid data and model synchronization mechanisms for efficient aggregation. By fully exploiting the opportunities of parallelism and pipeline modes in modern chips, the training efficiency can be further improved by carefully partitioning the training model and training data and allocating the pieces of them on heterogeneous nodes in edge learning.

9   Incentive Mechanisms in Edge Learning Systems

How to build a benign ecosystem for the sustainable development of edge learning is a critical issue. This chapter first introduces incentive mechanisms for edge learning to motivate mobile edge devices to contribute to model training. Specifically, in parameter server architecture, we introduce a deep reinforcement-learning-based incentive mechanism to determine the optimal pricing strategy for the parameter server and the optimal training strategies for mobile edge devices. Finally, we discuss future directions.

9.1   Fundamental Theory of Incentive Mechanisms

The theory of mechanism design takes a systematic look at the design of institutions and how these affect the outcomes of interactions. The main focus of mechanism design is on the design of institutions that satisfy certain objectives, assuming that the agents (i.e., the individuals that participate in the mechanism) interacting through the institution act strategically and may hold private information that is relevant to the decision at hand [123]. For example, in the bargaining game between buyers and sellers, the sellers want to raise the price of the item in order to maximize their revenue as much as possible, while the buyers want to pretend to have a low value for the item to lower down the price. One question is whether we can design an incentive mechanism through which bargaining occurs to induce efficient trade of the item, so that the trade can be successfully concluded whenever the buyer's valuation exceeds the seller's estimation. Another question is whether there exists such an incentive mechanism that encourage the buyer and seller to voluntarily participate in the mechanism.

Fig. 9.1 shows an illustration of mechanism design. The incentive mechanism design model shows the interaction of the agents using game theory tools. In this mechanism, each agent has a strategy space and a utility function of strategy chosen. For example, in an auction setting, the strategy space is the possible bids that can be submitted, and the outcome function specifies who gets the item and how much each agent pays as a function of the bids submitted. Different sorts of assumptions can be examined concerning how agents choose strategies as functions of their private information, and the analysis can be applied to a wide variety of contexts. The analysis also allows for the transfers to be made among the agents, so that some may be taxed and others may be subsidized to bring their incentives into alignment.

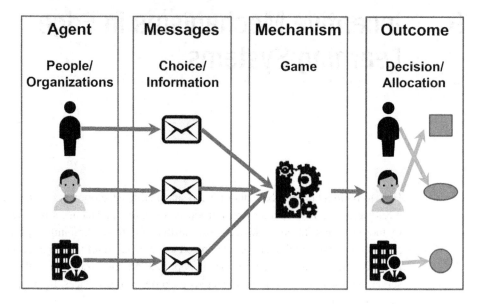

Figure 9.1 An illustration of mechanism design.

A general mechanism design setting includes a finite group of agents interacting. The set is denoted as $\mathcal{N} = \{1, 2, \cdots, N\}$, and a generic agent is represented as i. The set of agents' potential strategies is denoted as $\mathcal{D}$, and generic elements are represented as d and d'. The set of strategies may be finite or infinite depending on the real applications. Agents hold their own private information; for example, agent i's private information is represented as θ_i which lies in a set Θ_i. Agents have preferences over strategies that are represented by a utility function $u_i : \mathcal{D} \times \Theta_i \to \mathbb{R}$. Then, $u_i(d, \theta_i)$ denotes the utility that agent i of type $\theta_i \in \Theta_i$ receives from a strategy $d \in \mathcal{D}$. And $u_i(d, \theta_i) \geq u_i(d', \theta_i)$ indicates that agent i with type θ_i prefers strategy d to strategy d'. An incentive mechanism is often also referred to as a game form. The terminology game form distinguishes it from a game (i.e., game theory). As the consequence, a profile of messages is an outcome rather than a vector of utilities. Once the preferences of the agents are specified, then a game form or mechanism induces a game. Since the preference of agents often varies in the mechanism design, this distinction between mechanisms and games is critical.

The key issue is to design a mechanism so that when agents interact through the mechanism, they have incentives to select a function of their private information that leads to desired outcome. And the game theory is always used to model the mechanism design. Taking the dominant strategies as an example, it identifies situations in which agents have deterministic best strategies. A strategy d_i is a dominant strategy at $\theta_i \in \Theta_i$, if

$$u_i(d_i^*, \boldsymbol{d}_{-i}, \theta_i) \geq u_i(d_i, \boldsymbol{d}_{-i}, \theta_i),$$

where $d_{-i} = (d_1, d_2, \ldots, d_{i-1}, d_{i+1}, \ldots, d_N)$ is the strategies of other agents except agent i. A dominant strategy has the strong property that it is optimal for a agent no matter what the others do. When there exits a dominant strategy, all the agents should employ it.

9.2 Related Works

Incentive mechanism design has been widely studied in other areas. In this section, we first introduce some studies of incentive mechanism design in other areas, and then introduce the works of incentive mechanisms related to edge learning.

9.2.1 Incentive Mechanisms

Using game theory to design the incentive mechanism has been widely studied in many areas, such as crowdsourcing, edge computing, smart grid, etc. In [352], Yang et al. design the platform-centric and user-centric crowdsourcing applications based on the Stackelberg game and auction approaches, respectively. Li et al. [159] use the incentive mechanism to motivate users to use device-to-device communication. Two different markets named open markets and sealed markets are considered. In order to offload the time-critical applications to the edge computing platforms, incentive mechanisms have been designed to motivate the third-party edge computing platforms to contribute their computing power [181]. We can find that in the incentive mechanism design in aforementioned works, each participant's utility model can be built precisely; then the game theory is applied to analyze each participant's behavior. In edge learning, quantifying the value of each client's training data is challenging. At the same time, it is hard to model the final learning performance due to the complexity of the edge learning algorithm. Therefore, it is hard to model the utility of each participant in edge learning, which prevents the existing incentive mechanism design studies from being directly applied to edge learning.

9.2.2 Incentive Mechanisms for Edge Learning

The incentive mechanisms for edge learning can be divided into two categories: data perspective and system perspective.

9.2.2.1 Incentive Mechanisms from Data Perspective

In edge learning, the data for building a machine learning models are often provided by multiple entities. Further, the quality of the training data from different entities may vary widely. Therefore, a key question is how to fairly allocate the revenue generated by a machine learning model to the data contributors based on their contribution to the machine learning model. To attract self-interested mobile edge devices with high-quality training data, Song et al. [272] formally define the contribution index

(CI) to efficiently measure the contribution of differnet mobile edge devices in enterprise edge learning. The key is to record the intermediate results during the training process of edge learning and use thse results to compute the CIs approximately. Experiments based on MNIST dataset demonstrate the efficiency of the proposed methods. The auction mechanism has also been applied in edge learning. Authors in [383] present an incentive mechanism, FMore, which has a multidimensional procurement auction of K winners. FMore is not only lightweight and incentive compatible, but also can encourage more high-quality clients with low cost to participate in learning and eventually improve the performance of edge learning. To ensure security, Martinez et al. [194] aim to establish security, accuracy, and efficiency incentive mechanisms in rewarding clients' contributions, and ensure the scalability of data on the blockchain.

9.2.2.2   Incentive Mechanisms from System Perspective

Participating in the edge learning will consume computational and communication resources. Therefore, how to design an incentive mechanism for resource allocation among different clients becomes critical. In terms of computational resources, Sarikaya et al. first analyze the influence of heterogeneous mobile edge devices on edge learning convergence; based on that, they propose an incentive to balance the time of each iteration [248]. More specifically, the parameter server has a limited budget and distributes its budget among clients to motivate them to contribute their CPU power and achieve a fast convergence with a target accuracy. They present a Stackelberg game to improve its performance by optimizing the computational resource allocation strategy among clients as well as the budget allocation of the parameter server. The traditional theoretical analysis methods are inapplicable in edge learning due to the hardness of the learning algorithm and the dynamic learning environment, which makes it difficult to seek optimal solutions. Zhan et al. [385] propose a deep reinforcement-learning-based approach to design the incentive mechanism and find the optimal trade-off between model training time and the parameter server's payment in a dynamic network environment. Pandey et al. [226] propose a novel crowdsourcing platform by constructing a communication efficient cost model that considers the communication efficiency during the model parameter exchange. The Stackelberg game is applied to solve the primal-dual optimization problem where each side maximizes its own benefit.

9.3   A Learning-Based Incentive Mechanism for Edge Learning

In applications such as self-driving vehicles, video surveillance, and recommendation systems, mobile edge devices - e.g., smartphones, cameras, and wearable devices - generate large amounts of data at the network edge. Machine learning models are often built on these data to enable the detection, classification, and prediction of future events. Due to network bandwidth and storage, it is often impossible to send all the data generated at the edge to the data center for centralized model training.

Moreover, in many applications, training data are generated by mobile edge devices owned by individuals or different organizations, who hesitate to share their data and risk their privacy.

Private edge learning paradigm - i.e., federated learning over mobile devices - has been proposed to enable distributed computing nodes to collaboratively train models without exposing users' own data. Its basic idea is to let these computing nodes train local models using their own data, and then upload the local models, instead of data, to a logically centralized parameter server that synthesizes a global model.

Edge learning is a promising approach to enable collaborative learning over mobile devices while protecting data privacy. However, individual uses should contribute their data and consume their resources including wireless communication resources, computation resources, and battery when participating in the training process. Therefore, edge learning still faces a major challenge of how to incentivize individual devices to join the edge learning. Different from traditional incentive mechanisms, there are two main difficulties in edge learning. First, computing nodes do not share their decisions due to privacy concerns. Without the information of other nodes, it would be impossible for a participant to derive an optimal decision in a closed-form expression. Second, it is difficult to evaluate the contribution of participants to the accuracy of trained models. Evidence has shown that the relationship between model accuracy and the amount of training data is nonlinear, and this phenomenon is also illustrated in our preliminary experiments [385], as shown in Fig. 9.2.

On the other hand, the edge environment usually changes dynamically on many aspects - e.g., changing demands of users, and available resources - in which a statistical model cannot always satisfy the requirements. In order to adapt to the edge environment as well as the user requirements, the machine learning model usually is updated in real time. In many edge intelligence applications, using fresh data to update the machine learning model can provide services with high accuracy as the change of environment. For example, the recommendation services always prefer the latest

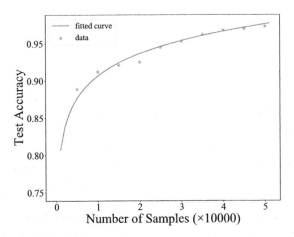

Figure 9.2 Test accuracy with varying the size of training data on MNIST dataset.

actions and scores submitted by users. It is difficult to design incentive mechanisms for edge learning systems with the consideration of the effect of fresh data.

In this section, we introduce a novel deep reinforcement learning-based incentive mechanism that integrates model updating using fresh data for edge learning [385]. In this scenario, a learning parameter server publishes an edge learning task with rewards dedicated to mobile devices participating in the learning process. The parameter server aims to minimize the total reward, while each participant aims to maximize its own profits, which are defined by the reward received from the parameter server minus the cost of data collection and model training. This optimization can be formulated as a Stackelberg game , and the objective is to derive the Nash equilibrium, which describes the steady state of the whole edge learning system. To address the challenges of unshared decisions and ambiguous contribution evaluation, a deep reinforcement learning based mechanism is employed to learn the system states from the historical training records. This algorithm is also adapted to dynamical environment by adjusting the strategies according to the environment changes - e.g, available resources - incremental data.

9.3.1   Problem Description

In this part, we briefly introduce the system model and problem formulation.

Edge learning is a promising distributed privacy-preserving machine learning technique that enables mobile edge devices to collaboratively train a shared global model without the need of uploading private local data to a central server. Assume that there are N mobile edge devices with local datasets $\{\mathcal{X}_1, \mathcal{X}_2, \ldots, \mathcal{X}_N\}$. Let x_n be the size of $\mathcal{X}_n$, and let ω be the machine learning model. The objective is to optimize the global loss function by minimizing the weighted average of every mobile device's local loss function on its local training samples; i.e.,

$$F(\omega) \triangleq \frac{\sum_{j \in \bigcup_n \mathcal{X}_n} f_j(\omega)}{|\bigcup_n \mathcal{X}_n|} = \frac{\sum_{n=1}^{N} x_n F_n(\omega)}{X}, \tag{9.1}$$

where $F(\omega)$ is the global loss function, $F_n(\omega)$ is the loss function on mobile device n, $f_j(\omega)$ is the loss function with respect to sample j, and $X = \sum_{n=1}^{N} x_n$ denotes the total number of samples.

Due to the inherent complexity of many machine learning models, it is impossible to find a closed-form solution of (9.1) for most learning problems. Gradient descent is a widely used algorithm to solve this problem. It runs in an iterative manner. In each iteration of gradient descent, each mobile device downloads a shared global model ω from the parameter server and trains the model using its local data. Then, mobile edge devices upload the new weights or gradients (i.e., local model update) to the parameter server that updates the global model.

9.3.2   System Model

We consider that there is a parameter server in the remote cloud, and it wants to incentivize a set $\mathcal{N} = \{1, 2, \ldots, N\}$ of mobile edge devices to participate in the edge learning. We assume that the edge learning system is in a quasi-static state, in which the mobile edge device will not join or leave the system.

The parameter server generates a training task by announcing a total reward $\tau > 0$; then each mobile edge device decides its training strategy based on the parameter server's reward. Without loss of generality, we assume that each mobile edge device $i \in \mathcal{N}$ maintains a dataset $\mathcal{D}_i$ and $\mathcal{D}_i \cap \mathcal{D}_j = \emptyset, \forall j \in \mathcal{N}, i \neq j$. If $\mathcal{D}_i = \emptyset$; mobile edge device i will not participate in the learning task. The training cost of mobile edge device i includes computational cost and communication cost, which are proportional to the amount of data used for local training. Let $c_{i,cmp}$ and $c_{i,com}$ indicate the unit computational cost amd communication cost, respectively. Assume that the training data in each mobile edge device has the same quality and is IID; then the reward of each mobile edge device i received from the parameter server is proportional to d_i. Thus, the utility of mobile edge device i is defined by

$$u_i(x_i) = \frac{x_i}{\sum_{i=1}^{N} x_i} \tau - c_{i,cmp} x_i - c_{i,com} x_i. \tag{9.2}$$

The data used for local training on each mobile edge device can help the learning task obtain a better model. Let $u(\tau)$ denote the utility of the parameter server, which indicates the gain of the model accuracy minus the total rewards paid to the edge devices. In Fig. 9.2, We show the model accuracy when varying the amount of training data. We observe that the model accuracy of machine learning model can be regarded as a concave function with respect to the size of training data. Therefore, the utility of parameter server is

$$u(\tau) = \lambda g(X) - \tau, \tag{9.3}$$

where $\lambda > 0$ is a system parameter, $g(d)$ is a concave function with respect to the size of training data, and $X = \sum_{i=1}^{N} x_i$.

The incentive mechanism for edge learning can be formulated as a Stackelberg game. There are two stages in the designed mechanism. In the first stage, the parameter server announces a total reward τ, followed by the second stage that each mobile edge device determines its training strategy to maximize its own utility. Hence, the paramter server is the leader and the mobile edge devices are the followers in the Stackelberg game. Game theory is a powerful framework to analyze the interactions among multiple players who act in their own interests, such that no player has the incentive to deviate unilaterally. Moreover, by using the intelligence of each player, game theory is a useful tool for designing decentralized mechanisms with low complexity, such that the players can self-organize into a mutually satisfactory solution. The strategy of parameter server and mobile edge devices are the reward τ and the size of training data x_i, respectively. The second stage of the incentive mechanism can be rewarded as a noncooperative game. For any reward τ and other mobile edge devices' decisions

x_{-i}, mobile edge device i would like to determine an optimal decision x_i to maximize its utility in terms of obtained reward and cost.

DEFINITION 9.1 (Nash Equilibrium)   **Nash Equilibrium:** *A set of strategies* $x^* = (x_1^*, x_2^*, \ldots, x_N^*)$ *is a Nash equilibrium of the second-stage game if for any mobile edge device i,*

$$u_i(x_i^*, x_{-i}*) \geq u_i(x_i, x_{-i}*),$$

for any $x_i \geq 0$.

The existence of the Nash equilibrium is important, since its strategy profile is stable whereas a non-Nash equilibrium is unstable.

9.3.3   Equilibrium Analysis

In this part, we first prove that, for any given τ, the second-stage game has a unique Nash equilibrium. For the parameter server in the first stage, it has a unique Stackelberg equilibrium.

9.3.3.1   Training Strategies of Mobile Edge Devices

To study the Nash equilibrium of the second-stage game in edge learning, we derive the first-order derivative of $u_i(x_i)$ with respect to x_i as

$$\frac{\partial u_i}{\partial x_i} = -\frac{\tau x_i}{\left(\sum_{i=1}^N x_i\right)^2} + \frac{\tau}{\sum_{i=1}^N x_i} - c_{i,cmp} - c_{i,com}. \tag{9.4}$$

Based on Eq. (9.4), we can derive the second-order derivative of u_i with respect to x_i as

$$\frac{\partial^2 u_i}{\partial x_i^2} = -\frac{2\tau \sum_{i \neq j} x_j}{\left(\sum_{j=1}^N x_j\right)^3} < 0.$$

LEMMA 9.1   *If the following conditions are satisfied, there exists a Nash equilibrium in the game [76].*

- *The player set is finite.*
- *The strategy sets are closed, bounded, and convex.*
- *The utility functions are continuous and quasi-concave in the strategy space.*

Based on Lemma 9.1, there exists a Nash equilibrium in the second-stage game. Setting $\frac{\partial u_i}{x_i} = 0$, we have

$$x_i = \sqrt{\frac{\tau \sum_{j \neq i} x_j}{c_{i,cmp} + c_{i,com}}} - \sum_{j \neq i} x_j. \tag{9.5}$$

If x_i in Eq. (9.5) is greater than 0, then mobile edge device i's best training strategy is x_i, or it will not participate in the edge learning. Further, if x_i in Eq. (9.5) is greater than d_i, then mobile edge device i executes the local model training with its best response by setting $x_i = d_i$. Therefore, we have

$$
x_i = \begin{cases}
0, if \ \tau \le (c_{i,cmp} + c_{i,com}) \sum_{j \ne i} x_j; \\[2mm]
\sqrt{\dfrac{\tau \sum_{j \ne i} x_j}{c_{i,cmp} + c_{i,com}}} - \sum_{j \ne i} x_j, x_i \in (0, d_i); \\[2mm]
d_i, otherwise.
\end{cases} \tag{9.6}
$$

THEOREM 9.1   *If all the mobile edge devices in $\mathcal{N}$, and $x_i < d_i$, then its optimal strategy is*

$$
x_i^* = \frac{(N-1)\tau}{\sum_{i \in \mathcal{N}} N(c_{i,cmp} + c_{i,com})} \left(1 - \frac{(M-1)(c_{i,cmp} + c_{i,com})}{\sum_i (c_{i,cmp} + c_{i,com})} \right). \tag{9.7}
$$

9.3.3.2   Parameter Server's Strategy Analysis

According to the analysis of mobile edge devices, the parameter sever knows there exists a unique Nash equilibrium among mobile edge devices under a given τ. Thus, the parameter server can maximize its utility by choosing the optimal τ according to mobile edge devices' training strategies. Plugging Eq. (9.7) into Eq. (9.3), we have

$$
u(\tau) = \lambda g \left(\sum_{i=1}^{N} x_i^* \right) - \tau. \tag{9.8}
$$

THEOREM 9.2 (Unique Stackelberg Equilibrium)   *There exists a unique Stackelberg equilibrium (τ^*, x^*), where τ^* is the unique solution to maximize the parameter server's utility.*

Proof   To prove that there exists a unique Stackelberg equilibrium that maximizes the utility of parameter server, we first derive the first-order derivative and second-order derivative of $u(\tau)$.

According to the formulation of $u(\tau)$ in (9.8), we have

$$
\frac{\partial u(\tau)}{\partial \tau} = \lambda g'(X) \frac{\partial X}{\partial \tau} - 1 = \lambda g'(X) \left(\frac{\partial x_1^*}{\partial \tau} + \frac{\partial x_2^*}{\partial \tau} + \cdots + \frac{\partial x_N^*}{\partial \tau} \right) - 1 \tag{9.9}
$$

$$
\frac{\partial^2 u(\tau)}{\partial \tau^2} = \lambda g''(X) \left(\frac{\partial x_1^*}{\partial \tau} + \frac{\partial x_2^*}{\partial \tau} + \cdots + \frac{\partial x_M^*}{\partial \tau} \right)^2 \tag{9.10}
$$

$$
+ \lambda g'(X) \left(\frac{\partial^2 x_1^*}{\partial \tau^2} + \frac{\partial^2 x_2^*}{\partial \tau^2} + \cdots + \frac{\partial^2 x_M^*}{\partial \tau^2} \right) \tag{9.11}
$$

$$
= \lambda g''(X) \left(\sum_{n=1}^{M} \frac{(M-1)}{\sum_{m \in \mathcal{M}} (c_m^{com} + c_m^{cmp})} \left(1 - \frac{(M-1) \left(c_n^{com} + c_n^{cmp} \right)}{\sum_{m \in \mathcal{M}} \left(c_m^{com} + c_m^{cmp} \right)} \right) \right)^2. \tag{9.12}
$$

We have $\frac{\partial^2 u(\tau)}{\partial \tau^2} < 0$ because $g(X)$ is a concave function of X. Therefore, the utility of the parameter server is a strictly concave function of τ for $\tau \geq 0$. Since $u(0) = 0$ and $u(\tau)$ goes to $-\infty$ with $\tau \to \infty$, there exists a unique Stackelberg equilibrium . The proof is completed.   □

9.3.4   A Deep Reinforcement Learning-Based Incentive Mechanism

In this section, we introduce the deep reinforcement learning-based incentive mechanism in edge learning. We first introduce the core idea of applying deep reinforcement learning in the incentive mechanism design in edge learning. Then, we describe the detailed design of deep reinforcement learning and show how the deep reinforcement learning-based mechanism determines the optimal strategies for the parameter and mobile devices.

Deep reinforcement learning aims to learn a general action decision from the past experiences based on the current state and the given reward. The process of deep reinforcement learning-based incentive mechanism is illustrated as follows. The parameter server as a leader who interacts with the environment in the deep reinforcement learning setting. At each training period t, the parameter server agent observes a state s_t and determines an action $\tau - t$. When this action is done, mobile edge devices interact with each other to determine their optimal participation level strategies. Since each mobile edge device does not know any information about decisions of other mobile edge devices, all devices need to learn the optimal strategy. We can use an offline mode to train the mobile edge devices. All the mobile edge devices interact with each other in a noncooperative game simulation environment to learn the Nash equilibrium. After each mobile edge device learn the Nash equilibrium, they update the model based on their local data and upload the updated model to the parameter server. The tth training period ends now. Then the current state transits to the next state s_{t+1}, and the parameter server agent receives a reward r_t. If the parameter server agent continues this process, it gets accumulated rewards after every action until the process is done. The objective of deep reinforcement learning is to find an optimal policy π mapping a state to an action that maximizes the expected discounted accumulated reward.

Then we describe how to map the optimization problem of the Stackelberg game into the deep reinforcement learning setting. Our deep reinforcement learning-based incentive mechanism uses an actor-critic deep reinforcement learning model. The key settings are summarized as follows.

- **State space of the parameter server.** The parameter server needs to train a machine learning model periodically. The parameter server can only observe the past strategies of mobile edge devices. Hence, the state space of the parameter server's deep reinforcement learning formulation consists of two components: its past payment strategy history $\{\tau_{t-L}, \tau_{t-L+1}, \ldots, \tau_{k-1}\}$ and participation level history of mobile edge devices $\{x_{t-L}, x_{t-L+1}, \ldots, x_{t-1}\}$.
- **State space of the mobile devices.** According to the previous formulation, the training strategies of mobile edge devices are affected by all the nodes' private

information and the parameter server's payment strategy. But for each mobile edge device, it could observe the history of other mobile edge devices' training strategies and current parameter server's payment. Therefore, the state input of mobile edge device n is $s_{t,k}^n = \{x_{-n}^{t,k-L}, x_{-n}^{t,k-L+1}, \ldots, x_{-n}^{t,k-1}, \tau^t\}$.

- **Policy of the parameter server.** According to the previous description, the action space can be represented as $\tau_t \in [0, +\infty)$. However, the action space of the parameter server agent is continuous, and there are infinite policy to be selected. To simplify this problem, we use the neural network to represent the policy, and the policy of the parameter server can be formulated as $\pi(\tau_t \mid s_t, \theta) \to [0, \infty)$.

- **Policies of the mobile devices.** Since the action space of each mobile edge device is also continuous, the neural network is also used to represent the policy $\pi_n(x_{t,k}^n \mid s_{t,k}^n, \theta_n) \to [0, \infty)$. Mobile edge devices continuously learn until they reach the Nash equilibrium under the current parameter server's payment strategy.

- **Reward of the parameter server.** According to (9.1), we define the reward r_t as the utility function of the parameter server in the tth training period, which satisfies $r_t = u(\tau_t)$.

- **Reward of the mobile devices.** In the tth training period, at the kth game, each mobile edge device determines a training strategy, which can be formulated as $r_{t,k}^n = u_n(x_{t,k}^n, x_{t,k}^{-n}, \tau_t)$.

The training process of parameter server agent and mobile edge device agent employs the state-of-the-art policy optimization approach, proximal policy optimization (PPO). Once the actor-critic network is trained, parameter server and mobile edge devices can determine their own strategies based on the output of their actor networks.

9.4   Conclusion and Future Directions

In this chapter, we introduce the incentive mechanism for edge learning. Though the edge learning has the advantage of data privacy, it is not clear how the incentive mechanism impacts on the utility of the parameter server. We address this issue by providing an incentive mechanism based on the Stackelberg game approach. First, we analyze the uniqueness of the Nash equilibrium in the second stage of the Stackelberg game and the uniqueness of the Stackelberg equilibrium in the first stage. Second, due to the unique challenges of unshared information and difficulties of contribution evaluation in edge learning, we propose the deep reinforcement learning-based incentive mechanism to address these issues.

Although incentive mechanisms for edge learning focus on how to motivate a large number of clients to participate to break the limitation of data in forms of isolated islands and guarantee learning performance, it still faces several research challenges including security issues, data assessment, and heterogeneous computational resource allocation. In what follows, we summarize the challenges and potential research directions in the future.

Security issues. Even though there are many works focusing on the incentive mechanism design for edge learning, they do not consider one of the critical issues: security. Considering a situation in which mobile edge devices may have malicious behaviors during edge learning. The edge learning system is vulnerable to be attacked, which will seriously degrade system performance. In order to keep a benign ecological environment for the edge learning system, the incentive mechanism can be applied. With incentive mechanism, the malicious mobile edge devices can be punished, thus reducing their probability of doing harm. This is a new but very important direction, and we believe that this is a very promising direction.

Data assessment. Given a set of clients with their own training data, how can the value of each client's data be evaluated so that the rewards are fairly distributed among the clients? In edge learning, each client collects the training data by itself. There is no doubt that data quality in different clients cannot be guaranteed. Consider a scenario of edge learning where client A has low-quality training data and client B has high-quality training data. In this case, it is obvious that with the same amount of training data, A's contribution for the edge learning model is higher than B. Therefore, it is unfair to give A and B the same reward. Therefore, it is important to evaluate the value of each clients' training data, which will directly impact the incentive mechanism design for edge learning.

Heterogeneous computational resource allocation. Suppose that each client has already prepared the data for local model training; however, training synchronization is also a critical problem. Edge learning consists of clients training local models in parallel in order to wait for the slowest client in each training round. The learning processes are often very slow - i.e., they suffer from the effect of straggler. It is crucial to optimize the computational resource allocation to different clients in such a heterogeneous environment. Furthermore, each client has limited computational resources, and all the running applications share the same resources. An incentive to motivate the rational clients is necessary.

The computational resource allocation problem can be even more challenging as more realistic factors are taken into consideration. First, there exists information asymmetry between the parameter server and clients since clients have more private information. Second, the communication time of each client also affects edge learning. Therefore, the parameter server also needs to consider the communication time in the incentive mechanism design. At the same time, the network quality of each client varies over time, which makes the incentive mechanism design in dynamic environment more complex.

10 Edge Learning Applications

Big data and AI are technologies that enable smart decision making, automation, and resource optimization. These technologies collectively promote intelligent services from concepts to practical applications. It is widely recognized that intelligent services facilitate the strategic development of emerging industries while enriching people's lifestyles with convenience and efficiency. This chapter introduces the popular programming frameworks for edge learning. We give some examples of emerging intelligent applications in the edge - e.g., smart healthcare, self-driving vehicles, smart surveillance, and smart transportation. Finally, we introduce an example of an edge intelligence application: the Dr.Body system for posture detection and rehabilitation tracking.

10.1 APIs, Libraries, and Platforms for Edge Learning

Basically, the workflow of the edge learning applications can be divided into the stages of a linear transformation, activation function, backward propagation, gradient optimization, etc. The corresponding algorithms of these stages can be packaged into independent modules to separate their functions from the programming. Therefore, large-scale edge learning frameworks can be built based on these modules to handle the deployment of real-world machine learning tasks and meet different kinds of requirements. Some common methodologies can be further abstracted into uniform application program interfaces (APIs) to simplify the implementation of various learning algorithms. Building the edge learning frameworks can help researchers and developers quickly evaluate their methods, promoting the research prototypes into production deployment. Overall, we will discuss the common machine learning frameworks, APIs, and libraries to build edge learning platforms.

10.1.1 General Programming Frameworks for Machine Learning

10.1.1.1 PyTorch

PyTorch (https://pytorch.org/) is a deep learning framework developed by Facebook. It stems from the project of Torch and uses Python as the programming language. PyTorch is an efficient developing software to define the core functions of building a model training procedure. For example, it provides the abstraction of tensors, layers, activations, loss functions, gradient optimizers, high-order partial derivatives, etc. This ensures PyTorch can handle the matrix operations and derivative chain rules effectively.

As to the model training in a distributed manner, PyTorch also provides good compatibility of parallel and heterogeneous computing. One can handle the distributed training via multiple GPUs and CPUs while not changing the programming logic. Also, we can use the multiprocessing library to fully exploit the processing capacity of multiple computation primitives. This property has been well embedded into the CuDNN library for learning in GPU-based clusters. In order to improve the communication efficiency, which often becomes the bottleneck of system performance, PyTorch provides the collective communication APIs based on NCCL (`https://developer.nvidia.com/nccl`) and MPI (`https://www.open-mpi.org/`) libraries.

Also, PyTorch provides the open neural network exchange format (ONMX) to export the neuron weights and network structures into the file format in order to interact with other machine learning frameworks to build complex learning applications. For example, ONMX supports the RNN, and it is possible to conduct inference for the time-series applications.

Besides, PyTorch employs the just-In-time (JIT) compiler to trace the variables and function stacks during the training runtime. PyTorch can compile the dynamic computation graphs into the static ones, so as to optimize the operation dependency for easy deployment. As the underlying implementation of PyTorch is based on the C++ library, it is possible to convert the PyTorch models to the format for other execution environments.

Recently, PyTorch has supported the learning scenarios on mobile devices, which is called the PyTorch Mobile (`https://pytorch.org/mobile/home/`). It provides an end-to-end solution to deploy the learning tasks for iOS and Android devices. We can get a seamless workflow from training to deployment within the same programming environment entirely. This property simplifies the development of on-device learning and protects the privacy for federated learning, which are important techniques to implement edge intelligence.

10.1.1.2   TensorFlow

TensorFlow (`https://www.tensorflow.org/`) is also a popular machine learning framework to develop and training machine learning models in various environments, including JavaScript, mobile phones, IoT devices, and domain-specific hardware. In realistic training, data are often organized in the format of high-dimensional matrices, which are called tensors. The name of TensorFlow indicates that the gist of its model training is to handle the dataflows inside the computation graphs. The execution engine transfers the learning tasks into the dataflows from one stage to the next. A stage is marked by the computational functions and local variables. The flows point out the operation dependency during the training procedure. Therefore, all the iterative optimization and task scheduling are handled based on these dataflows.

The dataflow characteristics inside TensorFlow provide good compatibility for the machine learning applications and are especially suitable to the iterative training pattern. Developers can build different machine learning models by using programming-friendly modular interfaces. Basically, an machine learning task is handled by the `Session` object, and the system will schedule all the sessions with proper resource assignment during the training runtime. All the initialization, suspension, resumption, and termination of machine learning tasks are controlled by the session manager.

The execution process of an machine learning task can be resolved into three modules: (1) the client, (2) the master, and (3) the worker. Basically, the client controls the initialization of a task, providing the interaction between the session and the master. The system will get the task runtime information via the client, including the resource requirements and training progress. Then, the master assigns the task with suitable resources and returns the computational results to the client. The master is an execution engine that optimizes the task scheduling according to the dependency of the dataflow graph. Finally, the worker is the workspace for different kinds of matrix operations, gradients, and derivatives. It receives the operator from the master and sends the intermediate results to the master.

Moreover, the recently developed TensorFlow Lite (`https://www.tensor flow.org/lite`) is a powerful lightweight machine learning framework that handles the model training and deployment entirely on the user end. It is specially designed for mobile and IoT devices. As all the operations and data are reserved on user devices, it provides good protection for user privacy. Also, TensorFlow Lite supports the transfer learning and quantization-aware training techniques, which can significantly reduce the memory footprint and computational overhead. This property makes TensorFlow Lite is a promising tool to build edge intelligence applications in the resource-constrained environment.

10.1.1.3 Apple Core ML

Apple Core ML (`https://developer.apple.com/machine-learning/ core-ml/`) is an on-device learning framework optimized for modern machine learning applications, supporting various models by exploiting Apple's neural chips. It aims to accelerate the learning performance while minimizing the memory footprint and energy consumption of the devices.

Core ML was first released with the iOS 11 system to provide machine learning frameworks for building the learning applications directly on iOS devices. It provides uniform APIs for creating the models of vision, neural language, speech, and sound analysis, with the underlying support of Apple hardware, Metal shaders (`https://developer.apple.com/metal/`), dedicated accelerators, and BNNs. Based on Core ML, it is possible to extract intelligent features from the on-device data. For example, we can recognize the dominant object in the photo via the user's camera. Starting at version of iOS 13, the latest Core ML 3 supports the model training on mobile phones. This unlocks a promising way to completely handle the end-to-end learning procedure on user devices, making the personalized model training possible for people's daily life.

Basically, there are two fundamental components to build the Core ML-based applications. The first the `mlmodel` file, which is an open file format storing the model structure and parameters. The second is the `CoreML` APIs, which interact with the model file to build different kinds of machine learning applications to support the environment of iOS, tvOS, watchOS, and macOS. The Core ML framework has the following advantages for on-device learning implementation:

- Core ML provides the programming-friendly APIs that can help developers quickly evaluate their ideas, enabling them to transfer the codes from research prototypes into production deployment.
- Core ML can run customized models on different kinds of computational environments - e.g., CPUs, GPUs, neural engines, and domain-specific hardware provided by the user's device. The capability of deploying on heterogeneous primitives can bring the optimized utilization of hardware resource utilization. For example, we can divide the model into different parts and assign the operations to these submodels in parallel. The computation-intensive parts can be deployed on neural engines, while the parts of workflow controlling can be handled by common CPUs.
- Core ML can be executed on both realistic devices and iOS simulators, which provides elastic developing tools to evaluate the learning performance on different devices. The machine learning applications built on mobile phones can be easily transferred to other systems, including watches, laptops, and televisions.
- Core ML can accelerate the processing speed of matrix operations, which often dominate the calculation during the model training and inference. By using the neural engine on iOS devices with the Apple A-series chips, it is possible to entirely handle the resource-hungry computation on user's mobile phones. For example, we can detect the user's feelings by analyzing the faces captured by the front-facing camera directly.

Overall, Apple Core ML is a powerful machine learning framework to build various on-device learning applications for mobile and edge devices.

10.1.1.4 Webank FATE

Considering the challenges of privacy leakage and distributed collaboration in edge intelligence applications, federated learning is a promising method to address these issues. Basically, federated learning aims to train a distributed model without exposing the user privacy or intensive information. The trained model can be shared across multiple participants. Therefore, it comes to the federated learning frameworks designed for this kind of training. In general, designing a high-performance federated learning framework needs to consider the following characteristics of federated learning applications.

First, there are often massive amount (thousands) of clients/workers in a federated learning cluster. These clients work together to finish the training of the global model. Each client holds a great amount personalized data for training the local model. The federated learning server collects all the local models and merges them as the global model. The global model will be assigned to the clients again, and future training will be conducted based on it. Note that the global model will keep updating until the convergence.

Second, although each client only holds a small-scale amount of data for local training, the global model is still established by aggregating plenty of local models from different clients. Therefore, the global model can learn rich knowledge from the local models, which extract various useful features from the local data. This property can avoid the over-fitting of the global model and maintain high training accuracy.

Third, all the local data of a client will not be exposed to other clients or servers, in order to protect user privacy during the training process. Regarding the aggregation of local models, the intensive information of model features can be encrypted for secure data exchanging. This encryption communication pattern ensures the primary data or model parameters will not be eavesdropped via attackers or malicious clients. Overall, the large-scale clients, model aggregation, and privacy protection are all crucial issues that significantly impact the effectiveness of federated learning frameworks.

In real-world implementations, one of the most famous federated learning platforms is the open-source Webank FATE framework (`https://fate.fedai.org/`), which is established by the AI Department of Webank. It supports common federated learning algorithms and provides secure computation for user devices. Based on the modular design of a scalable modeling pipeline, clear visual interface, and flexible scheduling management, FATE provides easy-to-use programming interfaces and an elastic learning library. Therefore, FATE is a high-performance federated learning platform to build edge intelligence applications. There are also other federated learning platforms that provide competitive performance, including Tencent AngelFL and TensorFlow Federated platforms (`https://www.tensorflow.org/federated`).

10.2 Application Scenarios

Edge learning can make use of massive scattered data to construct edge intelligent models, which have a wide application prospect in many fields, such as smart transportation , smart healthcare, smart grid, intelligent financial risk control [312–314, 381]. In this section, we introduce several potential application scenarios that can be implemented by using edge learning technology.

10.2.1 Smart Transportation

At the end of the last century, with the rapid development of social economy, science and technology, the level of urbanization and the number of motor vehicles are increasing rapidly. Traffic congestion, traffic accident rescue, traffic management, environmental pollution, energy shortages, and other issues have become common problems faced by all countries in the world. Smart transportation make full use of the IoT, cloud computing, edge computing, AI, automatic control, wireless communication, and other technologies in the field of transportation to alleviate these issues. It collects traffic information through new technologies to control and support all aspects of traffic management, transportation, public travel, and traffic construction management, to further expand transportation systems throughout cities and metropolitan areas. The large space-time range has the ability of perception, interconnection, analysis, prediction, and control. The main objectives are to fully guarantee traffic safety, increase the efficiency of transportation infrastructure, improve the operation efficiency and management level of transportation systems, ensure smooth public travel, and promote sustainable economic development.

The smart transportation system mainly solves the application requirements in the following four aspects:

- Real-time traffic monitoring. Using AI and big data analytic technologies, smart transportation monitors and predicts the locations of traffic accidents, traffic congestion, and fastest (unblocked) routes. The system will then provide this useful information to drivers and traffic management personnel.
- Public vehicle management. The two-way communication between drivers and dispatching management center improves the operation efficiency of commercial vehicles, buses, and taxis.
- Travel information service. Through multimedia and multiterminal, it can provide comprehensive traffic information to travelers.
- Vehicle auxiliary control. This feature uses real-time data to assist the driver or replace the driver's autopilot.

Data is the foundation of intelligent transportation. All of the aforementioned applications are based on real-time acquisition and analysis of massive amounts of data, including location information, traffic flow, speed, occupancy, queue length, travel time, interval speed as the most important traffic data. This information comes from a large number of sensors, cameras, and various applications. In [160], the authors propose to use heterogeneous unmanned vehicles for urban environment monitoring, which is a critical problem for smart transportation and smart cities. The vehicles include ground vehicles, air vehicles (also called drones), and water vehicles (also called unmanned boats), which can cover almost all areas within a city. Ground vehicles are powered by fuel or large batteries so that they can monitor streets for long periods of time. Air vehicles have limited energy but better moving capabilities and they are preferred for the monitoring of larger areas. Water vehicles can work in rivers and lakes to perform tasks like water pollution monitoring. These heterogeneous vehicles can work collaboratively to achieve large-scale and comprehensive urban environmental monitoring. However, in a smart transportation scenario, operating big data analytics only in the cloud cannot meet these requirements. Therefore, it is urgent to shift computing from cloud to edge. Besides, these data have various characteristics - including unstructured, quasistructured, and semistructured data - where the inherent scale, distribution, diversity, and velocity require huge computation overhead. Since the resources (e.g., battery power, CPU cycles, memory, and I/O data rate) of edge user devices are limited, this data cannot be processed via traditional mathematical methods due to a variety of drawbacks, such as severe delays, high costs, low accuracy, privacy leakages, etc. Fortunately, machine learning has been a promising technique to solve the previously discussed challenges. Thus, a smart transportation platform that controls transportation traffic in a highly efficient manner and promotes transportation safety in urban areas can be designed and implemented.

Existing centralized cloud-based approaches have not yet explored the great portion of data stored on edge devices - e.g., a large number of sensors in IoT, which can miss important and valuable information. The edge learning-based approach can leverage the computation capabilities of edge devices to fully exploit the data on edge devices, and hence, the developers of intelligent applications can build models by using sufficient data on both the cloud and the edge. The smart transportation application is a promising use case for the near future. Another important issue in the smart transportation system is data privacy and security protection. For example, the location information and surveillance videos gathered by developers from edge devices might cause privacy leakage issues, which have happened multiple times and caused severe consequences in the past few years. In this case, learning on edge without moving data to the cloud can significantly mitigate this issue. With the high level of security of data resources and user privacy, the platform can satisfy the strict requirements of modern machine learning applications. Moreover, by employing edge learning, the smart transportation system can provide a better quality of experience for users and offer promising application value for the industry.

With the support of sufficient computing resources in edge devices and the coordination of the cloud, any requirement of model construction can be satisfied. This is far more important in many domains. Consider autonomous vehicles as an example where all the vehicles need to learn the environment changes in real time. When there is a large number of vehicles, this process can incur a huge computational cost, and the cloud cannot afford it. While learning with the computing resource at the edge, this issue of insufficient computing resources of the cloud can be solved de-facto. In this way, the data producer does not need to transfer the data to the remote cloud as well but the rich data can still be utilized.

In Fig. 10.1, we give an example of a smart transportation system. The data sources are private vehicles and public road supervision devices. This data can be used to improve the efficiency of the public transportation system in urban areas. There are three promising aspects of smart transportation that can benefit from the platform: (1) the prediction of vehicle traffic, (2) the control of traffic lights, and (3) the detection of traffic accidents.

First, regarding the prediction of vehicle traffic, the purpose is to analyze the traffic patterns among different roads, intersections, and districts, so as to capture the global traffic patterns in a certain area. As shown in Fig. 10.1, a smart transportation platform can achieve flexible control and scheduling via integration with AI. The traffic patterns can be formulated as graph flows and use the graph computing technology to figure out which edges or vertices may become congested in the transportation system. Besides, we can dynamically adjust the road traffic scheduling strategy by controlling the traffic lights, so as to maximize the utilization of roads and alleviate potential traffic jams.

1) the prediction of vehicle traffic

2) the control of traffic lights   3) the detection of traffic accidents

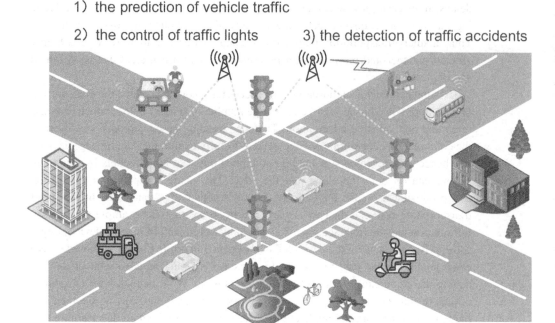

Figure 10.1 Illustration of smart transportation platform.

Instead of making a static scheduling strategy in advance, we intend to use the meta-learning technology to make the edge devices (e.g., the computation units in traffic lights) be able to determine the proper scheduling strategy automatically. This can effectively reduce the computation complexity because the devices do not need to consider all the traffic factors in advance. Also, this technology can make the edge device dynamically adjust the scheduling strategy, so as to adapt to the real-time transportation conditions since the surrounding circumstance may change quickly. Finally, detecting traffic accidents is also a crucial issue, as we need to cope with problems arising from the accidents and store the affected areas from failure to normal in time, which can be shown in Fig. 10.1. This requires our approach to respond promptly to the real-time images or videos collected from edge devices, such as monitors, radar chronographs, and other sensors. Features of traffic accidents can be recognized by the use of deep learning models like RNNs to capture the time-sequence-based characteristics and figure out the models.

Based on the three preceding pertinent application scenarios, by leveraging edge learning techniques, the learning component can be deployed in both vehicles and supervision devices. When a learning job is submitted, the vehicles calculate models locally with privacy protection while supervision devices calculate models with the assistance of edge servers, so as to accelerate the learning process. With the coordination of the cloud, the learning result can be aggregated such that all data from different sources can be fully utilized. Therefore, the preceding example of smart transportation is a data-driven platform with a series of integrated algorithms that provide a theoretical guarantee of system performance, which can process large-scale real-time data and holistically manage public resources by instantly detecting defects and promoting suitable operations in urban areas.

10.2.2   Smart Healthcare

With the development of AI and communication technology, the concept of smart healthcare has gradually come to the fore. Smart healthcare uses a new generation of information technologies - such as the IoT, big data, cloud, and edge computing, and AI - to transform the traditional medical system in an all-round way, making healthcare more efficient, more convenient, and more personalized.

AI will revolutionize the healthcare industry. As reported by Google Health, it has developed an AI program that is better at spotting breast cancer in mammograms than expert radiologists. In the COVID-19 pandemic, machine learning has been used to help the industry cope with sudden high patient volumes, connecting patients with reported data, diagnose and detect illnesses, and make general processes more efficient. One company even uses machine learning to detect disease outbreaks and was among the first organizations to alert the public about the respiratory virus in Wuhan. Beyond incredible practical uses, machine learning is also cost effective for healthcare – one report suggests that machine learning applications will save $150 billion annually for the US healthcare economy by 2026.

One of the most important applications in smart healthcare is assisting diagnosis and treatment. With the application of technologies such as AI, IoT, and medical cyber-physical systems, the diagnosis and treatment of diseases has become more intelligent. Among various approaches, medical cyber-physical systems that enable seamless and intelligent interaction between the computational elements and the medical devices is one of the enabling technologies for smart healthcare. Traditional medical cyber-physical systems rely on cloud resources to process the sensing data from medical devices, which will cause an intolerable delay. In [80], the authors propose integrating fog computation and medical cyber-physical systems to build a distributed medical data analytics platform in an edge environment.

In Fig. 10.2, we give an example of a smart healthcare application. Edge-based deployment of edge analytics and performance control applications support the creation of smart patient-monitoring systems, increase patient outcomes, and reduce healthcare staff workload. Smart healthcare should be adapted to different diseases of different persons (i.e., Fig. 10.2). In the construction of the model, two factors need to be considered: (1) model personalization: the model should be customized to fit the features (e.g., sex, age, race, etc.) of different patients; (2) model evolution: the model should evolve according to the changes of personal status and environment. Energy consumption is another challenge in smart healthcare. To enable green mobile AI chips via precision-aware computation, the NPU will be used

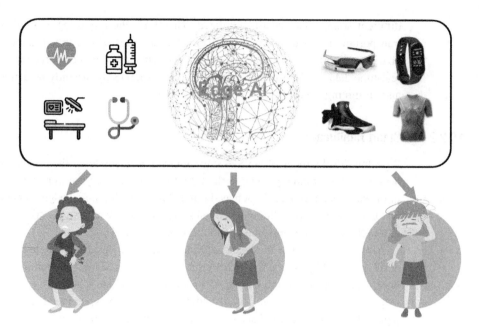

Figure 10.2 An example of edge-based healthcare application.

for AI-powered healthcare applications because of its fast speed and lower power consumption.

10.2.3   Intelligent Blockchain + Edge AI

Blockchain originated from Bitcoin, which was proposed in 2008 [210, 390, 404]. It is a technology that establishes a credible, transparent, complete, and tamper-proof distributed ledger between distrusting groups. It is a promising solution to security and privacy issues in distributed systems and has become an important supporting technology to promote new applications and industrial development for financial services, supply chain management, and credit investigation. In recent years, it has received extensive attention from the government and enterprises.

Blockchain organically integrates a variety of technologies such as distributed storage, point-to-point transmission, encryption mechanisms, consensus algorithms, etc., which can be used in digital currency, transaction records, identity authentication, and trusted storage. However, the existing blockchain system has low service quality, and limited service scope, and the resources are mainly concentrated in the backbone network. For example, in the Bitcoin system, about seven transactions are processed per second, the transaction confirmation delay is one hour, and all nodes are generally located in the Internet cloud. With the popularity of the IoT and mobile computing, the number of mobile terminals has increased exponentially and the massive amount of data generated by them is stored on a large number of edge nodes. Massive terminal devices at the edge of the network will gradually become the main service body and

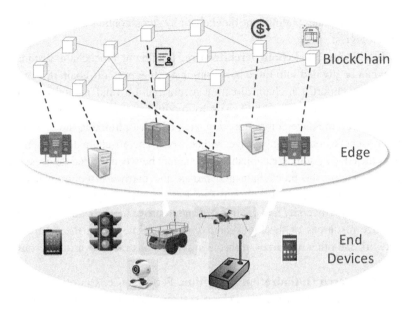

Figure 10.3 An example of edge-based Blockchain.

computing bearer of blockchain applications. According to Cisco's IoT forecast, there will be 500 billion terminal devices connected to the Internet in 2030, so the existing blockchain system cannot meet the application needs of edge scenarios. It is essential to achieve intelligent blockchain-based on edge learning (i.e., the architecture of an intelligent blockchain system can be illustrated in Fig. 10.3.).

Edge computing is based on the idea of making full use of edge computing, storage, and communication resources closer to terminal devices, effectively alleviating the pressure of data center, eliminating communication bottlenecks, and improving the quality of service. The decentralization concept of blockchain fits the edge computing architecture, and its distributed and credible features provide new solutions for the application design on the edge computing framework. Because there are a large number of service applications based on group decision making and interactive collaborative computing in the edge, the use of blockchain can ensure the privacy of service data, verifiable results, and tamper-proof. With the development of the edge computing paradigm and its enabling technologies, and the increasingly abundant edge device resources, new opportunities arise for building a blockchain system oriented to the edge environment.

Aiming to achieve a high-performance, high-reliability, and high-scalability intelligent blockchain system, it is of great importance to reconstruct the blockchain architecture and use edge resources to achieve the ternary integration and optimization of the performance, security, and scalability of the blockchain system. Furthermore, how to achieve the combination of software and hardware in the blockchain and how to design demo applications on the basis of architecture, theory, and implementation are also crucial issues. Intelligent blockchain systems contain the following three main technologies:

Intelligent Blockchain Architecture. Intelligent blockchain system reconstruction can be divided into three parts: on-chain direction, off-chain direction, and edge resource support. On-chain direction reconstruction fundamentally reconstructs the internal operation of the blockchain by modifying the consensus algorithm, storage mechanism, message communication, etc., and by optimizing the system in regard to three aspects: computing, storage, and network. The off-chain direction reconstruction uses the edge system to establish a fast channel between the end devices. It can reduce the burden on the blockchain and reduce the hardware requirements for terminal devices when using blockchain services. Edge resource support solves the problems of infrastructure diversity and complexity and improve the utilization ratio and efficiency of edge resources of the blockchain system by integrating the computing, storage, network and other resources of the edge system, abstracting various resource interface models.

AI-Powered Optimization Algorithm. Performance, security, and scalability are three main metrics in the blockchain system. They are independent of one another. The internal parameters of the blockchain system should be dynamically adjusted based on different service requirements and edge environments, providing a dynamic trade-off between performance, security, and scalability. At the same time, limited by the distribution, dynamics, and diversity of edge resources, the complexity of providing coordinated scheduling of computing, storage, and network resources for blockchain systems by edge computing has been increased. The interaction mechanism and internal trade-offs between performance, security, and scalability in the blockchain system will be studied, and a multi-objective evaluation system will be established. Based on the theoretical analysis on the intelligent blockchain architecture, we can use AI-powered algorithms to optimize the blockchain architecture, and finally realize a scalable, adaptive, and intelligent blockchain system.

Combination of Hardware-Software Implementation. Considering the characteristics of blockchain software and multiple types of hardware resources in the edge, the combination of software and hardware implementation is studied from three perspectives: (1) From the perspective of the trusted execution environment in the processor, we can use the trusted execution environment to protect the confidentiality and integrity of the execution code of security-sensitive functions. (2) From the perspective of resource-constrained hardware, we can design a blockchain microservice mechanism that is aware of edge hardware resources. (3) In terms of AI hardware resources, we can use edge AI hardware resources to improve the efficiency of the training and inference of the AI-powered blockchain.

10.2.4   Intelligent Financial Risk Control

While financial technology promotes the transformation and upgrading of the financial industry, it also brings a variety of new financial risks. For example, the risks of fraudulent loans, runaways, and cash-out refinances in the financial industry have successively surfaced, and nonperforming loan incidents happen frequently. Traditional financial risk control is faced with a single source of credit data, a large number of user applications, and partnership fraud problems.

With the continuous development of the financial industry, machine learning models are widely used in financial risk control. However, the analysis and application of financial big data are faced with the characteristics of large and diverse data sources and heterogeneous resource modes of nodes. The challenges in intelligent risk control are summarized as follows:

- **Privacy data exposure.** In order to improve the accuracy of an intelligent risk control model, a large amount of data is needed. However, some companies maliciously obtain the sensitive data of users by illegal means, resulting in negative social impacts. At present, the regulatory requirements for the compliance of intelligent risk control are becoming stricter and stricter. How to protect the security and privacy of personal data is the key problem to be solved.

- **Attack oriented to the AI model of financial risk control.** At present, the training cycle of the intelligent risk control model is long. Attackers can detect the tendency of the model through illegal ways, and can combine a large number of fraud attacks that can pass automatic approval in a short time, which makes financial institutions suffer heavy losses. In addition, a large number of nodes are required to participate in the training of the intelligent risk control model based on collaborative training frameworks such as federated learning. Malicious nodes can attack the training process, resulting in the inaccuracy of the risk control model.

- **Low efficiency in financial data processing.** Mass data processing efficiency is low. The real-time processing of massive amounts of complex data in intelligent risk control is a major difficulty. The anti-fraud information owned by financial enterprises has reached the level of billions of entities, and the existing technology has difficulties meeting the requirements of real-time processing. On the other hand, due to the diversity of sample sources and incomplete sample data of individual users, the efficiency of data processing is more challenging.

- **High complexity in model training and inference.** The core of intelligent risk control uses machine learning training model. The whole training process is very complex. Based on the traditional deep learning model, there are a lot of structures and parameters to be adjusted, and the threshold is very high. Financial institutions, especially small and medium-sized financial institutions, lack the human resources required to implement intelligent risk control.

Aiming to solve the pain points faced by traditional financial risk control industry such as the single source of credit data, high level of risk, the large number of user applications, and group fraud. In Fig. 10.4, we present an intelligent risk control system for risk perception, risk identification, and strategic intelligent recommendations. Intelligent risk control is a major innovation in both the technology and application of financial risk control. A variety of new technologies such as AI, big data, and cloud computing are integrated and applied to the risk control process, which emphasizes self-learning, self-optimization, and self-iteration of the system to accurately identify

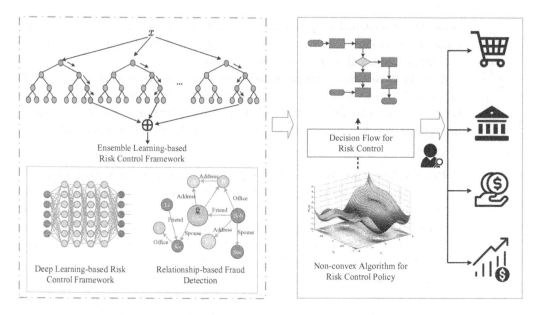

Figure 10.4 An example of intelligent risk control system.

risks. In terms of application, person-centred risk control has shifted to customer-centered risk control, which emphasizes data-driven control, reduces risk control costs, and improves user experience.

10.2.5   Edge AI + IoT

Trillions of IoT devices will be connected to the network to promote social production and human activities towards information, intelligence, and efficiency. According to Gartner, an IT market analysis agency, the number of global IoT will reach 25 billion by 2021, which will greatly improve the interconnection and innovation of the digital world. In the future, the development trend of the IoT will focus on smart cities; ecological livability; intelligent production; living, and other applications, and will move in important directions such as cross-domain interoperability and collaboration, high levels of adaptiveness and scalability.

At present, the development of the IoT is still in the early stage of applications and exploration. Most applications are limited to specific fields and to closed-loop application scenarios in local time and space. Large-scale IoT applications are faced with interoperability barriers, local resource imbalances, and high application costs. Furthermore, IoT platforms are often based on embedded lightweight devices with limited communication and computing capabilities, which limits the development and implementation of large-scale IoT to a certain extent. Although computation offloading through remote cloud service centers can reduce the computational overhead of IoT devices, the transmission of massive amounts of IoT data requires a large amount of communication bandwidth resources. However, there are often long

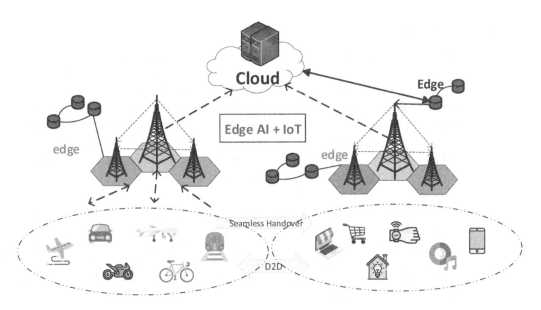

Figure 10.5 An example of edge-based IoT framework.

communication links between data centers and IoT devices, resulting in high defects such as communication delay and slow response time, which in turn affect the service quality of IoT applications.

The emergence of edge computing technology overcomes the conflict between the limitations of terminal equipment resources and the high response delay of cloud computing centers in large-scale IoT applications. Placing computing resources on edge devices/grids adjacent to the terminal business space not only splits the computing and communication tasks of IoT terminals but also greatly diminishes service delay, provides localization management, and ultimately improves service quality.

Although researchers around the world have conducted research on the IoT, edge computing, AI and other fields, large-scale research on the IoT empowered by edge learning is still in a blank stage. The large-scale AI-based IoT covers the intelligent management and the control of networks and data in the networks. At the same time, it needs to adapt to the diverse intelligent applications and perceptual data analysis in the IoT networks. Based on this innovative concept, researchers are encouraged to design of the AI-based IoT system: the network interconnection architecture of the large-scale AI-based IoT system, the advanced perception data preprocessing technology, and the collaborative learning framework for IoT devices. The edge-based IoT framework is illustrated in Fig. 10.5. Promoting the deep coupling of AI-oriented large-scale IoT and edge computing not only meets the dynamic demands for computation and communication resources, but also intelligently adjusts network resource management strategies to effectively improve the efficiency of the entire network. Moreover, it can provide superior service quality and a wide range of services, further deepening the information interaction and sharing in various fields.

10.2.6   Virtual Reality

Virtual reality (VR) panoramic video, or 360-degree video, is an immersive media service that provides users with a panoramic view and a personalized immersive viewing experience. In recent years, with the development of 360-degree omni-directional camera and panoramic video production software, the popularity of mobile intelligent devices and head-mounted display devices, and the wide release of the panoramic video on commercial video platforms (such as YouTube `https://support.google.com/youtube/answer/6396222`, Facebook `https://code.fb.com/virtual-reality/next-generation-video-encoding-techniques-for-360-video-and-vr/`, etc.), the popularity of VR panoramic video has increased significantly, forming an application with great commercial potential.

In traditional VR panoramic video applications, the head-mounted display is connected to a personal computer or a small console through a dedicated data cable, which greatly limits the mobility of users and affects the viewing experience. Users expect to enjoy VR video services anytime, anywhere, through mobile intelligent devices in a ubiquitous wireless environment. However, compared with traditional video, the data scale of VR panoramic video is larger and more sensitive to time delay. There are still many challenges to achieve high-quality VR panoramic video applications in the wireless environments.

Firstly, the transmission of VR panoramic video needs ultra-high bandwidth support and the ultra-low delay. In the same duration and with the same video quality, the size of VR panoramic video is about six times that of traditional video. For example, the bandwidth requirement of panoramic video with 4K resolution and 60 frame rate is 400 Mbps, and that of 8K resolution and 120 frame rate is more than 1 Gbps. Although only transmitting part of the video of the user's field of view (120 degrees horizontally and 90 degrees vertically) can effectively reduce the bandwidth overhead, the user can tolerate the image switching delay caused by head movement to be tens of milliseconds; otherwise, it causes dizziness and discomfort. The current cellular network transmission and Wi-Fi transmission cannot provide the guarantee of bandwidth and ultra-low delay. Secondly, the VR panoramic video needs huge storage space and diversified data modes. For example, an hour of 4K panoramic video requires about 200 GB of storage space, which would cause a great amount of cache pressure on edge intelligent devices and even cloud data centers. Additionally, the partial-view-based transmission mode would produce fragmented, incomplete video content, increasing the storage cost and maintenance cost in terms of data reliability and availability. In addition, in order to cope with bandwidth fluctuations, panoramic video usually adopts adaptive rate coding to save multiple rate versions, and the diversified data mode further increases the storage overhead and complexity. Finally, VR panoramic video rendering needs intensive computational overhead. The decoding of high-quality VR panoramic video usually faces large-scale data calculation, fragmentation, and multi-bit rate data sources. At the same time, the rendering of the panoramic video needs to

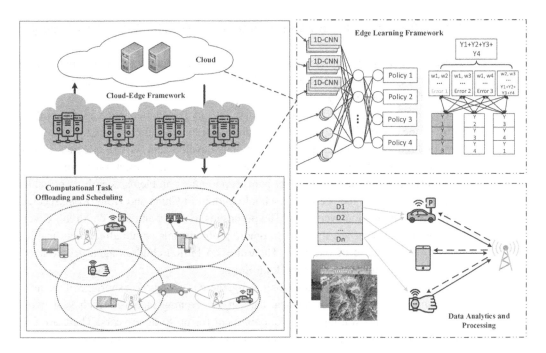

Figure 10.6 Intelligent video analysis framework in edge environment.

consume a lot of CPU and GPU resources. The real-time decoding and rendering mode will have an unbearable computing load on mobile intelligent devices. The round-trip delay of data in pre-decoding and pre-rendering modes assisted by a cloud data center has difficulty meeting the strict real-time guarantee. Meanwhile, centralized data processing cannot support large-scale simultaneous user requests, which limits the scalability of the system.

In a complex and dynamic cloud-side environment, the centralized processing of massive data cannot provide real-time guarantees. At the same time, processing computing tasks at the edge requires full consideration of equipment resource heterogeneity and resource bottlenecks. By employing edge learning, we introduce a VR video intelligent analysis platform in the edge environment, and an intelligent video processing service framework based on edge learning technology, as shown in Fig. 10.6. The deep reinforcement learning model is trained under the cloud-edge collaborative learning framework to achieve high-precision and real-time prediction of the user's field of view. On the other hand, the universal deployment of intelligent computing and processing service framework will be achieved in production nodes or edge nodes of the VR video. Based on the edge learning framework and video content perception, it achieves target detection and environmental analysis. The accuracy of tasks and the processing time will be guaranteed in intelligent driving, drone reconnaissance, and even field rescue.

10.3   The Dr. Body System for Posture Detection and Rehabilitation Tracking

There are many application examples of edge learning. Here we introduce one of representative systems in smart healthcare, i.e., the Dr. Body system for posture detection and rehabilitation tracking [350].

Physiological characteristics of children and adolescents change rapidly as they grow. If the skeleton is affected by any abnormal external force or bad posture, the growth direction will be changed and the bone development will be affected. If it is not corrected in time, it will eventually lead to bone skew and structural abnormalities. Therefore, it is important to discover bone development problems as early as possible. At present, primary and secondary school children in China and Hong Kong receive a physical examination every year. The purpose is to detect and treat children's development problems earlier, so as not to ignore problems that would affect their healthy growth in the course of one year. There are 2.5 billion children aged people aged 4 - 18 in China and one million in Hong Kong.

In some districts of China and Hong Kong, there is a long-term shortage of medical staff, and the wait time for medical care in the evening increases each year, with orthopedic patients waiting for an appointment for up to three years. There are not enough medical resources and systems in the second- and third-tier cities or rural areas to provide spinal health examinations for the public. It is urgent to develop rapid examination with instruments and preliminary screening of patients at night is needed to improve medical efficiency.

Traditional posture detection, especially scoliosis screening, is mainly carried out by traditional Chinese medicine bone touching or naked palpation, which involves several problems. For example, doctors need the subjects to take off their coats and must touch the skin of the subjects, which causes privacy problems; similarly, the experience of each doctor is different, leading to a large diagnostic errors. In addition, after spinal surgery, rehabilitation patients also need to maintain long-term exercise rehabilitation to restore muscle strength, and this process takes a long time. These patients also need to receive X-ray or CT irradiation regularly to evaluate the progress of their recovery, which has high costs, takes a long time, and exposes the body to a high amount of radiation. Long-term exposure to X-ray radiation induces complications and increases the risk of cancer.

In order to solve these problems, some teams have put forth a lot of effort. The DIERS team in Germany has developed a DIERS four-dimensional posture assessment system, based on projection three-dimensional imaging, through the establishment of a biomechanical model of the spine a three-dimensional reconstruction algorithm, a real-time reconstruction of the human spine three-dimensional shape, and finally, a calculation of the spine deformation parameters. This requires the subject to take off the back jacket, but the calculation method is in the cloud, which easily causes privacy leakage. In order to solve these problems, a team from Hong Kong Polytechnic University has developed a three-dimensional evaluation system of the spine based on infrared that uses infrared three-dimensional imaging to reconstruct the human body, extract the feature points of human back based on deep learning, establish a biomechanical model to reconstruct the three-dimensional spine, and, finally, carry out the parameters and diagnosis of the spine and other body problems. However, in order to solve the problem of privacy leakage, edge computing technologies are adopted, and the whole AI system is built into the detection equipment. While solving the problem of user privacy leakage, the system can work well even in areas without an Internet connection.

In addition, some teams, in order to better solve the problem of posture screening, developed a new algorithm, which can use a single photo of the back of the human body to conduct qualitative analysis on the spine shape and other issues. However, the algorithm is mainly based on deep learning, which requires users to take photos of their back and upload them to the cloud. The algorithm is placed in the cloud to conduct a qualitative evaluation of scoliosis, and feedback and an analysis report of scoliosis is provided to the user. However, using this method, users still need to upload their private photos to the cloud, which greatly reduces their enthusiasm. In order to solve this problem, the authors suggest that the AI algorithm model of scoliosis screening should be lightweight combined with edge calculation, so that it can be built into the user's mobile phone program, and the whole diagnosis process will be realized inside the terminal without uploading photos to the cloud [350]. Based on this idea, the authors designed and implemented the Dr. Body system and deployed the model training and inference for posture detection and rehabilitation tracking in the cloud-edge environment.

This system integrates offline 3-D posture detection along with online rehabilitation tracking to improve the physical condition of elderly people. The offline 3-D posture detection enables us to accurately measure the posture parameters with 3-D reconstruction and assigns suitable rehabilitation programs to users through big data analysis. Online rehabilitation tracking leverages the use of the smartphone to guide elderly people to perform systematic fitness and rehabilitation training in a convenient, safe, and low-cost way. During the training process, the intelligent application uses machine learning models to analyze and track posture in real time to ensure effectiveness and prevent the training damage caused by improper actions.

The traditional deep learning model needs a lot of computing resources, so it needs to use expensive hardware or maintain a continuous connection with the cloud to deploy on edge devices. If a general edge intelligent platform can be established, enterprise and individual developers can easily deploy an ultra-efficient deep learning model to edge devices. The models trained in advance for different scenarios are put on the platform, which can be adjusted according to the specific hardware platform, use cases, and performance requirements, to meet different requirements. For example, rich computer vision task models, such as object and human recognition, image segmentation, motion classification, can run on some low computational hardware such as Toradex's Apalis computer module with NXP I.mx6 and i.mx8 processors. For example, the building automation engineers can download object recognition models optimized for business office applications and run them on apalis modules that require speed and memory. The general edge intelligent platform can make the process as simple as possible, and can set up an edge model and run it in a short time. A few lines of code allow the model to run on the device.

Bibliography

[1] (2017). Baidu ring-allreduce: Bringing hpc techniques to deep learning. https://github.com/baidu-research/baidu-allreduce.

[2] (2020). Keras: the python deep learning api. https://keras.io/.

[3] (2020). Mpi forum: Message passing interface (mpi) forum home page. https://www.mpi-forum.org/.

[4] Abadi, M., Barham, P., Chen, J., Chen, Z., Davis, A., Dean, J., Devin, M., Ghemawat, S., Irving, G., Isard, M., Kudlur, M., Levenberg, J., Monga, R., Moore, S., Murray, D. G., Steiner, B., Tucker, P. A., Vasudevan, V., Warden, P., Wicke, M., Yu, Y., and Zheng, X. (2016). Tensorflow: A system for large-scale machine learning. In *Proc. OSDI*.

[5] Ablin, P., Moreau, T., Massias, M., and Gramfort, A. (2019). Learning step sizes for unfolded sparse coding. (NeurIPS).

[6] Addanki, R., Venkatakrishnan, S. B., Gupta, S., Mao, H., and Alizadeh, M. (2019). Placeto: Learning generalizable device placement algorithms for distributed machine learning. *CoRR*.

[7] Agarwal, N., Bullins, B., Chen, X., Hazan, E., Singh, K., Zhang, C., and Zhang, Y. (2019). Efficient full-matrix adaptive regularization. *in Proceedings of 36th International Conference on Machine Learning, ICML 2019*, 2019-June:139–147.

[8] Agarwal, N. and Singh, K. (2017). The price of differential privacy for online learning. In *Proceedings of the 34th International Conference on Machine Learning - Volume 70*.

[9] Aji, A. F. and Heafield, K. (2017). Sparse communication for distributed gradient descent. In *Proceedings of the 2017 Conference on Empirical Methods in Natural Language Processing, EMNLP 2017, Copenhagen, Denmark, September 9-11, 2017*, pages 440–445.

[10] Al-Fares, M., Loukissas, A., and Vahdat, A. (2008). A scalable, commodity data center network architecture. In *Proc. SIGCOMM*.

[11] Alistarh, D., Allen-Zhu, Z., and Li, J. (2018a). Byzantine stochastic gradient descent. In *Advances in Neural Information Processing Systems 31*.

[12] Alistarh, D., Grubic, D., Li, J., Tomioka, R., and Vojnovic, M. (2017a). QSGD: communication-efficient SGD via gradient quantization and encoding. In Guyon, I., von Luxburg, U., Bengio, S., Wallach, H. M., Fergus, R., Vishwanathan, S. V. N., and Garnett, R., editors, *Proceedings of Annual Conference on Neural Information Processing Systems, NeurIPS*.

[13] Alistarh, D., Grubic, D., Li, J., Tomioka, R., and Vojnovic, M. (2017b). QSGD: Communication-efficient SGD via gradient quantization and encoding. In *Proceedings of the Advances in Neural Information Processing Systems (NeurIPS)*, pages 1709–1720.

[14] Alistarh, D., Grubic, D., Li, J., Tomioka, R., and Vojnovic, M. (2017c). QSGD: communication-efficient SGD via gradient quantization and encoding. In *Proceedings of Conference on Neural Information Processing Systems (NeurIPS)*.

[15] Alistarh, D., Hoefler, T., Johansson, M., Konstantinov, N., Khirirat, S., and Renggli, C. (2018b). The convergence of sparsified gradient methods. In *Proceedings of Annual Conference on Neural Information Processing Systems, NeurIPS*.

[16] Alistarh, D., Hoefler, T., Johansson, M., Konstantinov, N., Khirirat, S., and Renggli, C. (2018c). The convergence of sparsified gradient methods. In *Proceedings of Neural Information Processing Systems (NeurIPS)*.

[17] Amiri, M. M. and Gunduz, D. (2019). Machine learning at the wireless edge: Distributed stochastic gradient descent over-the-air.

[18] Amiri, M. M., Gunduz, D., Kulkarni, S. R., and Poor, H. V. (2020a). Convergence of update aware device scheduling for federated learning at the wireless edge.

[19] Amiri, M. M., Gunduz, D., Kulkarni, S. R., and Poor, H. V. (2020b). Update aware device scheduling for federated learning at the wireless edge. *arXiv preprint arXiv:2001.10402*.

[20] Aydöre, S., Thirion, B., and Varoquaux, G. (2019). Feature grouping as a stochastic regularizer for high-dimensional structured data. *in Proceedings of 36th International Conference on Machine Learning, ICML 2019*, 2019-June:592–603.

[21] Banner, R., Hubara, I., Hoffer, E., and Soudry, D. (2018). Scalable methods for 8-bit training of neural networks. *Advances in Neural Information Processing Systems*, 2018-December(NeurIPS):5145–5153.

[22] Basu, D. D. (2019). *Qsparse-local-SGD: Communication Efficient Distributed SGD with Quantization, Sparsification, and Local Computations*. PhD thesis, University of California, Los Angeles, USA.

[23] Bernacchia, A., Lengyel, M., and Hennequin, G. (2018). Exact natural gradient in deep linear networks and application to the nonlinear case. *Advances in Neural Information Processing Systems*, 2018-Decem(NeurIPS):5941–5950.

[24] Bhagoji, A. N., Chakraborty, S., Mittal, P., and Calo, S. B. (2018). Analyzing federated learning through an adversarial lens. *CoRR*, abs/1811.12470.

[25] Bicheng Ying, Kun Yuan and Sayed, A. H. (2017). Variance-Reduced Stochastic Learning under Random Reshufflin. In *Advances in Neural Information Processing Systems*, volume 2017-Decem, pages 1624–1634.

[26] Blanchard, P., El Mhamdi, E. M., Guerraoui, R., and Stainer, J. (2017). Machine learning with adversaries: Byzantine tolerant gradient descent. In *Advances in Neural Information Processing Systems 30*.

[27] Bonawitz, K., Eichner, H., Grieskamp, W., Huba, D., Ingerman, A., Ivanov, V., Kiddon, C., Konecný, J., Mazzocchi, S., McMahan, H. B., Overveldt, T. V., Petrou, D., Ramage, D., and Roselander, J. (2019). Towards federated learning at scale: System design. *ArXiv*, abs/1902.01046.

[28] Bonawitz, K., Ivanov, V., Kreuter, B., Marcedone, A., McMahan, H. B., Patel, S., Ramage, D., Segal, A., and Seth, K. (2017). Practical secure aggregation for privacy-preserving machine learning. In *Proceedings of the 2017 ACM SIGSAC Conference on Computer and Communications Security*.

[29] Brendel, W., Rauber, J., and Bethge, M. (2017). Decision-based adversarial attacks: Reliable attacks against black-box machine learning models.

[30] Brutzkus, A., Elisha, O., and Gilad-Bachrach, R. (2018). Low latency privacy preserving inference. *CoRR*, abs/1812.10659.

[31] Buckman, J., Roy, A., Raffel, C., and Goodfellow, I. (2018). Thermometer encoding: One hot way to resist adversarial examples. In *International Conference on Learning Representations*.

[32] Canel, C., Kim, T., Zhou, G., Li, C., Lim, H., Andersen, D. G., Kaminsky, M., and Dulloor, S. R. (2019). Scaling video analytics on constrained edge nodes.

[33] Charles, Z., Papailiopoulos, D., and Ellenberg, J. (2017). Approximate gradient coding via sparse random graphs. *arXiv*.

[34] Chen, C., Choi, J., Brand, D., Agrawal, A., Zhang, W., and Gopalakrishnan, K. (2018a). Adacomp : Adaptive residual gradient compression for data-parallel distributed training. In *Proceedings of the Thirty-Second AAAI Conference on Artificial Intelligence, AAAI*.

[35] Chen, D., Leon, A. S., Engle, S. P., Fuentes, C., and Chen, Q. (2017a). Offline training for improving online performance of a genetic algorithm based optimization model for hourly multi-reservoir operation. *Environ. Model. Softw.*, 96:46–57.

[36] Chen, H., Wu, H. C., Chan, S. C., and Lam, W. H. (2019a). A stochastic quasi-newton method for large-scale nonconvex optimization with applications. *IEEE transactions on neural networks and learning systems*.

[37] Chen, J., Monga, R., Bengio, S., and Józefowicz, R. (2016). Revisiting distributed synchronous SGD. *arXiv*, abs/1604.00981.

[38] Chen, M., Yang, Z., Saad, W., Yin, C., Poor, H. V., and Cui, S. (2019b). A joint learning and communications framework for federated learning over wireless networks.

[39] Chen, T., Giannakis, G., Sun, T., and Yin, W. (2018b). LAG: Lazily aggregated gradient for communication-efficient distributed learning. In *Proceedings of the Advances in Neural Information Processing Systems (NeurIPS)*, pages 5050–5060.

[40] Chen, X., Liu, S., Xu, K., Li, X., Lin, X., Hong, M., and Cox, D. (2019c). ZO-AdaMM: Zeroth-Order Adaptive Momentum Method for Black-Box Optimization. (NeurIPS): 1–12.

[41] Chen, Y., Su, L., and Xu, J. (2017). Distributed statistical machine learning in adversarial settings: Byzantine gradient descent. *Proceedings of the ACM on Measurement and Analysis of Computing Systems (SIGMETRICS)*, 1(2), 1–25.

[42] Chen, Y.-K., Wu, A.-Y., Bayoumi, M. A., and Koushanfar, F. (2013). Editorial low-power, intelligent, and secure solutions for realization of internet of things. *IEEE Journal on Emerging and Selected Topics in Circuits and Systems*, 3(1):1–4.

[43] Chin, T.-W., Ding, R., and Marculescu, D. (2019). Adascale: Towards real-time video object detection using adaptive scaling. *arXiv preprint arXiv:1902.02910*.

[44] Chou, Y.-M., Chan, Y.-M., Lee, J.-H., Chiu, C.-Y., and Chen, C.-S. (2018). Unifying and merging well-trained deep neural networks for inference stage. *arXiv preprint arXiv:1805.04980*.

[45] Cipar, J., Ho, Q., Kim, J. K., Lee, S., Ganger, G. R., Gibson, G., Keeton, K., and Xing, E. (2013). Solving the straggler problem with bounded staleness. In *Presented as part of the 14th Workshop on Hot Topics in Operating Systems*.

[46] Cortes, C. and Vapnik, V. (2004). Support-vector networks. *Machine Learning*, 20:273–297.

[47] Daga, H., Nicholson, P. K., Gavrilovska, A., and Lugones, D. (2019). Cartel: A system for collaborative transfer learning at the edge. *Proceedings of the ACM Symposium on Cloud Computing*.

[48] Datta, S., Bhaduri, K., Giannella, C., Wolff, R., and Kargupta, H. (2006). Distributed data mining in peer-to-peer networks. *IEEE Internet Computing*, 10(4):18–26.

[49] Dean, J., Corrado, G., Monga, R., Chen, K., Devin, M., Mao, M., Ranzato, M., Senior, A., Tucker, P., Yang, K., et al. (2012). Large scale distributed deep networks. In *Advances in neural information processing systems*, pages 1223–1231.

[50] Defazio, A., Bach, F. R., and Lacoste-Julien, S. (2014). SAGA: A fast incremental gradient method with support for non-strongly convex composite objectives. In *Proceedings of Annual Conference on Neural Information Processing Systems*.

[51] Dekel, O., Gilad-Bachrach, R., Shamir, O., and Xiao, L. (2012). Optimal distributed online prediction using mini-batches. *J. Mach. Learn. Res.*, 13:165–202.

[52] Deng, J., Dong, W., Socher, R., Li, L.-J., Li, K., and Fei-Fei, L. (2009). Imagenet: A large-scale hierarchical image database. In *2009 IEEE conference on computer vision and pattern recognition*, pages 248–255. Ieee.

[53] Dennis, D. K., Pabbaraju, C., Simhadri, H. V., and Jain, P. (2018). Multiple instance learning for efficient sequential data classification on resource-constrained devices. *Advances in Neural Information Processing Systems*, 2018-December(NeurIPS):10953–10964.

[54] Denton, E. L., Zaremba, W., Bruna, J., LeCun, Y., and Fergus, R. (2014). Exploiting linear structure within convolutional networks for efficient evaluation. In *Advances in neural information processing systems*, pages 1269–1277.

[55] Devlin, J., Chang, M.-W., Lee, K., and Toutanova, K. (2018). Bert: Pre-training of deep bidirectional transformers for language understanding. *arXiv preprint arXiv:1810.04805*.

[56] Dhillon, G. S., Azizzadenesheli, K., Lipton, Z. C., Bernstein, J., Kossaifi, J., Khanna, A., and Anandkumar, A. (2018). Stochastic activation pruning for robust adversarial defense. *CoRR*, abs/1803.01442.

[57] Dieuleveut, A. and Patel, K. K. (2019). Communication trade-offs for local-sgd with large step size. In *Proceedings of Advances in Neural Information Processing Systems, NeurIPS*.

[58] Dong, X., Liu, L., Li, G., Li, J., Zhao, P., Wang, X., and Feng, X. (2019). Exploiting the input sparsity to accelerate deep neural networks: poster. In *Proceedings of the 24th Symposium on Principles and Practice of Parallel Programming*, pages 401–402.

[59] Dozat, T. (2016). Incorporating Nesterov Momentum into Adam. *in Proceedings of ICLR Workshop*, (1):2013–2016.

[60] Du, S. S. and Hu, W. (2019). Width provably matters in optimization for deep linear neural networks. *in Proceedings of 36th International Conference on Machine Learning, ICML 2019*, 2019-June:2956–2970.

[61] Du, Y. and Huang, K. (2018). Fast analog transmission for high-mobility wireless data acquisition in edge learning. *Arxiv Online Available: https://arxiv.org/abs/1807.11250*.

[62] Egan, K. J., Pinto-Bruno, Á. C., Bighelli, I., Berg-Weger, M., van Straten, A., Albanese, E., and Pot, A. (2018). Online training and support programs designed to improve mental health and reduce burden among caregivers of people with dementia: A systematic review. *Journal of the American Medical Directors Association*, 19 3:200–206.e1.

[63] Elgabli, A., Park, J., Issaid, C. B., and Bennis, M. (2020). Harnessing wireless channels for scalable and privacy-preserving federated learning. *ArXiv*, abs/2007.01790.

[64] Epasto, A., Esfandiari, H., and Mirrokni, V. (2019). On-device algorithms for public-private data with absolute privacy. In *The World Wide Web Conference*.

[65] Fang, B., Zeng, X., and Zhang, M. (2018). Nestdnn: Resource-aware multi-tenant on-device deep learning for continuous mobile vision. *Proceedings of the 24th Annual International Conference on Mobile Computing and Networking*.

[66] Faraji, I., Mirsadeghi, S. H., and Afsahi, A. (2016). Topology-aware GPU selection on multi-gpu nodes. In *2016 IEEE International Parallel and Distributed Processing Symposium Workshops, IPDPS Workshops*.

[67] Gao, Y., Chen, L., and Li, B. (2018a). Spotlight: Optimizing device placement for training deep neural networks. In *International Conference on Machine Learning*.

[68] Gao, Y., Chen, L., and Li, B. (2018b). Spotlight: Optimizing device placement for training deep neural networks. In *Proceedings of the 35th International Conference on Machine Learning, ICML*.

[69] Gaunt, A., Johnson, M., Riechert, M., Tarlow, D., Tomioka, R., Vytiniotis, D., and Webster, S. (2017). Ampnet: Asynchronous model-parallel training for dynamic neural networks. *arXiv*, abs/1705.09786.

[70] Gazagnadou, N., Gower, R. M., and Salmon, J. (2019). Optimal mini-batch and step sizes for SAGA. *in Proceedings of 36th International Conference on Machine Learning, ICML 2019*, 2019-June:3734–3742.

[71] Ge, J., Wang, Z., Wang, M., and Liu, H. (2018). Minimax-optimal privacy-preserving sparse pca in distributed systems. In *Proceedings of the Twenty-First International Conference on Artificial Intelligence and Statistics*.

[72] Geng, Y., Yang, Y., and Cao, G. (2018). Energy-efficient computation offloading for multicore-based mobile devices. *IEEE INFOCOM 2018 - IEEE Conference on Computer Communications*, pages 46–54.

[73] Ghadimi, S. and Lan, G. (2013). Stochastic first-and zeroth-order methods for nonconvex stochastic programming. *SIAM Journal on Optimization*, 23(4):2341–2368.

[74] Ghadimi, S. and Lan, G. (2016). Accelerated gradient methods for nonconvex nonlinear and stochastic programming. *Mathematical Programming*, 156:59–99.

[75] Giacomelli, I., Jha, S., Joye, M., Page, C. D., and Yoon, K. (2018). Privacy-preserving ridge regression with only linearly-homomorphic encryption. In *Applied Cryptography and Network Security*.

[76] Gibbons, R. (1992). *Primer in Game Theory*. Harvester Wheatsheaf.

[77] Gope, D., Dasika, G., and Mattina, M. (2019). Ternary hybrid neural-tree networks for highly constrained iot applications.

[78] Goyal, P., Dollár, P., Girshick, R., Noordhuis, P., Wesolowski, L., Kyrola, A., Tulloch, A., Jia, Y., and He, K. (2017). Accurate, large minibatch sgd: Training imagenet in 1 hour.

[79] Gu, J., Chowdhury, M., Shin, K. G., Zhu, Y., Jeon, M., Qian, J., Liu, H., and Guo, C. (2019a). Tiresias: A {GPU} cluster manager for distributed deep learning. In *16th {USENIX} Symposium on Networked Systems Design and Implementation ({NSDI} 19)*, pages 485–500.

[80] Gu, L., Zeng, D., Guo, S., Barnawi, A., and Xiang, Y. (2017). Cost efficient resource management in fog computing supported medical cyber-physical system. *IEEE Transactions on Emerging Topics in Computing*, 5(1):108–119.

[81] Gu, R., Yang, S., and Wu, F. (2019b). Distributed machine learning on mobile devices: A survey. *arXiv preprint arXiv:1909.08329*.

[82] Gunasekar, S., Lee, J. D., Soudry, D., and Srebro, N. (2018). Characterizing implicit bias in terms of optimization geometry. In *Proceedings of the 35th International Conference on Machine Learning, ICML*.

[83] Gündüz, D., de Kerret, P., Sidiropoulos, N. D., Gesbert, D., Murthy, C. R., and van der Schaar, M. (2019). Machine learning in the air. *IEEE J. Sel. Areas Commun.*, 37(10):2184–2199.

[84] Guo, C., Lu, G., Li, D., Wu, H., Zhang, X., Shi, Y., Tian, C., Zhang, Y., and Lu, S. (2009). Bcube: A high performance, server-centric network architecture for modular data centers. In *Proc. SIGCOMM*.

[85] Guo, P., Hu, B., Li, R., and Hu, W. (2018a). Foggycache: Cross-device approximate computation reuse. In *Proceedings of the 24th Annual International Conference on Mobile Computing and Networking*, pages 19–34. ACM.

[86] Guo, Y., Yao, A., and Chen, Y. (2016). Dynamic network surgery for efficient dnns. In *Annual Conference on Neural Information Processing Systems, NeurIPS, December 5-10, 2016, Barcelona, Spain*, pages 1379–1387.

[87] Guo, Y., Zhang, C., Zhang, C., and Chen, Y. (2018b). Sparse dnns with improved adversarial robustness. In *Advances in Neural Information Processing Systems 31*.

[88] Gupta, H., Srikant, R., and Ying, L. (2019). Finite-Time Performance Bounds and Adaptive Learning Rate Selection for Two Time-Scale Reinforcement Learning. (NeurIPS).

[89] Haddadpour, F., Kamani, M. M., Mahdavi, M., and Cadambe, V. R. (2019a). Local SGD with periodic averaging: Tighter analysis and adaptive synchronization. In *Proceedings of Advances in Neural Information Processing Systems, NeurIPS*.

[90] Haddadpour, F., Kamani, M. M., Mahdavi, M., and Cadambe, V. R. (2019b). Trading redundancy for communication: Speeding up distributed SGD for non-convex optimization. In *Proceedings of the 36th International Conference on Machine Learning, ICML*.

[91] Hadjis, S., Zhang, C., Mitliagkas, I., Iter, D., and Ré, C. (2016). Omnivore: An optimizer for multi-device deep learning on cpus and gpus. *arXiv*.

[92] Han, K., Wang, Y., Tian, Q., Guo, J., Xu, C., and Xu, C. (2019). Ghostnet: More features from cheap operations. *arXiv preprint arXiv:1911.11907*.

[93] Han, P., Wang, S., and Leung, K. K. (2020). Adaptive gradient sparsification for efficient federated learning: An online learning approach. *CoRR*, abs/2001.04756.

[94] Han, S., Mao, H., and Dally, W. J. (2015a). Deep compression: Compressing deep neural networks with pruning, trained quantization and huffman coding. *arXiv preprint arXiv:1510.00149*.

[95] Han, S., Mao, H., and Dally, W. J. (2016). Deep compression: Compressing deep neural network with pruning, trained quantization and huffman coding. *arXiv*.

[96] Han, S., Pool, J., Tran, J., and Dally, W. (2015b). Learning both weights and connections for efficient neural network. In *Advances in neural information processing systems*, pages 1135–1143.

[97] Han, S., Pool, J., Tran, J., and Dally, W. J. (2015c). Learning both weights and connections for efficient neural network. In *Annual Conference on Neural Information Processing Systems, NeurIPS, December 7-12, 2015, Montreal, Quebec, Canada*, pages 1135–1143.

[98] Harlap, A., Narayanan, D., Phanishayee, A., Seshadri, V., Devanur, N. R., Ganger, G. R., and Gibbons, P. B. (2018). Pipedream: Fast and efficient pipeline parallel DNN training. *arXiv*, abs/1806.03377.

[99] He, F., Liu, T., and Tao, D. (2019). Control Batch Size and Learning Rate to Generalize Well: Theoretical and Empirical Evidence. *NeurIPS*, (NeurIPS):10.

[100] He, J., Chen, Y., Fu, T. Z. J., Long, X., Winslett, M., You, L., and Zhang, Z. (2018a). Haas: Cloud-based real-time data analytics with heterogeneity-aware scheduling. In *38th IEEE International Conference on Distributed Computing Systems, ICDCS*.

[101] He, K., Zhang, X., Ren, S., and Sun, J. (2016). Deep residual learning for image recognition. In *Proc. CVPR*, pages 770–778.

[102] He, W., Li, B., and Song, D. (2018b). Decision boundary analysis of adversarial examples. In *International Conference on Learning Representations*.

[103] Hearst, M. A., Dumais, S. T., Osuna, E., Platt, J., and Scholkopf, B. (1998). Support vector machines. *IEEE Intelligent Systems and their applications*, 13(4):18–28.

[104] Heikkilä, M., Lagerspetz, E., Kaski, S., Shimizu, K., Tarkoma, S., and Honkela, A. (2017). Differentially private bayesian learning on distributed data. In *Advances in Neural Information Processing Systems 30*.

[105] Hesamifard, E., Takabi, H., and Ghasemi, M. (2017). Cryptodl: Deep neural networks over encrypted data. *CoRR*, abs/1711.05189.

[106] Hinton, G., Vinyals, O., and Dean, J. (2015). Distilling the knowledge in a neural network. *arXiv preprint arXiv:1503.02531*.

[107] Hitaj, B., Ateniese, G., and Perez-Cruz, F. (2017). Deep models under the gan: Information leakage from collaborative deep learning. In *Proceedings of the 2017 ACM SIGSAC Conference on Computer and Communications Security*.

[108] Hochreiter, S. and Schmidhuber, J. (1997). Long short-term memory. *Neural computation*, 9(8):1735–1780.

[109] Holmes, C., Mawhirter, D., He, Y., Yan, F., and Wu, B. (2019). Grnn: Low-latency and scalable rnn inference on gpus. *Proceedings of the 14th EuroSys Conference 2019*.

[110] Hosmer, D. W. and Lemeshow, S. (1989). Applied logistic regression.

[111] Hsieh, K., Harlap, A., Vijaykumar, N., Konomis, D., Ganger, G. R., Gibbons, P. B., and Mutlu, O. (2017a). Gaia: Geo-distributed machine learning approaching LAN speeds. In *Proceedings of the 14th USENIX Symposium on Networked Systems Design and Implementation, NSDI*.

[112] Hsieh, K., Harlap, A., Vijaykumar, N., Konomis, D., Ganger, G. R., Gibbons, P. B., and Mutlu, O. (2017b). Gaia: Geo-distributed machine learning approaching {LAN} speeds. In *14th {USENIX} Symposium on Networked Systems Design and Implementation ({NSDI} 17)*, pages 629–647.

[113] Hsieh, K., Harlap, A., Vijaykumar, N., Konomis, D., Ganger, G. R., Gibbons, P. B., and Mutlu, O. (2017c). Gaia: Geo-distributed machine learning approaching lan speeds. In *Proc. NSDI*.

[114] Hu, J., Shen, L., and Sun, G. (2018). Squeeze-and-excitation networks. In *Proceedings of the IEEE conference on computer vision and pattern recognition*, pages 7132–7141.

[115] Huang, C., Zhai, S., Talbott, W., Bautista, M. A., Sun, S. Y., Guestrin, C., and Susskind, J. (2019a). Addressing the loss-metric mismatch with adaptive loss alignment. *in Proceedings of 36th International Conference on Machine Learning, ICML 2019*, 2019-June:5145–5154.

[116] Huang, H., Wang, C., and Dong, B. (2019b). Nostalgic ADAM: Weighting more of the past gradients when designing the adaptive learning rate. *in Proceedings of IJCAI International Joint Conference on Artificial Intelligence*, 2019-Augus:2556–2562.

[117] Huang, J., Qian, F., Guo, Y., Zhou, Y., Xu, Q., Mao, Z. M., Sen, S., and Spatscheck, O. (2013). An in-depth study of lte: effect of network protocol and application behavior on performance. *ACM SIGCOMM Computer Communication Review*, 43(4):363–374.

[118] Huang, L., Yin, Y., Fu, Z., Zhang, S., Deng, H., and Liu, D. (2018). Loadaboost: Loss-based adaboost federated machine learning on medical data. *arXiv preprint arXiv:1811.12629*.

[119] Huang, T., Ye, B., Qu, Z., Tang, B., Xie, L., and Lu, S. (2020). Physical-layer arithmetic for federated learning in uplink mu-mimo enabled wireless networks. In *Proceedings of IEEE Conference on Computer Communications, INFOCOM.*

[120] Huang, Y., Cheng, Y., Chen, D., Lee, H., Ngiam, J., Le, Q. V., and Chen, Z. (2019c). Gpipe: Efficient training of giant neural networks using pipeline parallelism. In *Proc. NeurIPS.*

[121] Hui, L., Li, X., Gong, C., Fang, M., Zhou, J. T., and Yang, J. (2019). Inter-Class Angular Loss for Convolutional Neural Networks. *in Proceedings of the AAAI Conference on Artificial Intelligence*, 33:3894–3901.

[122] Iandola, F. N., Han, S., Moskewicz, M. W., Ashraf, K., Dally, W. J., and Keutzer, K. (2016). Squeezenet: Alexnet-level accuracy with 50x fewer parameters and< 0.5 mb model size. *arXiv preprint arXiv:1602.07360.*

[123] Jackson, M. O. (2014). Mechanism theory. *Available at SSRN 2542983.*

[124] Jaggi, M., Smith, V., Takác, M., Terhorst, J., Krishnan, S., Hofmann, T., and Jordan, M. I. (2014). Communication-efficient distributed dual coordinate ascent. In *Proc. NIPS.*

[125] Jain, P., Thakkar, O., and Thakurta, A. (2017). Differentially private matrix completion, revisited. *CoRR*, abs/1712.09765.

[126] Jayaraman, B., Wang, L., Evans, D., and Gu, Q. (2018). Distributed learning without distress: Privacy-preserving empirical risk minimization. In *Advances in Neural Information Processing Systems 31.*

[127] Jeon, Y.-S., Amiri, M. M., Li, J., and Poor, H. V. (2020). Gradient estimation for federated learning over massive mimo communication systems.

[128] Jeong, E., Oh, S., Kim, H., Park, J., Bennis, M., and Kim, S.-L. (2018a). Communication-efficient on-device machine learning: Federated distillation and augmentation under non-iid private data. *arXiv preprint arXiv:1811.11479.*

[129] Jeong, H.-J., Lee, H.-J., Shin, C. H., and Moon, S.-M. (2018b). Ionn: Incremental offloading of neural network computations from mobile devices to edge servers. In *Proceedings of the ACM Symposium on Cloud Computing*, pages 401–411.

[130] Jia, Q., Guo, L., Jin, Z., and Fang, Y. (2018). Preserving model privacy for machine learning in distributed systems. *IEEE Transactions on Parallel and Distributed Systems*, 29(8):1808–1822.

[131] Jiang, J., Cui, B., Zhang, C., and Yu, L. (2017a). Heterogeneity-aware distributed parameter servers. *Proceedings of the ACM SIGMOD International Conference on Management of Data*, Part F127746:463–478.

[132] Jiang, J., Cui, B., Zhang, C., and Yu, L. (2017b). Heterogeneity-aware distributed parameter servers. In *Proc. SIGMOD.*

[133] Jiang, R. and Zhou, S. (2020). Cluster-based cooperative digital over-the-air aggregation for wireless federated edge learning. *ArXiv*, abs/2008.00994.

[134] Jin, S., Di, S., Liang, X., Tian, J., Tao, D., and Cappello, F. (2019). Deepsz: A novel framework to compress deep neural networks by using error-bounded lossy compression. In *Proceedings of the 28th International Symposium on High-Performance Parallel and Distributed Computing*, pages 159–170.

[135] Johnson, R. and Zhang, T. (2013). Accelerating stochastic gradient descent using predictive variance reduction. In *Proceedings of 27th Annual Conference on Neural Information Processing Systems, NeurIPS.*

[136] Jouppi, N. P., Young, C., Patil, N., Patterson, D. A., Agrawal, G., Bajwa, R., Bates, S., Bhatia, S., Boden, N., Borchers, A., Boyle, R., Cantin, P., Chao, C., Clark, C., Coriell,

J., Daley, M., Dau, M., Dean, J., Gelb, B., Ghaemmaghami, T. V., Gottipati, R., Gulland, W., Hagmann, R., Ho, C. R., Hogberg, D., Hu, J., Hundt, R., Hurt, D., Ibarz, J., Jaffey, A., Jaworski, A., Kaplan, A., Khaitan, H., Killebrew, D., Koch, A., Kumar, N., Lacy, S., Laudon, J., Law, J., Le, D., Leary, C., Liu, Z., Lucke, K., Lundin, A., MacKean, G., Maggiore, A., Mahony, M., Miller, K., Nagarajan, R., Narayanaswami, R., Ni, R., Nix, K., Norrie, T., Omernick, M., Penukonda, N., Phelps, A., Ross, J., Ross, M., Salek, A., Samadiani, E., Severn, C., Sizikov, G., Snelham, M., Souter, J., Steinberg, D., Swing, A., Tan, M., Thorson, G., Tian, B., Toma, H., Tuttle, E., Vasudevan, V., Walter, R., Wang, W., Wilcox, E., and Yoon, D. H. (2017). In-datacenter performance analysis of a tensor processing unit. In *Proceedings of the 44th Annual International Symposium on Computer Architecture, ISCA, Toronto, ON, Canada, June 24-28, 2017*, pages 1–12.

[137] Kalchbrenner, N., Danihelka, I., and Graves, A. (2015). Grid long short-term memory. *arXiv*.

[138] Karimireddy, S. P., Rebjock, Q., Stich, S. U., and Jaggi, M. (2019). Error feedback fixes signsgd and other gradient compression schemes. *arXiv preprint arXiv:1901.09847*.

[139] Ke, G., Meng, Q., Finley, T., Wang, T., Chen, W., Ma, W., Ye, Q., and Liu, T.-Y. (2017). Lightgbm: A highly efficient gradient boosting decision tree. In *Proc. NeurIPS*.

[140] Kim, Y., Kim, J., Chae, D., Kim, D., and Kim, J. (2019). μlayer: Low latency on-device inference using cooperative single-layer acceleration and processor-friendly quantization. In *Proceedings of the Fourteenth EuroSys Conference 2019*, pages 1–15.

[141] Kingma, D. P. and Ba, J. (2014). Adam: A method for stochastic optimization. *arXiv preprint arXiv:1412.6980*.

[142] Koda, Y., Yamamoto, K., Nishio, T., and Morikura, M. (2020). Differentially private aircomp federated learning with power adaptation harnessing receiver noise. *ArXiv*, abs/2004.06337.

[143] Koloskova, A., Lin, T., Stich, S. U., and Jaggi, M. (2019a). Decentralized deep learning with arbitrary communication compression. *arXiv preprint arXiv:1907.09356*.

[144] Koloskova, A., Stich, S. U., and Jaggi, M. (2019b). Decentralized stochastic optimization and gossip algorithms with compressed communication. *arXiv preprint arXiv:1902.00340*.

[145] Konecný, J., McMahan, H. B., and Ramage, D. (2015). Federated optimization: Distributed optimization beyond the datacenter. *ArXiv*, abs/1511.03575.

[146] Koutnik, J., Greff, K., Gomez, F., and Schmidhuber, J. (2014). A clockwork rnn. *arXiv*.

[147] Krizhevsky, A., Sutskever, I., and Hinton, G. E. (2012). Imagenet classification with deep convolutional neural networks. In *Advances in neural information processing systems*, pages 1097–1105.

[148] Kumar, A., Fu, J., Tucker, G., and Levine, S. (2019). Stabilizing off-policy q-learning via bootstrapping error reduction. In *NeurIPS*.

[149] Kusupati, A., Singh, M., Bhatia, K., Kumar, A., Jain, P., and Varma, M. (2018). Fastgrnn: A fast, accurate, stable and tiny kilobyte sized gated recurrent neural network. In *Advances in Neural Information Processing Systems*, pages 9017–9028.

[150] Lathauwer, L. D., Moor, B. D., and Vandewalle, J. (2000). A multilinear singular value decomposition. *SIAM J. Matrix Analysis Applications*, 21:1253–1278.

[151] LeCun, Y. (1998). The mnist database of handwritten digits. *http://yann.lecun.com/exdb/mnist/*.

[152] Lee, K., Lam, M., Pedarsani, R., Papailiopoulos, D., and Ramchandran, K. (2018). Speeding up distributed machine learning using codes. *IEEE Transactions on Information Theory*, 64(3):1514–1529.

[153] Lee, S., Kim, J. K., Zheng, X., Ho, Q., Gibson, G. A., and Xing, E. P. (Canada, 2014). On model parallelization and scheduling strategies for distributed machine learning. In *Proc. NeurIPS*.

[154] Lei, L., Tan, Y., Liu, S., Zheng, K., et al. (2019). Deep reinforcement learning for autonomous internet of things: Model, applications and challenges. *arXiv preprint arXiv:1907.09059*.

[155] Li, M., Andersen, D. G., Park, J. W., Smola, A. J., Ahmed, A., Josifovski, V., Long, J., Shekita, E. J., and Su, B. (2014a). Scaling distributed machine learning with the parameter server. In *Proceedings of 11th USENIX Symposium on Operating Systems Design and Implementation, OSDI*.

[156] Li, M., Andersen, D. G., Park, J. W., Smola, A. J., Ahmed, A., Josifovski, V., Long, J., Shekita, E. J., and Su, B. Y. (2014b). Scaling distributed machine learning with the parameter server. *in Proceedings of the 11th USENIX Symposium on Operating Systems Design and Implementation, OSDI 2014*, pages 583–598.

[157] Li, M., Andersen, D. G., Park, J. W., Smola, A. J., Ahmed, A., Josifovski, V., Long, J., Shekita, E. J., and Su, B.-Y. (2014c). Scaling distributed machine learning with the parameter server. pages 583–598.

[158] Li, M., Zhang, T., Chen, Y., and Smola, A. J. (New York, 2014d). Efficient mini-batch training for stochastic optimization. In *Proc. SIGKDD*.

[159] Li, P. and Guo, S. (2015). Incentive mechanisms for device-to-device communications. *IEEE Network*, 29(4):75–79.

[160] Li, P., Wu, X., Shen, W., Tong, W., and Guo, S. (2019a). Collaboration of heterogeneous unmanned vehicles for smart cities. *IEEE Network*, 33(4):133–137.

[161] Li, S., Kalan, S. M. M., Yu, Q., Soltanolkotabi, M., and Avestimehr, A. S. (2018a). Polynomially coded regression: Optimal straggler mitigation via data encoding. *arXiv*.

[162] Li, T., Sahu, A. K., Zaheer, M., Sanjabi, M., Talwalkar, A., and Smith, V. (2018b). Federated optimization in heterogeneous networks. *arXiv preprint arXiv:1812.06127*.

[163] Li, T., Sanjabi, M., Beirami, A., and Smith, V. (2019b). Fair resource allocation in federated learning.

[164] Li, X. and Orabona, F. (2018). On the Convergence of Stochastic Gradient Descent with Adaptive Stepsizes. 89.

[165] Li, X., Wang, W., Hu, X., and Yang, J. (2019c). Selective kernel networks. In *Proceedings of the IEEE conference on computer vision and pattern recognition*, pages 510–519.

[166] Li, Y., Ma, T., and Zhang, H. (2018c). Algorithmic regularization in over-parameterized matrix sensing and neural networks with quadratic activations. In Bubeck, S., Perchet, V., and Rigollet, P., editors, *Proceedings of Conference On Learning Theory, COLT*.

[167] Li, Y., Wei, C., and Ma, T. (2019d). Towards Explaining the Regularization Effect of Initial Large Learning Rate in Training Neural Networks. (NeurIPS):1–12.

[168] Li, Z., Brendel, W., Walker, E. Y., Cobos, E., Muhammad, T., Reimer, J., Bethge, M., Sinz, F. H., Pitkow, X., and Tolias, A. S. (2019e). Learning From Brains How to Regularize Machines. (NeurIPS):1–11.

[169] Li, Z., Xu, C., and Leng, B. (2018d). Rethinking Loss Design for Large-scale 3D Shape Retrieval. pages 840–846.

[170] Li, Z., Xu, C., and Leng, B. (2019f). Angular Triplet-Center Loss for Multi-View 3D Shape Retrieval. *in Proceedings of the AAAI Conference on Artificial Intelligence, AAAI.*

[171] Lian, X., Zhang, C., Zhang, H., Hsieh, C.-J., Zhang, W., and Liu, J. (2017). Can decentralized algorithms outperform centralized algorithms? a case study for decentralized parallel stochastic gradient descent. In *Advances in Neural Information Processing Systems*, pages 5330–5340.

[172] Lian, X., Zhang, W., Zhang, C., and Liu, J. (2018). Asynchronous decentralized parallel stochastic gradient descent. In Dy, J. G. and Krause, A., editors, *Proceedings of the 35th International Conference on Machine Learning, ICML.*

[173] Ligett, K., Neel, S., Roth, A., Waggoner, B., and Wu, S. Z. (2017). Accuracy first: Selecting a differential privacy level for accuracy constrained erm. In *Advances in Neural Information Processing Systems 30.*

[174] Lim, W. Y. B., Luong, N. C., Hoang, D. T., Jiao, Y., Liang, Y.-C., Yang, Q., Niyato, D., and Miao, C. (2019). Federated learning in mobile edge networks: A comprehensive survey. *arXiv preprint arXiv:1909.11875.*

[175] Lin, T., Stich, S. U., Patel, K. K., and Jaggi, M. (2020). Don't use large mini-batches, use local SGD. In *Proceedings of 8th International Conference on Learning Representations, ICLR.*

[176] Lin, T.-Y., Maire, M., Belongie, S., Hays, J., Perona, P., Ramanan, D., Dollár, P., and Zitnick, C. L. (2014). Microsoft coco: Common objects in context. In *European conference on computer vision*, pages 740–755. Springer.

[177] Lin, Y., Han, S., Mao, H., Wang, Y., and Dally, B. (2018). Deep gradient compression: Reducing the communication bandwidth for distributed training. In *Proceedings of 6th International Conference on Learning Representations, ICLR.*

[178] Liu, F. and Shroff, N. B. (2019). Data poisoning attacks on stochastic bandits. In *Proceedings of the 36th International Conference on Machine Learning.*

[179] Liu, W., Zang, X., Li, Y., and Vucetic, B. (2020). Over-the-air computation systems: Optimization, analysis and scaling laws. *IEEE Transactions on Wireless Communications*, 19(8):5488–5502.

[180] Liu, Y., Shang, F., and Jiao, L. (2019). Accelerated incremental gradient descent using momentum acceleration with scaling factor. *In Proceedings of IJCAI International Joint Conference on Artificial Intelligence*, 2019-Augus:3045–3051.

[181] Liu, Y., Xu, C., Zhan, Y., Liu, Z., Guan, J., and Zhang, H. (2017). Incentive mechanism for computation offloading using edge computing: A stackelberg game approach. *Computer Networks*, 129:399–409.

[182] Loshchilov, I. and Hutter, F. (2017). FIXING WEIGHT DECAY REGULARIZATION IN ADAM.

[183] Louizos, C., Reisser, M., Blankevoort, T., Gavves, E., and Welling, M. (2019). Relaxed quantization for discretized neural networks. In *7th International Conference on Learning Representations, ICLR, New Orleans, LA, USA, May 6-9, 2019.* OpenReview.net.

[184] Lu, Y. and Sa, C. D. (2020). Moniqua: Modulo quantized communication in decentralized SGD.

[185] Luo, L., Xiong, Y., Liu, Y., and Sun, X. (2019). Adaptive gradient methods with dynamic bound of learning rate. *In Proceedings of 7th International Conference on Learning Representations, ICLR 2019*, (2018):1–19.

[186] Luping, W., Wei, W., and Bo, L. (2019). Cmfl: Mitigating communication overhead for federated learning. In *Proceedings of IEEE 39th International Conference on Distributed Computing Systems, ICDCS*.

[187] M. Jagielski, A. Oprea, B. B. C. L. C. N.-R. and Li, B. (2018). Manipulating machine learning: Poisoning attacks and countermeasures for regression learning. In *2018 IEEE Symposium on Security and Privacy (SP)*.

[188] Ma, X., Sun, H., and Qingyang Hu, R. (2020). Scheduling Policy and Power Allocation for Federated Learning in NOMA Based MEC. *arXiv e-prints*, page arXiv:2006.13044.

[189] Madry, A., Makelov, A., Schmidt, L., Tsipras, D., and Vladu, A. (2017). Towards deep learning models resistant to adversarial attacks.

[190] Mahloujifar, S., Mahmoody, M., and Mohammed, A. (2019). Data poisoning attacks in multi-party learning. In *Proceedings of the 36th International Conference on Machine Learning*.

[191] Maity, R. K., Rawa, A. S., and Mazumdar, A. (2019). Robust gradient descent via moment encoding and ldpc codes. In *Proceedings of IEEE International Symposium on Information Theory (ISIT)*.

[192] Malewicz, G., Austern, M. H., Bik, A. J., Dehnert, J. C., Horn, I., Leiser, N., and Czajkowski, G. (2010). Pregel: A system for large-scale graph processing. In *Proc. SIGMOD*.

[193] Manessi, F., Rozza, A., Bianco, S., Napoletano, P., and Schettini, R. (2018). Automated pruning for deep neural network compression. In *24th International Conference on Pattern Recognition, ICPR*.

[194] Martinez, I., Francis, S., and Hafid, A. S. (2019). Record and reward federated learning contributions with blockchain. In *Proc of IEEE CyberC*, pages 50–57.

[195] Mathur, A., Lane, N. D., Bhattacharya, S., Boran, A., Forlivesi, C., and Kawsar, F. (2017). Deepeye: Resource efficient local execution of multiple deep vision models using wearable commodity hardware. *Proceedings of the 15th Annual International Conference on Mobile Systems, MobiSys, Applications, and Services*.

[196] McMahan, B., Moore, E., Ramage, D., Hampson, S., and Arcas, B. A. (2017a). Communication-efficient learning of deep networks from decentralized data. In *Proceedings of International Conference on Artificial Intelligence and Statistics (AISTATS)*.

[197] McMahan, B., Moore, E., Ramage, D., Hampson, S., and y Arcas, B. A. (2017b). Communication-efficient learning of deep networks from decentralized data. In *Proceedings of Artificial Intelligence and Statistics, AISTATS*.

[198] McMahan, H. B., Moore, E., Ramage, D., Hampson, S., et al. (2017c). Communication-efficient learning of deep networks from decentralized data. In *Proceedings of the 20th International Conference on Artificial Intelligence and Statistics (AISTATS)*.

[199] McMahan, H. B., Moore, E., Ramage, D., Hampson, S., and y Arcas, B. A. (2017d). Communication-efficient learning of deep networks from decentralized data. In *Proc. AISTATS*.

[200] McMahan, H. B., Ramage, D., Talwar, K., and Zhang, L. (2017e). Learning differentially private language models without losing accuracy. *CoRR*, abs/1710.06963.

[201] Melis, L., Song, C., De Cristofaro, E., and Shmatikov, V. (2019). Exploiting unintended feature leakage in collaborative learning. In *2019 IEEE Symposium on Security and Privacy (SP)*.

[202] Meng, Q., Chen, W., Wang, Y., Ma, Z.-M., and Liu, T.-Y. (2019). Convergence analysis of distributed stochastic gradient descent with shuffling. *ArXiv*, abs/1709.10432.

[203] Mirhoseini, A., Goldie, A., Pham, H., Steiner, B., Le, Q. V., and Dean, J. (2018). A hierarchical model for device placement.

[204] Mirza, M. and Osindero, S. (2014). Conditional generative adversarial nets. *arXiv preprint arXiv:1411.1784*.

[205] Mohammadi, M., Al-Fuqaha, A., Sorour, S., and Guizani, M. (2018). Deep learning for iot big data and streaming analytics: A survey. *IEEE Communications Surveys & Tutorials*, 20(4):2923–2960.

[206] Mohassel, P. and Rindal, P. (2018). Aby3: A mixed protocol framework for machine learning. In *Proceedings of the 2018 ACM SIGSAC Conference on Computer and Communications Security*.

[207] Mohri, M., Sivek, G., and Suresh, A. T. (2019). Agnostic federated learning. *arXiv preprint arXiv:1902.00146*.

[208] Mokhtari, A. and Ribeiro, A. (2016). DSA: decentralized double stochastic averaging gradient algorithm. *J. Mach. Learn. Res.*, 17:61:1–61:35.

[209] Murshed, M. G. S., Murphy, C., Hou, D., Khan, N., Ananthanarayanan, G., and Hussain, F. (2019). Machine learning at the network edge: A survey. pages 1–28.

[210] Nakamoto, S. (2009). Bitcoin: A peer-to-peer electronic cash system. *[Online] Available: https://bitcoin.org/bitcoin.pdf*.

[211] Nakandala, S., Kumar, A., and Papakonstantinou, Y. (2019). Incremental and approximate inference for faster occlusion-based deep cnn explanations. In *Proceedings of the 2019 International Conference on Management of Data*, pages 1589–1606.

[212] Nar, K. and Shankar Sastry, S. (2018). Step size matters in deep learning. *Advances in Neural Information Processing Systems*, 2018-Decem(NeurIPS):3436–3444.

[213] Narayanan, D., Harlap, A., Phanishayee, A., Seshadri, V., Devanur, N. R., Ganger, G. R., Gibbons, P. B., and Zaharia, M. (2019). Pipedream: generalized pipeline parallelism for DNN training. In *Proceedings of the 27th ACM Symposium on Operating Systems Principles, SOSP, Huntsville, ON, Canada, October 27-30, 2019*, pages 1–15.

[214] Nasr, M., Shokri, R., and Houmansadr, A. (2018). Machine learning with membership privacy using adversarial regularization. In *Proceedings of the 2018 ACM SIGSAC Conference on Computer and Communications Security*.

[215] Nasr, M., Shokri, R., and Houmansadr, A. (2019). Comprehensive privacy analysis of deep learning: Passive and active white-box inference attacks against centralized and federated learning. In *2019 IEEE Symposium on Security and Privacy (SP)*.

[216] Neel, S. and Roth, A. (2018). Mitigating bias in adaptive data gathering via differential privacy. *CoRR*, abs/1806.02329.

[217] Nesterov, Y. (2012a). Efficiency of coordinate descent methods on huge-scale optimization problems. *SIAM J. Optimization*, 22:341–362.

[218] Nesterov, Y. E. (2012b). Efficiency of coordinate descent methods on huge-scale optimization problems. *SIAM J. Optimization*, 22(2):341–362.

[219] Neter, J., Wasserman, W. J., and Kutner, M. H. (1974). Applied linear statistical models : regression, analysis of variance, and experimental designs.

[220] Nguyen, L. M., van Dijk, M., Phan, D. T., Nguyen, P. H., Weng, T.-w., and Kalagnanam, J. R. (2019). Finite-Sum Smooth Optimization with SARAH. pages 1–26.

[221] Niknam, S., Dhillon, H. S., and Reed, J. H. (2019). Federated learning for wireless communications: Motivation, opportunities and challenges. *arXiv preprint arXiv: 1908.06847*.

[222] Nishio, T. and Yonetani, R. (2019a). Client selection for federated learning with hetero-geneous resources in mobile edge. *ICC 2019 - 2019 IEEE International Conference on Communications (ICC)*.

[223] Nishio, T. and Yonetani, R. (2019b). Client selection for federated learning with hetero-geneous resources in mobile edge. In *ICC 2019-2019 IEEE International Conference on Communications (ICC)*, pages 1–7. IEEE.

[224] Ozfatura, E., Gündüz, D., and Ulukus, S. (2019). Speeding up distributed gradient descent by utilizing non-persistent stragglers. In *Proceedings of IEEE International Symposium on Information Theory, ISIT*.

[225] Panageas, I., Piliouras, G., and Wang, X. (2019). First-order methods almost always avoid saddle points: the case of vanishing step-sizes. (NeurIPS):1–10.

[226] Pandey, S. R., Tran, N. H., Bennis, M., Tun, Y. K., Manzoor, A., and Hong, C. S. (2020). A crowdsourcing framework for on-device federated learning. *IEEE Transactions on Wireless Communications*, 19(5):3241–3256.

[227] Pang, T., Du, C., Dong, Y., and Zhu, J. (2018). Towards robust detection of adversarial examples. In *Advances in Neural Information Processing Systems 31*.

[228] Papernot, N., Abadi, M., ÂÍÂšlfar Erlingsson, Goodfellow, I., and Talwar, K. (2016). Semi-supervised knowledge transfer for deep learning from private training data.

[229] Parashar, A., Rhu, M., Mukkara, A., Puglielli, A., Venkatesan, R., Khailany, B., Emer, J. S., Keckler, S. W., and Dally, W. J. (2017). SCNN: an accelerator for compressed-sparse convolutional neural networks. In *Proceedings of the 44th Annual International Symposium on Computer Architecture, ISCA*.

[230] Park, H., Zhai, S., Lu, L., and Lin, F. X. (2019). Streambox-tz: Secure stream analytics at the edge with trustzone. In *2019 USENIX Annual Technical Conference (USENIX ATC 19)*.

[231] Park, J. H., Yun, G., Chang, M. Y., Nguyen, N. T., Lee, S., Choi, J., Noh, S. H., and Choi, Y.-r. (2020). Hetpipe: Enabling large {DNN} training on (whimpy) heterogeneous {GPU} clusters through integration of pipelined model parallelism and data parallelism. In *2020 {USENIX} Annual Technical Conference ({USENIX} {ATC} 20)*, pages 307–321.

[232] Park, N., Mohammadi, M., Gorde, K., Jajodia, S., Park, H., and Kim, Y. (2018). Data synthesis based on generative adversarial networks. *Proc. VLDB Endow.*, 11(10):1071–1083.

[233] Patel, K. K. and Dieuleveut, A. (2019). Communication trade-offs for synchronized distributed SGD with large step size. (NeurIPS):1–12.

[234] Payman Mohassel, Y. Z. (2017). Secureml: A system for scalable privacy-preserving machine learning. In *2017 IEEE Symposium on Security and Privacy (SP)*.

[235] Peng, Y., Bao, Y., Chen, Y., Wu, C., and Guo, C. (2018). Optimus: an efficient dynamic resource scheduler for deep learning clusters. In *Proceedings of the Thirteenth EuroSys Conference, EuroSys*.

[236] Peteiro-Barral, D. and Guijarro-Berdiñas, B. (2013). A survey of methods for distributed machine learning. *Progress in Artificial Intelligence*, 2(1):1–11.

[237] Pilla, L. (2020). Optimal task assignment to heterogeneous federated learning devices. *ArXiv*, abs/2010.00239.

[238] Prokhorenkova, L., Gusev, G., Vorobev, A., Dorogush, A. V., and Gulin, A. (2018). Catboost: unbiased boosting with categorical features. In *Advances in neural information processing systems*, pages 6638–6648.

[239] Qiao, A., Aragam, B., Zhang, B., and Xing, E. P. (2019). Fault tolerance in iterative-convergent machine learning. In *Proceedings of the 36th International Conference on Machine Learning ICML*, pages 5220–5230.

[240] Raviv, N., Tandon, R., Dimakis, A., and Tamo, I. (2018). Gradient coding from cyclic MDS codes and expander graphs. In *Proceedings of the 35th International Conference on Machine Learning, ICML*, pages 4302–4310.

[241] Reddi, S. J., Kale, S., and Kumar, S. (2018). On the convergence of Adam and beyond. *in Proceedings of 6th International Conference on Learning Representations, ICLR*, pages 1–23.

[242] Ren, J., Yu, G., and Ding, G. (2019a). Accelerating dnn training in wireless federated edge learning system.

[243] Ren, S., Zhang, Z., Liu, S., Zhou, M., and Ma, S. (2019b). Unsupervised Neural Machine Translation with SMT as Posterior Regularization. *in Proceedings of the AAAI Conference on Artificial Intelligence*, 33:241–248.

[244] Rob Hall, S. E. F. and Nardi, Y. (2011). Secure multiple linear regression based on homomorphic encryption. *Journal of Official Statistics*, 27(4):669–691.

[245] Robbins, H. E. (2007). A stochastic approximation method. *Annals of Mathematical Statistics*, 22:400–407.

[246] Sakr, C., Wang, N., Chen, C., Choi, J., Agrawal, A., Shanbhag, N. R., and Gopalakrishnan, K. (2019). Accumulation bit-width scaling for ultra-low precision training of deep networks. In *7th International Conference on Learning Representations, ICLR, New Orleans, LA, USA, May 6-9, 2019*. OpenReview.net.

[247] Sandler, M., Howard, A., Zhu, M., Zhmoginov, A., and Chen, L.-C. (2018). Mobilenetv2: Inverted residuals and linear bottlenecks. In *Proceedings of the IEEE conference on computer vision and pattern recognition*, pages 4510–4520.

[248] Sarikaya, Y. and Ercetin, O. (2019). Motivating workers in federated learning: A stackelberg game perspective. *IEEE Networking Letters*, 2(1):23–27.

[249] Sattler, F., Müller, K.-R., and Samek, W. (2019a). Clustered federated learning: Model-agnostic distributed multi-task optimization under privacy constraints. *arXiv preprint arXiv:1910.01991*.

[250] Sattler, F., Wiedemann, S., Müller, K.-R., and Samek, W. (2019b). Robust and communication-efficient federated learning from non-iid data. *IEEE transactions on neural networks and learning systems*.

[251] Schein, A., Wu, Z. S., Schofield, A., Zhou, M., and Wallach, H. (2018). Locally private bayesian inference for count models.

[252] Schmidt, M. W., Roux, N. L., and Bach, F. R. (2017). Minimizing finite sums with the stochastic average gradient. *Mathematical Programming*, 162:83–112.

[253] Seide, F., Fu, H., Droppo, J., Li, G., and Yu, D. (2014a). 1-bit stochastic gradient descent and its application to data-parallel distributed training of speech dnns. In *Proceedings of 15th Annual Conference of the International Speech Communication Association, INTERSPEECH*.

[254] Seide, F., Fu, H., Droppo, J., Li, G., and Yu, D. (2014b). 1-bit stochastic gradient descent and its application to data-parallel distributed training of speech dnns. In *Fifteenth Annual Conference of the International Speech Communication Association*.

[255] Sergeev, A. and Balso, M. D. (2018). Horovod: fast and easy distributed deep learning in tensorflow. *ArXiv*, abs/1802.05799.

[256] Sery, T., Shlezinger, N., Cohen, K., and Eldar, Y. C. (2020). Over-the-air federated learning from heterogeneous data. *ArXiv*, abs/2009.12787.

[257] Sharif-Nassab, A., Salehkaleybar, S., and Golestani, S. J. (2019). Order optimal one-shot distributed learning. In *Proceedings of Advances in Neural Information Processing Systems, NeurIPS*.

[258] Shen, Y. and Sanghavi, S. (2018). Iteratively learning from the best. *CoRR*, abs/1810.11874.

[259] Shi, S., Zhao, K., Wang, Q., Tang, Z., and Chu, X. (2019a). A convergence analysis of distributed SGD with communication-efficient gradient sparsification. In Kraus, S., editor, *Proceedings of the Twenty-Eighth International Joint Conference on Artificial Intelligence, IJCAI 2019, Macao, China, August 10-16, 2019*, pages 3411–3417. ijcai.org.

[260] Shi, S., Zhao, K., Wang, Q., Tang, Z., and Chu, X. (2019b). A convergence analysis of distributed SGD with communication-efficient gradient sparsification. In *Proceedings of the 28th International Joint Conference on Artificial Intelligence (IJCAI)*.

[261] Shi, W., Cao, J., Zhang, Q., Li, Y., and Xu, L. (2016). Edge computing: Vision and challenges. *IEEE Internet of Things Journal*, 3:637–646.

[262] Shi, W., Ling, Q., Wu, G., and Yin, W. (2015). EXTRA: an exact first-order algorithm for decentralized consensus optimization. *SIAM J. Optim.*, 25(2):944–966.

[263] Shi, W., Ling, Q., Yuan, K., Wu, G., and Yin, W. (2014). On the linear convergence of the ADMM in decentralized consensus optimization. *IEEE Trans. Signal Process.*, 62(7):1750–1761.

[264] Shi, W., Zhou, S., and Niu, Z. (2019c). Device scheduling with fast convergence for wireless federated learning.

[265] Shoham, N., Avidor, T., Keren, A., Israel, N., Benditkis, D., Mor-Yosef, L., and Zeitak, I. (2019). Overcoming forgetting in federated learning on non-iid data. *arXiv preprint arXiv:1910.07796*.

[266] Shokri, R., Stronati, M., Song, C., and Shmatikov, V. (2017). Membership inference attacks against machine learning models. In *2017 IEEE Symposium on Security and Privacy (SP)*.

[267] Simonyan, K. and Zisserman, A. (2014). Very deep convolutional networks for large-scale image recognition. *arXiv preprint arXiv:1409.1556*.

[268] Singh, N., Data, D., George, J., and Diggavi, S. (2020). Squarm-sgd: Communication-efficient momentum sgd for decentralized optimization. *arXiv preprint arXiv: 2005.07041*.

[269] Smith, A., Thakurta, A., and Upadhyay, J. (2017). Is interaction necessary for distributed private learning? In *2017 IEEE Symposium on Security and Privacy (SP)*.

[270] Song, C., Ristenpart, T., and Shmatikov, V. (2017). Machine learning models that remember too much. In *Proceedings of the 2017 ACM SIGSAC Conference on Computer and Communications Security*.

[271] Song, S., Lichtenberg, S. P., and Xiao, J. (2015). Sun rgb-d: A rgb-d scene understanding benchmark suite. In *Proceedings of the IEEE conference on computer vision and pattern recognition*, pages 567–576.

[272] Song, T., Tong, Y., and Wei, S. (2019). Profit allocation for federated learning. In *Proc. of IEEE Big Data*, pages 2577–2586.

[273] Staib, M., Reddi, S., Kale, S., Kumar, S., and Sra, S. (2019). Escaping saddle points with adaptive gradient methods. *in Proceedings of 36th International Conference on Machine Learning, ICML 2019*, 2019-June:10420–10454.

[274] Steinhardt, J., Koh, P. W. W., and Liang, P. S. (2017). Certified defenses for data poisoning attacks. In *Advances in Neural Information Processing Systems 30*.

[275] Stich, S. U. (2019). Local SGD converges fast and communicates little. In *Proceedings of 7th International Conference on Learning Representations, ICLR*.

[276] Stich, S. U., Cordonnier, J., and Jaggi, M. (2018a). Sparsified SGD with memory. In *Proceedings of Annual Conference on Neural Information Processing Systems, NeurIPS*.

[277] Stich, S. U., Cordonnier, J.-B., and Jaggi, M. (2018b). Sparsified sgd with memory. In *Advances in Neural Information Processing Systems*, pages 4447–4458.

[278] Streeter, M. (2019). Learning optimal linear regularizers. *in Proceedings of 36th International Conference on Machine Learning, ICML 2019*, 2019-June:10489–10498.

[279] Sun, J., Chen, T., Giannakis, G., and Yang, Z. (2019). Communication-efficient distributed learning via lazily aggregated quantized gradients. In *Proceedings of Advances in Neural Information Processing Systems, NeurIPS*.

[280] Sun, S., Chen, W., Bian, J., Liu, X., and Liu, T. (2018). Slim-dp: A multi-agent system for communication-efficient distributed deep learning. In *Proceedings of the 17th International Conference on Autonomous Agents and MultiAgent Systems, AAMAS 2018, Stockholm, Sweden, July 10-15, 2018*, pages 721–729.

[281] Sun, Y., Zhou, S., and GÃijndÃijz, D. (2020). Energy-aware analog aggregation for federated learning with redundant data. In *ICC 2020 - 2020 IEEE International Conference on Communications (ICC)*, pages 1–7.

[282] Szegedy, C., Liu, W., Jia, Y., Sermanet, P., Reed, S., Anguelov, D., Erhan, D., Vanhoucke, V., and Rabinovich, A. (2015). Going deeper with convolutions. In *Proceedings of the IEEE conference on computer vision and pattern recognition*, pages 1–9.

[283] Tan, T., Yin, S., Liu, K., and Wan, M. (2019). On the convergence speed of AMSGRAD and beyond. *in Proceedings of International Conference on Tools with Artificial Intelligence, ICTAI*, 2019-Novem:464–470.

[284] Tandon, R., Lei, Q., Dimakis, A. G., and Karampatziakis, N. (2017). Gradient coding: Avoiding stragglers in distributed learning. In *Proceedings of the 34th International Conference on Machine Learning, ICML*.

[285] Tang, H., Gan, S., Zhang, C., Zhang, T., and Liu, J. (2018a). Communication compression for decentralized training. In Bengio, S., Wallach, H. M., Larochelle, H., Grauman, K., Cesa-Bianchi, N., and Garnett, R., editors, *Advances in Neural Information Processing Systems 31: Annual Conference on Neural Information Processing Systems 2018, NeurIPS 2018, 3-8 December 2018, Montréal, Canada*, pages 7663–7673.

[286] Tang, H., Gan, S., Zhang, C., Zhang, T., and Liu, J. (2018b). Communication compression for decentralized training. In *Advances in Neural Information Processing Systems*, pages 7652–7662.

[287] Tang, H., Lian, X., Qiu, S., Yuan, L., Zhang, C., Zhang, T., and Liu, J. (2019a). Deepsqueeze: Decentralization meets error-compensated compression. *arXiv*, pages arXiv–1907.

[288] Tang, H., Yu, C., Lian, X., Zhang, T., and Liu, J. (2019b). Doublesqueeze: Parallel stochastic gradient descent with double-pass error-compensated compression. In Chaudhuri, K. and Salakhutdinov, R., editors, *Proceedings of the 36th International Conference on Machine Learning, ICML*.

[289] Tang, H., Yu, C., Lian, X., Zhang, T., and Liu, J. (2019c). Doublesqueeze: Parallel stochastic gradient descent with double-pass error-compensated compression. In *International Conference on Machine Learning*, pages 6155–6165. PMLR.

[290] Tao, G., Ma, S., Liu, Y., and Zhang, X. (2018). Attacks meet interpretability: Attribute-steered detection of adversarial samples. In *Advances in Neural Information Processing Systems 31*.

[291] Tian, L. and Gu, Q. (2017). Communication-efficient distributed sparse linear discriminant analysis. In Singh, A. and Zhu, X. J., editors, *Proceedings of the 20th International Conference on Artificial Intelligence and Statistics, AISTATS 2017, 20-22 April 2017, Fort Lauderdale, FL, USA*, volume 54 of *Proceedings of Machine Learning Research*, pages 1178–1187. PMLR.

[292] Tong, L., Yu, S., Alfeld, S., and Vorobeychik, Y. (2018). Adversarial regression with multiple learners. *CoRR*, abs/1806.02256.

[293] TramÂÍÂĺr, F., Kurakin, A., Papernot, N., Goodfellow, I., Boneh, D., and McDaniel, P. (2017). Ensemble adversarial training: Attacks and defenses.

[294] Tran, N. H., Bao, W., Zomaya, A., Nguyen, M. N. H., and Hong, C. S. (2019). Federated learning over wireless networks: Optimization model design and analysis. In *IEEE INFOCOM 2019 - IEEE Conference on Computer Communications*, pages 1387–1395.

[295] Tuncer, O., Leung, V. J., and Coskun, A. K. (2015). Pacmap: Topology mapping of unstructured communication patterns onto non-contiguous allocations. In *Proceedings of the 29th ACM on International Conference on Supercomputing, ICS*.

[296] Vaswani, A., Shazeer, N., Parmar, N., Uszkoreit, J., Jones, L., Gomez, A. N., Kaiser, Ł., and Polosukhin, I. (2017). Attention is all you need. In *Advances in neural information processing systems*, pages 5998–6008.

[297] Venkataramani, S., Ranjan, A., Banerjee, S., Das, D., Avancha, S., Jagannathan, A., Durg, A., Nagaraj, D., Kaul, B., Dubey, P., and Raghunathan, A. (2017). Scaledeep: A scalable compute architecture for learning and evaluating deep networks. In *Proc. ISCA*.

[298] Vepakomma, P., Swedish, T., Raskar, R., Gupta, O., and Dubey, A. (2018). No peek: A survey of private distributed deep learning.

[299] Verbeke, J., Nadgir, N., Ruetsch, G., and Sharapov, I. (2002). Framework for peer-to-peer distributed computing in a heterogeneous, decentralized environment. In Parashar, M., editor, *Grid Computing — GRID 2002*, pages 1–12, Berlin, Heidelberg. Springer Berlin Heidelberg.

[300] Viswanathan, R., Ananthanarayanan, G., and Akella, A. (2016). Clarinet: Wan-aware optimization for analytics queries. In *12th USENIX Symposium on Operating Systems Design and Implementation (OSDI 16)*, pages 435–450.

[301] Vogels, T., Karimireddy, S. P., and Jaggi, M. (2019). Powersgd: Practical low-rank gradient compression for distributed optimization. In *Proceedings of Annual Conference on Neural Information Processing Systems, NeurIPS*.

[302] Vu, T. T., Ngo, D. T., Tran, N. H., Ngo, H. Q., Dao, M. N., and Middleton, R. H. (2020). Cell-free massive MIMO for wireless federated learning. *IEEE Transactions on Wireless Communications, Early Access*.

[303] Wadu, M. M., Samarakoon, S., and Bennis, M. (2020). Federated learning under channel uncertainty: Joint client scheduling and resource allocation. In *2020 IEEE Wireless Communications and Networking Conference (WCNC)*, pages 1–6.

[304] Wang, D., Chen, C., and Xu, J. (2019a). Differentially private empirical risk minimization with non-convex loss functions. In *Proceedings of the 36th International Conference on Machine Learning*.

[305] Wang, D., Gaboardi, M., and Xu, J. (2018a). Empirical risk minimization in non-interactive local differential privacy revisited. In *Advances in Neural Information Processing Systems 31*.

[306] Wang, D., Ye, M., and Xu, J. (2017a). Differentially private empirical risk minimization revisited: Faster and more general. In *Advances in Neural Information Processing Systems 30*.

[307] Wang, H., Guo, S., Tang, B., Li, R., and Li, C. (2019b). Heterogeneity-aware gradient coding for straggler tolerance. In *39th IEEE International Conference on Distributed Computing Systems, ICDCS*.

[308] Wang, H., Qu, Z., Guo, S., Gao, X., Li, R., and Ye, B. "Intermittent Pulling with Local Compensation for Communication-Efficient Distributed Learning," *IEEE Transactions on Emerging Topics in Computing*, 2020, DOI: 10.1109/TETC.2020.3043300, Preprint.

[309] Wang, H., Zhou, R., and Shen, Y.-D. (2019c). Bounding Uncertainty for Active Batch Selection. *in Proceedings of the AAAI Conference on Artificial Intelligence*, 33:5240–5247.

[310] Wang, J., Tantia, V., Ballas, N., and Rabbat, M. (2019d). SlowMo: Improving Communication-Efficient Distributed SGD with Slow Momentum.

[311] Wang, J., Tantia, V., Ballas, N., and Rabbat, M. (2019e). Slowmo: Improving communication-efficient distributed sgd with slow momentum. *arXiv preprint arXiv:1910.00643*.

[312] Wang, K., Li, H., Maharjan, S., Zhang, Y., and Guo, S. (2018b). Green energy scheduling for demand side management in the smart grid. *IEEE Transactions on Green Communications & Networking*, pages 596–611.

[313] Wang, K., Xu, C., and Guo, S. (2017b). Big data analytics for price forecasting in smart grids. In *Global Communications Conference*.

[314] Wang, K., Xu, C., Zhang, Y., Guo, S., and Zomaya, A. Y. (2019f). Robust big data analytics for electricity price forecasting in the smart grid. *IEEE Transactions on Big Data*, 5(1):34–45.

[315] Wang, L., Yang, Y., Min, R., and Chakradhar, S. (2017c). Accelerating deep neural network training with inconsistent stochastic gradient descent. *Neural Networks*, 93:219–229.

[316] Wang, M., Fang, E. X., and Liu, H. (2017d). Stochastic compositional gradient descent: algorithms for minimizing compositions of expected-value functions. *Mathematical Programming*, 161:419–449.

[317] Wang, M., Liu, J., and Fang, E. X. (2017e). Accelerating stochastic composition optimization. *J. Mach. Learn. Res.*, 18:105:1–105:23.

[318] Wang, S., Chen, M., Yin, C., Saad, W., Hong, C. S., Cui, S., and Poor, H. V. (2020b). Federated learning for task and resource allocation in wireless high altitude balloon networks.

[319] Wang, S., Li, D., Cheng, Y., Geng, J., Wang, Y., Wang, S., Xia, S.-T., and Wu, J. (2018c). Bml: A high-performance, low-cost gradient synchronization algorithm for dml training. In *Advances in Neural Information Processing Systems*, pages 4238–4248.

[320] Wang, S., Li, D., Cheng, Y., Geng, J., Wang, Y., Wang, S., Xia, S.-T., and Wu, J. (2018d). Bml: A high-performance, low-cost gradient synchronization algorithm for dml training. In *Proc. NeurIPS*.

[321] Wang, S., Pi, A., and Zhou, X. (2019g). Scalable Distributed DL Training: Batching Communication and Computation. *In Proceedings of the AAAI Conference on Artificial Intelligence*, 33:5289–5296.

[322] Wang, S., Pi, A., and Zhou, X. (2019h). Scalable distributed dl training: Batching communication and computation. In *Proceedings of the AAAI Conference on Artificial Intelligence*, volume 33, pages 5289–5296.

[323] Wang, S., Sun, J., and Xu, Z. (2019i). HyperAdam: A Learnable Task-Adaptive Adam for Network Training. *In Proceedings of the AAAI Conference on Artificial Intelligence*, 33:5297–5304.

[324] Wang, Z. (2019). SpiderBoost and Momentum : Faster Stochastic Variance Reduction Algorithms. *In Proceedings of NeurIPS2019*, (NeurIPS).

[325] Wangni, J., Wang, J., Liu, J., and Zhang, T. (2018a). Gradient sparsification for communication-efficient distributed optimization. In *Proceedings of the Advances in Neural Information Processing Systems (NeurIPS)*.

[326] Wangni, J., Wang, J., Liu, J., and Zhang, T. (2018b). Gradient sparsification for communication-efficient distributed optimization. In *Advances in Neural Information Processing Systems*, pages 1299–1309.

[327] Ward, R., Wu, X., and Bottou, L. (2019). Adagrad stepsizes: Sharp convergence over nonconvex landscapes. *In Proceedings of 36th International Conference on Machine Learning, ICML 2019*, 2019-June:11574–11583.

[328] Wen, W., Xu, C., Yan, F., Wu, C., Wang, Y., Chen, Y., and Li, H. (2017a). Terngrad: Ternary gradients to reduce communication in distributed deep learning. In Guyon, I., von Luxburg, U., Bengio, S., Wallach, H. M., Fergus, R., Vishwanathan, S. V. N., and Garnett, R., editors, *Proceedings of Annual Conference on Neural Information Processing Systems, NeurIPS*.

[329] Wen, W., Xu, C., Yan, F., Wu, C., Wang, Y., Chen, Y., and Li, H. (2017b). Terngrad: Ternary gradients to reduce communication in distributed deep learning. In *Advances in neural information processing systems*, pages 1509–1519.

[330] Williams, R. J. and Zipser, D. (1989). A learning algorithm for continually running fully recurrent neural networks. *Neural computation*, 1(2):270–280.

[331] Woodworth, B. E., Patel, K. K., Stich, S. U., Dai, Z., Bullins, B., McMahan, H. B., Shamir, O., and Srebro, N. (2020). Is local SGD better than minibatch sgd? *CoRR*.

[332] Wu, F., He, S., Yang, Y., Wang, H., Qu, Z., and Guo, S. (2020a). On the convergence of quantized parallel restarted sgd for serverless learning. *CoRR*.

[333] Wu, J., Huang, W., Huang, J., and Zhang, T. (2018a). Error compensated quantized sgd and its applications to large-scale distributed optimization. *arXiv preprint arXiv:1806.08054*.

[334] Wu, L., Li, S., Hsieh, C.-J., and Sharpnack, J. (2019). Stochastic Shared Embeddings: Data-driven Regularization of Embedding Layers. (NeurIPS):1–11.

[335] Wu, T., Yuan, K., Ling, Q., Yin, W., and Sayed, A. H. (2018b). Decentralized consensus optimization with asynchrony and delays. *IEEE Trans. Signal Inf. Process. over Networks*, 4(2):293–307.

[336] Wu, X., Ward, R., and Bottou, L. (2018c). WNGrad: Learn the Learning Rate in Gradient Descent. pages 1–16.

[337] Xia, W., Quek, T. Q. S., Guo, K., Wen, W., Yang, H. H., and Zhu, H. (2020). Multi-armed bandit based client scheduling for federated learning. *IEEE Transactions on Wireless Communications*, pages 1–1.

[338] Xiao, L. and Zhang, T. (2014). A proximal stochastic gradient method with progressive variance reduction. *SIAM J. Optimization*, 24:2057–2075.

[339] Xiao, W., Bhardwaj, R., Ramjee, R., Sivathanu, M., Kwatra, N., Han, Z., Patel, P., Peng, X., Zhao, H., Zhang, Q., Yang, F., and Zhou, L. (2018). Gandiva: Introspective cluster scheduling for deep learning. In *Proc. OSDI*.

[340] Xie, C., Koyejo, O., and Gupta, I. (2018). Zeno: Byzantine-suspicious stochastic gradient descent. *CoRR*, abs/1805.10032.

[341] Xie, P., Kim, J. K., Zhou, Y., Ho, Q., Kumar, A., Yu, Y., and Xing, E. (2016). Lighter-communication distributed machine learning via sufficient factor broadcasting. In *Proc. UAI*.

[342] Xie, P., Kim, J. K., Zhou, Y., Ho, Q., Kumar, A., Yu, Y., and Xing, E. P. (2014). Distributed machine learning via sufficient factor broadcasting. *arXiv*, abs/1511.08486.

[343] Xie, S., Girshick, R. B., Dollár, P., Tu, Z., and He, K. (2017). Aggregated residual transformations for deep neural networks. In *Proc. CVPR*, pages 5987–5995.

[344] Xing, E. P., Ho, Q., Xie, P., and Dai, W. (2015). Strategies and principles of distributed machine learning on big data. *CoRR*.

[345] Xing, E. P., Ho, Q., Xie, P., and Wei, D. (2016). Strategies and principles of distributed machine learning on big data. *Engineering*, 2(2):179–195.

[346] Xing, H., Simeone, O., and Bi, S. (2020). Decentralized federated learning via sgd over wireless d2d networks. In *2020 IEEE 21st International Workshop on Signal Processing Advances in Wireless Communications (SPAWC)*, pages 1–5.

[347] Xu, J. and Wang, H. (2020). Client selection and bandwidth allocation in wireless federated learning networks: A long-term perspective.

[348] Xu, S., Zhang, H., Neubig, G., Dai, W., Kim, J. K., Deng, Z., Ho, Q., Yang, G., and Xing, E. P. (2018). Cavs: An efficient runtime system for dynamic neural networks. In *2018 USENIX Annual Technical Conference (USENIX ATC 18)*, pages 937–950.

[349] Xu, Y., Dong, X., Li, Y., and Su, H. (2019). A main/subsidiary network framework for simplifying binary neural networks. In *in Proceedings of IEEE Conference on Computer Vision and Pattern Recognition, CVPR*, pages 7154–7162.

[350] Xu, Z., Zhang, Y., Fu, C., Liu, L., and Guo, S. (2020). Back shape measurement and three-dimensional reconstruction of spinal shape using one kinect sensor. In *2020 IEEE 17th International Symposium on Biomedical Imaging (ISBI)*.

[351] Yan, Z., Guo, Y., and Zhang, C. (2018). Deep defense: Training dnns with improved adversarial robustness. In *Advances in Neural Information Processing Systems 31*.

[352] Yang, D., Xue, G., Fang, X., and Tang, J. (2016). Incentive mechanisms for crowd-sensing: Crowdsourcing with smartphones. *IEEE/ACM Transactions on Networking*, 24(3):1732–1744.

[353] Yang, H. H., Arafa, A., Quek, T. Q. S., and Vincent Poor, H. (2020). Age-based scheduling policy for federated learning in mobile edge networks. In *ICASSP 2020 - 2020 IEEE International Conference on Acoustics, Speech and Signal Processing (ICASSP)*, pages 8743–8747.

[354] Yang, H. H., Liu, Z., Quek, T. Q. S., and Poor, H. V. (2019a). Scheduling policies for federated learning in wireless networks.

[355] Yang, K., Jiang, T., Shi, Y., and Ding, Z. (2020). Federated learning via over-the-air computation. *IEEE Transactions on Wireless Communications*, 19(3):2022–2035.

[356] Yang, K., Shi, Y., Zhou, Y., Yang, Z., Fu, L., and Chen, W. (2020). Federated machine learning for intelligent iot via reconfigurable intelligent surface. *IEEE Network*, 34(5):16–22.

[357] Yang, Q., Liu, Y., Chen, T., and Tong, Y. (2019b). Federated machine learning: Concept and applications. *ACM Transactions on Intelligent Systems and Technology (TIST)*, 10(2):1–19.

[358] Yang, Y., Zhang, G., Katabi, D., and Xu, Z. (2019c). Me-net: Towards effective adversarial robustness with matrix estimation. *CoRR*, abs/1905.11971.

[359] Yang, Z., Chen, M., Saad, W., Hong, C. S., and Shikh-Bahaei, M. (2019d). Energy efficient federated learning over wireless communication networks.

[360] Yang, Z., Dai, Z., Yang, Y., Carbonell, J., Salakhutdinov, R. R., and Le, Q. V. (2019e). Xlnet: Generalized autoregressive pretraining for language understanding. In *Advances in neural information processing systems*, pages 5754–5764.

[361] Yeganeh, Y., Farshad, A., Navab, N., and Albarqouni, S. (2020). Inverse distance aggregation for federated learning with non-iid data. *arXiv preprint arXiv:2008.07665*.

[362] Yeh, T. T., Sabne, A., Sakdhnagool, P., Eigenmann, R., and Rogers, T. G. (2019). Pagoda: A gpu runtime system for narrow tasks. *ACM Transactions on Parallel Computing (TOPC)*, 6(4):1–23.

[363] Yin, D., Chen, Y., Ramchandran, K., and Bartlett, P. L. (2018a). Byzantine-robust distributed learning: Towards optimal statistical rates. *CoRR*, abs/1803.01498.

[364] Yin, D., Chen, Y., Ramchandran, K., and Bartlett, P. L. (2018b). Defending against saddle point attack in byzantine-robust distributed learning. *CoRR*, abs/1806.05358.

[365] Yin, D., Pananjady, A., Lam, M., Papailiopoulos, D. S., Ramchandran, K., and Bartlett, P. L. (2018c). Gradient diversity: a key ingredient for scalable distributed learning. In *Proceedings of International Conference on Artificial Intelligence and Statistics, AISTATS*.

[366] Ying, B., Yuan, K., Vlaski, S., and Sayed, A. H. (2019). Stochastic Learning Under Random Reshuffling With Constant Step-Sizes. In *IEEE Transactions on Signal Processing*, volume 67, pages 474–489.

[367] Yong, H., Huang, J., Hua, X., and Zhang, L. (2020). Gradient Centralization: A New Optimization Technique for Deep Neural Networks.

[368] You, K., Long, M., Wang, J., and Jordan, M. I. (2019). How Does Learning Rate Decay Help Modern Neural Networks?

[369] You, Y., Li, J., Reddi, S. J., Hseu, J., Kumar, S., Bhojanapalli, S., Song, X., Demmel, J., Keutzer, K., and Hsieh, C. (2020a). Large batch optimization for deep learning: Training BERT in 76 minutes. In *Proceedings of 8th International Conference on Learning Representations, ICLR*.

[370] You, Y., Wang, Y., Zhang, H., Zhang, Z., Demmel, J., and Hsieh, C. (2020b). The limit of the batch size. *CoRR*.

[371] You, Y., Zhang, Z., Hsieh, C.-J., Demmel, J., and Keutzer, K. (2018). Imagenet training in minutes. In *Proceedings of the 47th International Conference on Parallel Processing, ICPP*.

[372] Yu, L., Liu, L., Pu, C., Gursoy, M. E., and Truex, S. (2019). Differentially private model publishing for deep learning. In *2019 IEEE Symposium on Security and Privacy (SP)*.

[373] Yu, P. and Chowdhury, M. (2019). Salus: Fine-grained gpu sharing primitives for deep learning applications. *CoRR*.

[374] Yu, Q., Li, S., Raviv, N., Kalan, S. M. M., Soltanolkotabi, M., and Avestimehr, A. S. (2019). Lagrange coded computing: Optimal design for resiliency, security, and privacy. In *Proceedings of The 22nd International Conference on Artificial Intelligence and Statistics, AISTATS*.

[375] Yuan, J. and Yu, S. (2014). Privacy preserving back-propagation neural network learning made practical with cloud computing. *IEEE Transactions on Parallel and Distributed Systems*, 25(1):212–221.

[376] Yuan, K., Ling, Q., and Yin, W. (2016). On the convergence of decentralized gradient descent. *SIAM J. Optim.*, 26(3):1835–1854.

[377] Yuan, X., Feng, Z., Norton, M., and Li, X. (2019). Generalized Batch Normalization: Towards Accelerating Deep Neural Networks. *in Proceedings of the AAAI Conference on Artificial Intelligence*, 33:1682–1689.

[378] Yue Yu, Jiaxiang Wu, L. H. (2019). Double quantization for communication-efficient distributed optimization. In *Proceedings of the Advances in Neural Information Processing Systems (NeurIPS)*, pages 4440–4451.

[379] Yurochkin, M., Agarwal, M., Ghosh, S., Greenewald, K. H., Hoang, T. N., and Khazaeni, Y. (2019). Bayesian nonparametric federated learning of neural networks. In *Proceedings of the 36th International Conference on Machine Learning, ICML*.

[380] Zaheer, M., Reddi, S. J., Sachan, D., Kale, S., and Kumar, S. (2018). Adaptive methods for nonconvex optimization. *Advances in Neural Information Processing Systems*, 2018-Decem(NeurIPS):9793–9803.

[381] Zeng, D., Gu, L., Lian, L., Guo, S., Yao, H., and Hu, J. (2016). On cost-efficient sensor placement for contaminant detection in water distribution systems. *IEEE Transactions on Industrial Informatics*, 12(6):2177–2185.

[382] Zeng, Q., Du, Y., Leung, K. K., and Huang, K. (2019). Energy-efficient radio resource allocation for federated edge learning.

[383] Zeng, R., Zhang, S., Wang, J., and Chu, X. (2020a). Fmore: An incentive scheme of multidimensional auction for federated learning in mec. *arXiv preprint arXiv:2002.09699*.

[384] Zeng, T., Semiari, O., Mozaffari, M., Chen, M., Saad, W., and Bennis, M. (2020b). Federated learning in the sky: Joint power allocation and scheduling with uav swarms.

[385] Zhan, Y. and Zhang, J. (2020). An incentive mechanism design for efficient edge learning by deep reinforcement learning approach. In *Proc. of IEEE INFOCOM*, pages 2489–2498.

[386] Zhang, C., Öztireli, C., Mandt, S., and Salvi, G. (2019a). Active Mini-Batch Sampling Using Repulsive Point Processes. *in Proceedings of the AAAI Conference on Artificial Intelligence*, 33:5741–5748.

[387] Zhang, G., Li, L., Nado, Z., Martens, J., Sachdeva, S., Dahl, G. E., Shallue, C. J., and Grosse, R. (2019b). Which Algorithmic Choices Matter at Which Batch Sizes? Insights From a Noisy Quadratic Model. (NeurIPS):1–12.

[388] Zhang, H., Li, J., Kara, K., Alistarh, D., Liu, J., and Zhang, C. (2017a). Zipml: Training linear models with end-to-end low precision, and a little bit of deep learning. In Precup, D. and Teh, Y. W., editors, *Proceedings of the 34th International Conference on Machine Learning, ICML*.

[389] Zhang, H., Zheng, Z., Xu, S., Dai, W., Ho, Q., Liang, X., Hu, Z., Wei, J., Xie, P., and Xing, E. P. (2017b). Poseidon: An efficient communication architecture for distributed deep learning on GPU clusters. In *Proc. ATC*.

[390] Zhang, J., Hong, Z., Qiu, X., Zhan, Y., Guo, S., and Chen, W. (2020). Skychain: A deep reinforcement learning-empowered dynamic blockchain sharding system. In *International Conference on Parallel Processing (ICPP*.

[391] Zhang, M., Rajbhandari, S., Wang, W., and He, Y. (2018). Deepcpu: Serving rnn-based deep learning models 10x faster. In *2018 USENIX Annual Technical Conference (USENIX ATC 18)*, pages 951–965.

[392] Zhang, N. and Tao, M. (2020). Gradient statistics aware power control for over-the-air federated learning.

[393] Zhang, N. and Tao, M. (2020). Gradient statistics aware power control for over-the-air federated learning in fading channels. In *2020 IEEE International Conference on Communications Workshops (ICC Workshops)*, pages 1–6.

[394] Zhang, Q., Yang, L. T., and Chen, Z. (2016). Privacy preserving deep computation model on cloud for big data feature learning. *IEEE Transactions on Computers*, 65(5):1351–1362.

[395] Zhang, X., Zhao, R., Yan, J., Gao, M., Qiao, Y., Wang, X., and Li, H. (2019c). P2SGRAD: Refined gradients for optimizing deep face models. *in Proceedings of the IEEE Computer Society Conference on Computer Vision and Pattern Recognition*, 2019-June:9898–9906.

[396] Zhang, Y., Qu, H., Chen, C., and Metaxas, D. (2019d). Taming the noisy gradient: Train deep neural networks with small batch sizes. *in Proceedings of IJCAI International Joint Conference on Artificial Intelligence*, 2019-Augus:4348–4354.

[397] Zhao, J. (2018). Distributed deep learning under differential privacy with the teacher-student paradigm. In *Workshops at the Thirty-Second AAAI Conference on Artificial Intelligence*.

[398] Zhao, S., Xie, Y., Gao, H., and Li, W. (2019a). Global momentum compression for sparse communication in distributed SGD. *CoRR*, abs/1905.12948.

[399] Zhao, T., Zhang, Y., and Olukotun, K. (2019b). Serving recurrent neural networks efficiently with a spatial accelerator.

[400] Zheng, K., Mou, W., and Wang, L. (2017a). Collect at once, use effectively: Making non-interactive locally private learning possible. In *Proceedings of the 34th International Conference on Machine Learning - Volume 70*.

[401] Zheng, S., Huang, Z., and Kwok, J. (2019). Communication-efficient distributed block-wise momentum sgd with error-feedback. In *Advances in Neural Information Processing Systems*, pages 11450–11460.

[402] Zheng, W., Popa, R. A., Gonzalez, J. E., and Stoica, I. (2019). Helen: Maliciously secure coopetitive learning for linear models. In *2019 IEEE Symposium on Security and Privacy (SP)*.

[403] Zheng, Z. and Hong, P. (2018). Robust detection of adversarial attacks by modeling the intrinsic properties of deep neural networks. In *Advances in Neural Information Processing Systems 31*.

[404] Zheng, Z., Xie, S., Dai, H., Chen, X., and Wang, H. (2017b). An overview of blockchain technology: Architecture, consensus, and future trends. In *2017 IEEE International Congress on Big Data (BigData Congress)*.

[405] Zhou, F. and Cong, G. (2018). On the convergence properties of a k-step averaging stochastic gradient descent algorithm for nonconvex optimization. In *Proceedings of the Twenty-Seventh International Joint Conference on Artificial Intelligence, IJCAI*.

[406] Zhou, Z., Chen, X., Li, E., Zeng, L., Luo, K., and Zhang, J. (2019). Edge intelligence: Paving the last mile of artificial intelligence with edge computing. *Proceedings of the IEEE*, 107(8):1738–1762.

[407] Zhu, G., Du, Y., Gündüz, D., and Huang, K. (2020). One-bit over-the-air aggregation for communication-efficient federated edge learning: Design and convergence analysis. *CoRR*, abs/2001.05713.

[408] Zhu, G., Liu, D., Du, Y., You, C., Zhang, J., and Huang, K. (2018). Towards an intelligent edge: Wireless communication meets machine learning. *CoRR*, abs/1809.00343.

[409] Zinkevich, M., Weimer, M., Li, L., and Smola, A. J. (2010). Parallelized stochastic gradient descent. In *Advances in neural information processing systems*, pages 2595–2603.

[410] Zou, F., Shen, L., Jie, Z., Zhang, W., and Liu, W. (2019). A sufficient condition for convergences of adam and rmsprop. *in Proceedings of the IEEE Computer Society Conference on Computer Vision and Pattern Recognition*, 2019-June(1):11119–11127.

Index